Serving with Calvin

Leading and Planning Services of Worship in the Reformed Church

Terry L. Johnson

EP BOOKS
First Floor Venture House, 6 Silver Court, Watchmead,
Welwyn Garden City, UK, AL7 1TS

web: http://www.epbooks.org

e-mail: sales@epbooks.org

EP Books are distributed in the USA by:
JPL Distribution
3741 Linden Avenue Southeast
Grand Rapids, MI 49548
E-mail: orders@jpldistribution.com
Tel: 877.683.6935

© Terry L. Johnson 2015. All rights reserved. No part of this publication may be reproduced, stored in a retrieval system or transmitted, in any form, or by any means, electronic, mechanical, photocopying, recording or otherwise, without the prior permission of the publishers.

First published 2015

British Library Cataloguing in Publication Data available

ISBN: 978-1-78397-117-6

*Unless otherwise indicated, Scripture quotations are taken from the Holy Bible, New American Standard Version. Copyright © 1960, 1962, 1963, 1968, 1971, 1972, 1973, 1075, 1977 by The Lockman Foundation.

Contents

Preface		11
Acknowledgements		13
1	**Introduction**	**15**
	Our vision	21
	Building wisely	25
2	**Preparing the Minister**	**29**
	Pastoral Leadership	29
	Piety	38
	Humility	48
	Wisdom	50
3	**Preparing the Services**	**59**
	General considerations	60
	Public Services of Worship	60
	Ordinary means	64
	Frequency	65
	Specific characteristics	71
	Catholicity	71
	Excellence	73
	Order	74
	Praise	74
	Confession	77

Serving with Calvin

Means of Grace	79
Thanksgiving & Benediction	80
Form and freedom	81
Reverence	85
Pace	90
Economy	92
Length	93
Aesthetics	93
Simplicity	107
4 Administering the Elements—1	**113**
Reading Scripture	114
What to read	115
How to read	117
Preaching	120
What to preach	121
1. Preach the lectio continua	124
2. Preach topically as prudence dictates	129
3. Preach grammatical-historical-redemptive sermons	131
4. Preach the text	132
5. Preach Christocentrically	145
6. Preach simple content	175
7. Begin preaching those books of the Bible that are the most accessible	177
8. Vary the sermon diet	177
How to preach	178
1. Preach persuasively	178
2. Preach with urgency	180
3. Preach authentically	183
4. Review and repeat constantly	185
5. Apply the text throughout	187
6. Include exhortation	189

Contents 5

7. Explain the context but don't dwell on it	193
8. Use quotations sparingly	193
9. Preach sermons of moderate length	196

5 Administering the Elements—2 199

Prayer 199

What to pray 200

How to pray 210

Singing 229

Criteria for evaluation 231

Practical helps 249

Sacraments 250

6 Preparing the Setting **275**

External Style 276

Interior Arrangement 277

Central Pulpit 278

Table and Font 279

Choir & Organ 280

The furnishings, decorations, and the arts 284

Devotional art 287

Decorative art 288

Illustrative & didactic art 291

Graphic art 292

Performing arts 293

Modern Innovations 294

Facilities & Appearances 296

Regarding buildings & grounds 297

Regarding members 298

Regarding the environment of the service 299

7 Preparing the Congregation **303**

Savannah background 303

Savannah ministry 304

Growth	305
Ministry today	307
Getting there	308
Worship services	309
Inquirers' Class	310
Officers' Training Class	311
Pastor's writings	311
Reformation & Heritage Sundays	312
8 Mistakes to Avoid	**315**
General concerns	319
Faith or presumption?	319
Faithfulness or failure?	322
Pace or imprudence?	323
Specific concerns	325
Reverential or liturgical?	325
Depth or length?	326
Fervency or frequency?	327
Spirit or form?	328
Primary means or only means?	329
9 Epilogue: Final Considerations	**333**
Scripture	334
Gospel	334
Church	335
Spirit	337
God	337
Appendix A: Our Order of Service	**339**
Appendix B: Charts	**355**
Bibliography of Cited Works	**361**
Bibliography	**363**
Scripture Index	**381**
Index of names	**395**

Serving with Calvin

*Leading and planning services of
worship in the Reformed Church*

8

Dedication

This work is dedicated to the members of the Twin Lakes Fellowship, the ministerial fraternal of the Presbyterian Church in America, along with all those who long to see the revival of the historic ministry and worship of Reformed Protestantism.

10

Preface

The concluding sentence of *Worshipping with Calvin* promised a follow-up work that would focus on implementation.[1] *Serving with Calvin* is that work. Whereas *Worshipping with Calvin* argued for the revival of historic Reformed ministry and worship by focusing on its biblical, theological, and historical foundations, *Serving with Calvin* will focus on the nuts and bolts, the "how-to's," the application of historic Reformed ministry and worship today. Our hope is that many will be convinced that it can be done, and should be. The Word read, preached, sung, prayed, and seen is as effective today as it ever was. When practiced by faith, in the power of the Holy Spirit, ordinary means ministry may be the instrument by which Christ once again builds His church, against which even the gates of hell shall not prevail.

---

[1]   *Worshipping with Calvin: Recovering the Historic Ministry & Worship of Reformed Protestantism* (Darlington, England: EP Books, 2014).

12

Acknowledgements

I am indebted to the many sources I mentioned in *Worshipping with Calvin*. I only wish to repeat my gratitude to Debbie Parker, my secretary for nearly fifteen years, apart from whose extraordinary skill on a keyboard many of my projects would never have been completed.

14

❧ Chapter 1 ❧

Introduction

We labor today in the era of the "gimmick-driven church." In addition to the eye-popping stunts we discussed in our previous work,[1] mailers cross the desks of ministers on a nearly weekly basis promising slightly more mundane silver bullets which will slay the dragons of non-growth and invigorate a season of super-growth. We can recall the yellow Sunday School bus ministry, "Here's Life America," hand-bell choirs, Evangelism Explosion, small group discipleship, telemarketing, the seeker-friendly church, the church for the unchurched, the Toronto Blessing, the Laughing Revival, and the Brownsville Revival, each presented as a panacea that would cure what ails the church. Since the advent of the twenty-first century we've seen Promise Keepers, Wild at Heart, WWJD, The Prayer of Jabez, Forty

---

1   See *Worshipping with Calvin*, Chapter 9.

Days of Purpose, the Passion of Christ, the Florida Outpouring, Xtreme Ministries ("where Feet, Fist and Faith Collide"), the "Emergent Church," "Deep Church," "Secret Church," and so on.[2] "The One Month to Live Challenge," endorsed by Warren & Hybels, promises to "help your church experience exponential growth" and "double your small groups and Sunday School."[3] *Synergize 2! Pastors Conference* appeals to those "who wish to double their impact and influence."[4] Marketing concerns have led to churches branding themselves with increasingly unusual names: Elevation, Envision, Restoration, enCompass, Journey, The River, Tapestry, Celebration, Oasis, Crossings, Crosspointe, Sandals, Harvest, Impact, The Refinery, Mosaic, Relate Church, and Liquid Church, among many others. There is an almost compulsive desire among our contemporaries to reinvent the church and reconstruct its ministry. The "change" mantra gets politicians elected and books published. "Work on their horror of the Same Old Thing," Screwtape tells his demon-in-training.[5] Contrast regularly is made between the "traditional" church (usually left undefined: traditional Southern Baptist and tradition Presbyterian are very different creatures; which do they mean?) and the new and improved alternative for new and exceptional times.[6] Tomorrow another cure-all will be unveiled, another

---

2   Belcher, *Deep Church: A Third Way Beyond Emerging & Traditional* (Downers Grove, Ill: InterVarsity Press, 2009),; "Secret Church," *Christianity Today*, May 2010, Vol. 54, No. 5, 40.

3   "One Month to Live Challenge" brochure.

4   Synergize2! Pastors Conference letter of 12/28/09.

5   C. S. Lewis, *The Screwtape Letters*, Revised Edition (New York: Macmillan Publishing Company, 1982), 116, 118.

6   T. David Gordon complains that "My students routinely assume that I am defending Bill Gaither or Fanny Crosby when I express reluctance about praise choruses" (*Why Johnny Can't Sing Hymns: How Pop Culture Rewrote the Hymnal* [Phillipsburg, New Jersey: P&R Publishing Company, 2010], 42).

"can't miss" program that will tip the scales. "Like a gambler looking for a winning ticket, (congregations) search for a program that will 'turn their church around,'" Harry Reeder, pastor of the Briarwood Presbyterian Church in Birmingham, Alabama, observes.[7]

The seeker-churches have become great promoters of new forms of ministry. Their assumption: the old forms don't work. For Randy Pope, the gifted founding pastor of the Perimeter Presbyterian Church and Perimeter ministries in Atlanta, small groups are the "primary method of making mature and equipped followers of Christ."[8] His TEAMS (Truth, Equipping, Accountability, Mission, Supplication) are the primary place where nurture, education, and equipping take place, among other things. Rick Warren has a similar small group program at his Saddleback Church. Pope provides a survey of church history which might lead one to conclude that Perimeter Church's structure of the church gathered (on Sundays) and scattered (in small groups on weekdays) is a breakthrough which restores the ministry pattern of the New Testament church for the first time since the days of the Apostles. Perimeter Church is "suggesting a radical change in the way church is done."[9] "Radical change" is assumed to be necessary.

In addition to reaching the lost, Pope says that seeker-churches are eager "to answer the question of how to make mature followers of Christ."[10] The church catholic has had some experience in

---

7   Harry Reeder, *From Embers to a Flame: How God Can Revitalize Your Church* (Phillipsburg, NJ: P&R Publishing, 2004), 9.

8   Randy Pope, *The Prevailing Church: An Alternative Approach to Ministry* (Chicago: Moody Press, 2005), 113.

9   Ibid. 123.

10   Ibid. 123.

answering this question, but not to the satisfaction of the seeker churches. The old ways will not work for them. Ministry must be reinvented. Why? Because for them, all previous forms of ministry are inadequate.

However, we would suggest one reason for this perception of the inadequacy of all that precedes them is so little of consequence occurs in a typical "contemporary" Sunday service. The ordinary means of grace have been watered down to the point of impotence. Necessity has forced them to become experts at mid-week ministry alternatives. Pope's subtitle is, "An Alternative Approach to Ministry." Warren's book-cover comments extol him for "a new paradigm for ministry." Apparently 2000 years of church history and nearly 500 years of Protestant ministry provide no viable models for the twenty-first century. All previous ministries were in one way or another incomplete, or inadequate, or lacking. The dynamic church of the Patristic era, the missional church of the Middle Ages, the transformational church of the Reformation era, the faithful churches of Protestant orthodoxy (seventeenth and eighteenth centuries) and the evangelizing churches of the Awakenings (eighteenth and nineteenth centuries) provide no pattern for ministry for contemporary churches. The primary means of making "mature followers of Christ" during each of these historic periods primarily was through the use of the ordinary means of grace in the public assembly of the whole church on the Lord's Day for morning and evening prayer. The Scripture reading, preaching, psalm-singing, praying, and even the eucharist (yes, even the eucharist, as Jungmann pointed out of the Patristic Church[11] and Schmidt

---

11   Joseph A.Jungmann, S.J., *The Early Liturgy: To the Time of Gregory the Great*, Liturgical Studies Volume VI (Notre Dame, Indiana: University of Notre Dame Press, 1959); see chapter 1 of *Worshipping with Calvin*.

did of the Scottish Presbyterian churches[12]) of the Patristic, Reformation, Puritan and evangelical churches transformed their worlds. We are not opposed to alternative forms of ministry. Sometimes innovation may be necessary and helpful. However, it is all too typical of Baby-boomer's imagined self-importance to think that the historic means employed by the church in all its eras of health and growth are no longer workable and new structures must be created. Boomers, Gen-Xers, Millennials and the like are so unique, so distinctive from every previous generation! The post-modern world is so different! The old ways will no longer work. Yet here's what will: and out rolls the latest, the best, the greatest program, technique, organization, ministry yet devised.

Have the new paradigms worked? We and others are persuaded they have not (see chapter 1, *Worshipping with Calvin*). "My first Sunday back from some time away, I sat in the worship service and wept," writes Walt Kallestad, pastor of Phoenix-area megachurch, Community Church of Joy. It was not the emotional impact of the service that moved him. Quite the contrary. Rather, the service "struck me as such a production, so performance driven. In a word, it was shallow ... I was mortified at what we'd become."[13] Kallestad built a market-driven, seeker-friendly church based on the principles espoused by Bill Hybels and Rick Warren (whom he names) and others. Attendance skyrocketed, he says, but "we became a program-driven church attracting consumers looking

---

12   Leigh Eric Schmidt, *Holy Fairs Scottish Communions and American Revivals in the Early Modern Period* (Princeton, New Jersey: Princeton University Press, 1989); see chapter 6 of *Worshipping with Calvin*.

13   Walt Kallestad, "'Showtime!' No More," in *Leadership Journal.net*, http://www.christianitytoday.com/le/2008/fall/13.39.html, posted November 26, 2008, 1.

for the latest and greatest religious presentations."[14] "Worship was a show," he admits, "and we'd produced consumers."[15] "Why weren't we producing empowered disciples?" he asks. "What were we missing?"[16] He later answers his own question. "We were entertaining people as a substitute for leading them into the presence of God."[17]

"We made a mistake," Bill Hybels admits in light of the disappointing levels of commitment indicated by members of the Willow Creek Church, the Vatican City of seeker-sensitive services. Dale Buss, writing in *The Wall Street Journal*, labels this "a megadevelopment in the world of megachurches." Hybels and his staff have found that significant numbers of their flock "consider themselves 'stalled' or 'dissatisfied' with the role of the church in their spiritual growth and huge portions of these groups were considering leaving Willow Creek because of it."[18] David Wells speaks of "the failure of the market-driven, seeker-sensitive churches to produce serious Christian life." "*Forget rethinking the church*," he insists.[19]

The extent to which the problems encountered by the market-driven churches leads to a re-evaluation of their revamping of the primary services of "seeker-sensitive" churches remains to be seen.[20] Some advocates of contemporary worship see the need for

---

14 Ibid. 2.
15 Ibid. 2,3.
16 Ibid. 4,5.
17 Ibid. 7.
18 Dale Buss, "Less Seeking, More Thrills," *The Wall Street Journal*, June 27, 2008, W11.
19 David Wells, *The Courage to be Protestant: Truth Lovers, Marketers, and Emergents in the Postmodern World* (Grand Rapids, Michigan: Wm. B. Eerdmans Publishing Co., 2008), 216.
20 This admission is in Greg Hawkins & Cally Parkinson's *Reveal: Where Are You?* (Barrington, Illinois: Willow Creek Association, 2007) has been much

worship that is God-centered, gospel-driven, Spirit-dependent, word-filled. However, the forms they presently employ are not conducive of these goals (see *Worshipping with Calvin*, chapter 1). For example, Bob Kauflin admits to not reading extended texts of Scripture in worship.[21] Snippets of verses may be read in the call to worship, or read between stanzas of a song, or projected on a screen, or printed on a bulletin cover.[22] But systematic Bible reading is not envisioned, nor is expository preaching, nor is metrical psalm singing, nor is classic hymnody, nor is a full-diet of prayer.

Our vision

We are opposed to a seeker-driven, market-driven philosophy, not because of a party-spirit or overall meanness, but because we have a different vision of the church, its worship, and its ministry.

First, the Sunday services of the church should be, and indeed are, de facto, the primary place where Christian ministry occurs. "The place of public assembling to worship should be highly prized," says the Puritan Nathanael Vincent (1638–1697), "*for the sake of the work that is performed here.*" Here the Triune God is "publicly owned and acknowledged." The public assembly he says, citing Psalm 42:2 and 73:17–19, "is, as it were, the suburbs of the city of God in heaven."[23] We concede that it seems otherwise;

---

commented upon. See Chuck Colson, "Rethinking Church" in Prison Fellowship's Breakpoint Commentaries.

21 See Bob Kauflin, *Worship Matters: Leading Others to Encounter the Greatness of God* (Wheaton, IL: Crossway Books, 2008), chapters 8–11, 15. He urges keeping the word central "by treasuring, singing, reading, showing and praying God's word."

22 Ibid. 94–95.

23 Nathanael Vincent, *Attending Upon God Without Distraction* (1695; Grand Rapids, Michigan: Soli Deo Gloria Publications, 2010), 20.

that the most visible and exciting ministry is occurring "out there" among the para-church groups and in the specialized discipleship groups of the church. We maintain that this perception is wrong, and for two reasons.

1. The church assembles primarily on Sunday. The numbers participating in ministry once one moves outside the public assemblies of the Lord's Day drop off dramatically. Only a fraction of the Sunday crowd reappears for ministry of any sort at any other time. Sunday is when the overwhelming number of our people are present, and the Sunday services are the only opportunity we have to minister the gospel to the great majority of them.

2. Only at the Lord's Day assembly of the church are the means of grace fully operative. Nowhere else may the sacraments be administered. It is unlikely that the ministry of preaching of those ordained, commissioned, and "sent" into ministry will occur at alternative gatherings (Romans 10:15). It is doubtful that a full-diet of prayer will be experienced, or that there will be a commitment to biblical psalmody and hymnody, or extended Scripture reading outside of the public assembly of the church. The means of grace are operative for the whole people of God in the Sunday services in ways they are not at any other time in the life of God's people. These services should be the primary focus of the church's ministering energies.

Second, the public assembly of the church should be characterized by God-centered reverence. We are opposed to turning worship services into entertaining evangelistic meetings. For 2000 years the Lord's Day has been the day of Christian worship. Voices are being raised within the contemporary

Christian worship movement against "performancism."[24] We are convinced that the character of the Sunday assembly as a service of worship must be maintained (see chapter 3 of this work, "Public Services"). The Sunday services are intended for the worship of God and the edification of the saints. This is why the word of God is read, preached, sung, prayed, and administered (Acts 2:42). These are acts of worship that edify God's people. They also carry the content of the evangel, as we've seen. However, evangelism is a by-product of worship, not a central or governing principle.

Third, the ministry of the church should target the community as a whole. We are opposed to targeting a selected demographic within a community and tailoring the services of the church to appeal to the cultural preferences of that demographic or sub-culture. A demographically specific strategy implicitly excludes those outside the boundaries of the targeted group, an exclusion that cannot be biblically justified (Galatians 3:28).

Fourth, the congregation that develops as a result of the Christian ministry should be a cross-section of the whole community. We are opposed to the intentional building of homogenous churches, which, it must be admitted, are the inevitable result of a seeker-driven philosophy. We insist that churches were never meant to attract one kind of person or be composed of one kind of person (Galatians 3:28).

Fifth, the regular ministry of the church should focus on "ordinary" and "primary" means of grace. We are opposed to a philosophy that places so much emphasis on external, relatively superficial, and often extra-biblical methodology. Churches are built, we maintain, not by pop format, media, drama, praise

---

24   James Brown of Falls Church, Anglican, "Are We Headed For a Crash: Reflections on the Current State of Evangelical Worship" (posted May 19, 2014).

bands, "practical" messages, and assorted entertainment-driven gimmicks, but by the word, prayer, and sacraments. "Men's inventions in religion, though often followed with great eagerness, are found unprofitable and vain to them who have been zealous for them," warns Nathanael Vincent. His perspective represents that of the older Reformed tradition: "But the ordinance which the Lord Himself has appointed, He is ready to own and make effectual to them who attend upon Him in the use of them."[25] Stanley Hauerwas, a man whom *Time* once called "America's Best Theologian," responded to a question about his view of new church movements, especially emergent church trends, saying, "The future of the church is not found in things like this, the future is doing the same thing Sunday after Sunday."[26] If by "the same thing" is meant the regular ministry of the word, prayer, and sacraments, we couldn't agree more.

Sixth, the regular ministry of the church should be simple, one which depends on the Holy Spirit, not human ingenuity. We are opposed to a philosophy which diminishes the Lordship of Christ and sovereignty of God in the building of the church. "I will build My church," Jesus says (Matthew 16:18). "God causes the growth," says the Apostle Paul (1 Corinthians 3:6–8).

While we do not denigrate the numerical success that the seeker churches have seen, and the lost souls that they have won, we do wonder what might have been if extremely talented and energetic ministers like Warren, Hybels, and Pope, and perceptive observers like Barna, had poured their lives into historic patterns of Protestant ministry. We suspect they would have dynamic ministries every bit as large and influential as they have today and

---

25 Vincent, *Attending Upon God*, 21.
26 Anthony D. Baker, "Learning to Read the Gospel Again," *Christianity Today*, Vol. 55, No. 12, December 2011.

perhaps even more so, given the greater attention to the ministry of the word read, preached, sung, prayed, and administered that this would have involved.

Reformed worship and ministry has the potential to restore sanity and fruitfulness to the church life of evangelical Christianity. It is true that God can work whenever and where He wishes, with or without means. It is true that God has used the above named programs and movements to bring the lost to Christ and sanctify saints. We wouldn't deny this for a moment. It is also true that we are wise to invest our energies in the expectation that He will work *in those places where He has promised and through those means that He has ordained*. Reformed ministry and worship places confidence in the word, sacraments, and prayer as promised means of grace. They are the "golden pipes," (from Zechariah 4:12) says Nathanael Vincent, "that convey the grace of the Spirit into the hearts of men."[27] This confidence results in a congregational life that is simplified. The frenetic multiplication of programs gives way to the ordinary services of the church in a ministry that takes Reformed ministry and worship seriously.

Moreover, Reformed ministry and worship has the potential to unite the whole people of God in a common worship. It centers on God, Father, Son, and Holy Spirit. It honors the word and Spirit. It respects catholicity and tradition. It claims its own ecclesiastical culture around which the diversity of worldly cultures are encouraged to gather. It makes the communion of the saints, past, present, and future, possible.

Building wisely

Yet it is important to recognize that the circumstances of each

---

27   Vincent, *Attending Upon God*, 21.

congregation are different. Those who are building churches must proceed as "wise master builders" (1 Corinthians 3:10). Our cures must not kill the patient. Some may need merely to maintain and improve the historic Reformed worship that they are now conducting, fending off rivals in the process. Others may be able immediately to transform their current practice and implement the elements and forms of Reformed worship and ministry. Still others will need to proceed slowly and cautiously, only gradually introducing reforms. God's people, whoever they are, need to live and worship in a manner that is God, Bible, Christ, Church, and Spirit-centered. Reformed worship will help them to do so.

Traditionalists would do well to acknowledge that we have not always applied our principles wisely. Reformed theology as well as Reformed practice has sometimes been a blunt instrument, taught and implemented without the "special prudence and care" commended by the *Westminster Confession of Faith* (III.8.). Regrettably the anecdotal evidence indicates that our ecclesiastical communions are polarized, with the *pragmatists* on one end and the *purists* on the other. The former stand ready to abandon historic practices at a whim, seemingly only to care about what "works." The latter appear intent on importing the seventeenth century into the twenty-first without any adjustment at all, content, it seems, with remnant churches that never grow beyond a few dozen members. Long services with long prayers and long sermons sometimes have tried otherwise sympathetic observers; new and strange practices (difficult music, weekly communion, exclusive use of communion wine, intinction) have alienated others. Neither the pragmatists nor the purists are building wisely. The foundation is Jesus Christ, we all agree (1 Corinthians 3:11). We are, we trust, in substantial theological agreement regarding God, man, sin, salvation, Christian living, ecclesiology and eschatology. We stand ready to preach "Christ crucified" (1 Corinthians 2:2). Yet like the Apostle Paul's first century readers, we must "be careful how (we) build upon" that foundation (1 Corinthians 3:10). A "wise master builder" must be a shrewd observer of principles, people, and context. He must be alert, sensitive as to when to push ahead and when to back off. (See more on this theme in Chapter 8). It must be frankly admitted that some of the more pragmatically oriented writers, even seeker-oriented authors such as Rick Warren, *Purpose-Driven Church* and Randy Pope, *The Prevailing Church*, display more discernment about twenty-first century ministry than do the purists.[28] Reformed worship and ministry is what Christ's disciples need. The word read, preached, sung, prayed, and administered is indeed what cures the ailing patient. However (to continue the medical metaphor) an overdose may prove lethal. How then ought we to proceed? We need to prepare the minister, prepare the setting, prepare the services, and prepare the congregation.

---

28   Rick Warren, *The Purpose-Driven Church* (Grand Rapids, Michigan: Zondervan, 1995), 256–277, has a number of good ideas; Pope, *The Prevailing Church*, 45–49. I have to admit, however, that I find myself overwhelmed by their points and subpoints, lost in a sea of acronyms and acrostics.

28

❧ Chapter 2 ❦

Preparing the Minister

We begin our implementation of historic Reformed ministry and worship with the preparation of those who will lead the church's public services. The worship of Reformed Protestantism is weighty. It is substantial and spiritual. It cannot properly be led casually, thoughtlessly, spontaneously, or mechanically. Effective leadership cannot be reduced to technique, or structure, or even content. If today's church is to "worship with Calvin," the theological, ethical, devotional, and practical preparation of those who lead the church's public services must be given priority attention. We recommend the following, that spiritual services might have spiritual men to lead them.

Pastoral Leadership
First, those who lead the church in its worship should be ordained.

30   *Serving with Calvin*

Why ordained? Because ordination is a process whereby, over time, the theological and moral qualifications of church leaders are assessed and finally approved. "Not a novice," the Apostle Paul insists (KJV). "Not a new convert" (NASV), lest he fall prey to the temptations of the immature and uninstructed (1 Timothy 3:6). Ministry is to be entrusted to those known to be "faithful men" (2 Timothy 2:2).

"Anabaptist thinking has invaded *our* churches," lamented the great Dutch theologian and statesman, Abraham Kuyper, a hundred years ago. "In almost all Reformed and Presbyterian churches," he said, an understanding of office and ordination "is disappearing."[1] We confess to being uncomfortable with the growing practice of turning over the leadership of worship to "worship teams" made up of (often very young) unordained musicians and others. A few years ago the General Assembly of the Presbyterian Church in America featured a worship service in which a praise team comprised of teenagers and 20-somethings led the service. The irony of an assembly hall full of highly qualified ministers and thoroughly vetted elders being led by unordained, under-qualified, youthful novices was rich, and disorienting. What are ministers if they are not worship leaders? D. A. Carson has urged that we "abolish forever the notion of a 'worship leader,'" because the title implies that preaching, reading, and applying God's word are not worship.[2] Can our discomfort with unordained leadership be justified as anything other than unwarranted clericalism? We think so. Limiting worship leadership to ordained ministers can be justified in precisely the

---

1   Abraham Kuyper, *Our Worship*, ed. Harry Boonstra (1911; Grand Rapids: Wm. B. Eerdmans Publishing Co., 2009), 120.

2   Tony Payne, interview with D. A. Carson, *The Briefing*, Issue #232, Matthias Media, 2000; cited in Kauflin, *Worship Matters*, 53.

same way in which regular preaching and the administration of the sacraments in traditional Protestant churches are restricted to those who had been examined both in theology and character and approved for licensure or ordination by the responsible authorities.

Focus for a moment on the administration of the sacraments. Who may administer the sacraments in historic Protestant churches? The consistent practice both among the continental Reformed and the Anglo-American Reformed tradition has been to limit their administration to the ordained clergy in the context of the gathered church under the authority of the church session (board of elders). *Not even lay elders may administer the sacraments.* The reason is simple: the warnings against abuse of the Lord's Table are so strong in Scripture (e.g. 1 Corinthians 11:23–34), and the errors surrounding the sacraments that have plagued the church throughout its history are so serious that this safeguard is necessary. Wisdom requires that only those theologically educated, examined, and approved at the highest level should administer them. Even though lay elders are examined theologically and for their character and spiritual maturity, they may not administer the sacraments because they have not been educated or examined at a level sufficient to ensure their competence to do so. They lack the benefit of three years of seminary education. They have not served in a ministerial internship. They have not submitted to oral and written examinations in Bible, theology, church government, and Christian experience. They have not been prepared sufficiently to explain the subtleties of the church's sacramental theology (e.g. meaning and mode of baptism, the meaning of Jesus' eucharistic words, the nature of Christ's presence in the eucharist, etc.) or to fence the table. Sacramentalism lurks at one extreme, memorialism at another, and desecration of the table through unworthy partaking is an ever present danger. Hence the church historically has placed this limit on their administration. Only the ordained clergy (that is, those observed, educated, tested, and approved) may do so.

What about preaching? The practice in the Reformed churches has been (whatever others have thought) to apply the stringent requirements of 1 Timothy 3 and Titus 1 by limiting regular preaching to those who are theologically trained and examined, whose character has been observed and known to be of superior quality, and finally approved by the assembly of ministers and elders. Through the safeguard of licensure and ordination the church has protected itself from the theological errors and ethical lapses of the inexperienced and immature (1 Timothy 3:6). The high privilege of regular public proclamation ought to be entrusted only to those who have been observed, educated, examined, and approved at the highest levels.

If it is wise to limit the administration of the sacraments and preaching to ordained clergy, then who ought to do the public praying? Likewise, who ought to be selecting the hymns? It is only because we no longer are as careful as we once were to pray and sing biblical language and sound theology that we have forgotten the need for rigorous theological qualifications for those who lead in worship through prayer and song as well as those who preach. So much error was spread in the early church through the hymns of heretics that the liturgy was purged of virtually all non-scriptural language around the fifth century. Hymns were not readmitted to the regular worship of the church until the twelfth century.[3] We mention this, we repeat again, not to advocate exclusive psalm singing (though we do venerate the tradition), but to illustrate the point: leadership in worship ought to be left in the hands of those with thorough theological training and carefully assessed character. In other words, in the hands of the ordained clergy.

What is true of preaching and the sacraments ought also be recognized of the other elements of worship and of the service as a whole.[4] The extended and difficult ordination process is

---

3 See Mary Berry, "Hymns," in J. G. Davies (ed.), *The New Westminster Dictionary of Liturgy & Worship* (Philadelphia: The Westminster Press, 1986), 262; Jones, *et al* (eds), *The Study of Liturgy*, 509. See *Worshipping with Calvin*, Chapter 5 "Sing the Word."

4 The Reformed tradition has consistently insisted upon ministerial leadership in worship. The current position of the Christian Reformed Church is "the minister of the Word serving as pastor of a congregation shall preach the Word, administer the sacraments, conduct public worship services ..." (Church Order, Article 12). The Orthodox Presbyterian Church's *Form of Government* states, "It is [the minister's] task to conduct the public worship of God," and identifies specifically prayer, reading and preaching the Scriptures, the administration of the sacraments, and the blessing (chapter VIII). The current "Directory for Worship" of the Presbyterian Church in America requires that the public reading of Scripture, public prayer, preaching and the administration of the sacraments all be conducted by the minster. This was true of the Westminster Assembly's original Directory as well, and reflects the historic Reformed understanding. The *Westminster Confession of Faith* (Glasgow: Free Presbyterian Publications, 1985) requires that neither sacrament "be dispensed by any, but by a minister of the Word, lawfully ordained" (XXVII.4). Dr. Robert Godfrey reminds us that this conviction "is implied in the Belgic confession." He writes, "Article 30 reads, 'we believe that this true church ought to be governed according to the spiritual order that our Lord has taught us in his Word. There should be ministers or pastors to preach the Word of God and administer the Sacraments.' It is also implicit in Article 16 of the Dort Church Order (1619), 'The office of the Minister is to continue in prayer and in the Ministry of the Word, to dispense the Sacraments, to watch over his fellow-brethren, Elders and Deacons, as well as the Congregation ...' There is no provision in either of these documents for anyone other than the minister to lead in worship" [W. Robert Godfrey, "Leading in Worship," (unpublished paper, n.d.);

an important though imperfect mechanism for weeding-out candidates for worship leadership that would otherwise prove theologically and morally unstable. The church is wise to retain it. Worship is ministry and ministers ought to lead it. Even if one rejects our argument for ordained public leadership, the implications of the qualifications for ministry found in Acts 6:1–5, 1 Timothy 3, and Titus 1 would require at least that all who take a public role in the public services of the church, from gathering the collection to ushering to leading the singing to reading Scripture, be subject to some form of careful examination in Christian experience, character, knowledge, and ethics. No one should be given a public role in the ministry of the church who is not known to be qualified doctrinally and morally to do so. The more public the responsibilities, the more thorough should be the examination. The danger of dishonor being brought to the name of Christ through the moral lapses of the immature or the theological errors of the uninstructed must be minimized. Careful examination of public servants will not eliminate the occasions of public reproach for the church, but it may reduce the frequency of those occasions.

Consistent with this, *ordained ministers ought to plan Reformed worship services.* Scottish theologian, W. G. Blaikie, writing in the 1890s of tendencies that, if anything, have become more pronounced today, explained that "the devotional part of the service is often conducted with little care and preparation." He asks, "is it conscientious, is it respectful to God, is it fair to the congregation, for the man who is to be their mouthpiece at the throne of grace, to rush into so solemn and momentous a

---

see also Charles G. Dennison, "Worship and Office," in Mark R. Brown, ed., *Order in the Offices* (Classic Presbyterian Government Resources: Duncansville, PA 1993), 157–79.

service with hardly a thought of it beforehand?"[5] Leading requires planning. Ministers ought to plan the order of service. They ought to decide which items to include and which to exclude. They ought to determine the Scripture readings and sermon texts. They ought to determine the placement of the six prayers (praise, confession of sin, thanksgiving, intercessions, illumination, and benediction), and how to distribute them (singularly or in combination). They ought to explain the transitions between the items in the service. They ought to decide which psalms and hymns to sing.

Some ministers make the mistake of turning over this responsibility to the music director or musician.[6] We question why this should be thought necessary or desirable. Is the musician better trained theologically to do so? Does he have greater knowledge of the content of the sermon and what would better tie in with it? Is he more aware of the needs of the congregation? We trust that the answer to these questions would be no. The only reasonable justification might be the obvious one, that the musician knows the hymnal better than the minister. This points out a larger problem. We have noted that many of the ministers serving Reformed churches today are men who were converted in high school or college through campus ministries.[7] Their formative spiritual experiences occurred in the context of para-church organizations. Many of these men went directly from college to seminary, and from there into the churches.

---

5   William G. Blaikie, *For the Work of the Ministry: A Manual of Homiletical and Pastoral Theology* (1896; Birmingham, Alabama: Solid Ground Christian Books, 2005), 166–167.

6   "The choice of hymns will, of course, be absolutely in your own hands," R. W. Dale, *Nine Lectures on Preaching* (London: Hodder and Stoughton, n.d.), 277.

7   See *Worshipping with Calvin*, Chapter 1.

Consequently they bring with them a vast ignorance of the church, its life, and its devotional forms.

We can think of a fine minister for whom the above description fits, who never attended Sunday night services, and when he became a solo pastor, had no interest in having a Sunday night service. He had no background and consequently no understanding of the ways in which Sunday night services function in the life of a congregation. The same is true for the order of service and hymnody. Many are pastoring churches who have never participated in a traditional Protestant service. Their experience of public devotional gatherings is limited to youth functions and college fellowships. Many are ignorant of the rich treasury of hymns that is the heritage of the church. I console myself in thinking that worship services sometimes look as they do because those leading them just don't know any better.

Consequently, we urge Reformed ministers to be students of the hymnal and psalter. W. G. T. Shedd (1820–1894), one of the outstanding American Reformed theologians of the nineteenth century whose *Dogmatic Theology* remains in print today, devoted considerable space to hymn-selection in his *Homiletics and Pastoral Theology* (1867). He urged the minister to study the hymnody of the church, and specifically the hymnbook of the church to which he ministers so that he will "obtain that taste and feeling for sacred lyric poetry which will guide him, as by a sure instinct, to the choice of the best and most appropriate hymns."[8] When I first began to lead worship services I asked a pianist in the church to play for me every single selection in the hymnal. I rated the words and tunes of the hymns on a scale of one to ten,

---

8   W. G. T. Shedd, *Homiletics and Pastoral Theology* (1867; Edinburgh: The Banner of Truth Trust, 1965), 270.

recorded my ratings, and then created a list of the several hundred earning a score seven or greater. On a similar list I continue to record the dates when hymns are used, color-coding the year for easy reference. The result has been not only a vast expansion of my knowledge of available and useful hymns, but a much broader exposure to outstanding hymnody for the congregation I serve. Both the new and old *Trinity Hymnal* are gold mines of devotional material. Study them. Covenant Seminary's Robert G. Rayburn (1915–1990), in his very useful study, *O Come, Let Us Worship*, estimates that the average congregation uses about thirty or thirty-five songs or hymns in a year.[9] Our congregation uses over 200 different hymns and psalms each year. This wider exposure enriches the worship of the church as well as the personal devotional life of the members of the congregation.

The minister himself also ought to control the worship service. He ought to control the service for all the reasons stated above. Given all the variables in the typical worship service and the constraints of time, he should be in a position to make instant adjustments, cutting and deleting, that will keep the service on schedule. How often do sermons get crowded out because the various "worship leaders" are pursuing their own agendas without an eye to the whole? The minister must keep the reins on the entire service.

Pastoral concern drives our insistence on ordained leadership in the church's public services. All of the foregoing decisions about the content and order of the church's public services directly impact the spiritual welfare of the church's members. The reading, preaching, praying, singing, and administering is all for the edification of the congregation. All of the safeguards

---

9   Robert Rayburn, *O Come Let Us Worship: Corporate Worship in the Evangelical Church* (Grand Rapids: Baker Book House, 1980), 226.

implicit in ordination protect the congregation from the likelihood of doctrinal or moral scandal, or even the loss incurred, the opportunities missed, the time squandered because of unprepared and incompetent leadership. Noel Due, in concluding his "Genesis to Revelation" survey of the biblical theology of worship, makes this same point. He argues that "the leading of worship in the public assembly must be seen as a facet of the pastoral care of the congregation ... For this reason," he continues, "the whole idea of a 'worship leader' who is a non-elder of the congregation (or at least directly accountable to the eldership) must be held up to question."[10] Pastors must lead in order to ensure that Christ's sheep are being fed the proper content and that the elements are being administered in their proper proportions.

Piety

Second, we must insist upon exemplary *piety* on the part of those who lead worship services. Years ago my brother-in-law, an elder in the Presbyterian Church of American, served on his church's search committee for an assistant minister. After interviewing half-a-dozen candidates he made an interesting comment. He noted that all of the candidates were young, sharp, and impressive. He said they all displayed keen wit, winsome personalities, and pastoral competence. However, he went on to observe, none of them seemed to be particularly devout. He didn't perceive much spiritual passion. Or disciplined devotion. Or ethical precision. Or a burden for souls. Or love for Christ. Or a zeal for the glory of God. They were well-educated, well-dressed, thoroughly trained

---

10   Noel Due, *Created for Worship: From Genesis to Revelation to You* (Geanies House, Fearn, Ross-shire, Scotland: Christian Focus Publications, 2005), 234,235.

for ministry, and skilled managers and program organizers. They were groomed for success. All the necessary ingredients were present. Yet they lacked spiritual *gravitas*, the seriousness and focus, the intensity and carefulness that comes from knowing the God of the Bible.

Deep piety, we would argue, is a necessary concomitant of supernatural religion. Spiritual worship requires spiritual leadership. The single most important factor in the leading of effective worship services is the spiritual maturity, the intensity, the zeal, and the depth of piety of those leading these services. Put negatively, one cannot effectively lead in prayer publicly if one is not devoted to prayer in the closet ("be much in secret prayer," urges Baxter)[11]; one cannot effectively lead in the study of God's word through its reading and preaching in public if one is not disciplined in the study of God's word in private; one cannot effectively lead the people of God into communion with Christ at the Table unless one pursues communion with Him as a habit of life. Exemplary piety is essential.[12]

What David Wells has called the "managerial revolution," coupled with a market-driven philosophy of church growth, has been tragically misleading at this point. The impression has been made that "success" in ministry is almost entirely a matter of

---

11 Richard Baxter, *The Reformed Pastor* (1656, reprint; Edinburgh: The Banner of Truth Trust, 1974), 61.

12 The vows for ordination for the Presbyterian Church in America include this: "Do you engage to be faithful and diligent in the exercise of all your duties as a Christian and a minister of the Gospel, whether personal or relational, private or public; and to endeavor by the grace of God to adorn the profession of the Gospel in your manner of life, and to *walk with exemplary piety* before the flock of which God shall make you overseer?" (*The Book of Church Order of the Presbyterian Church in America*, Office of the Stated Clerk, Sixth Edition, 2005, Sec. 21–5, my emphasis).

external factors. This may not have been said in so many words. Rather it has been implied by the emphasis that has been placed on everything but piety in discussions of growth. The keys to success, one might have thought, are to be found in discovering one's market niche, creative advertising, establishing a culture (e.g. casual), a format (late-night talk show), a style of music (pop), a type of building (non-churchy), and kind of message (topical sermons addressing felt needs). Success for the church (it has been implied) is to be found in programs and services, promotion and marketing, top-of-the-line sound and light systems, therapeutic or "practical" messages, managerial skill and professional leadership. The godliness of those leading the church is almost entirely overlooked. This is nowhere more obvious than in the aforementioned prevalence of young people, often teenagers, up front, leading worship services with instruments, music, and not infrequently painful transitional comments, who, unlike the ministers of yesteryear, are untested, untrained, and spiritually unqualified for the task. Attempts are being made to correct the problem of immaturity and carnality in "worship leaders," but the predominance of the young and theologically ignorant makes a solution unlikely.[13] Personality, it would seem, has been allowed to trump piety; format, faithfulness; style, substance; and technique, character. If John Angell James thought in 1847 that "An Earnest Ministry" was "the want of the times," one can scarcely imagine his response to the state of the public ministry of the church at the beginning of the twenty-first century.[14]

Previous generations of commentators are unanimous in their insistence that the single most important factor in worship

---

13   Kauflin, *Worship Matters*, 43–48; 252–253.

14   John Angell James, *An Earnest Ministry: The Want of the Times* (1847, Edinburgh: The Banner of Truth Trust, 1993).

leadership is the piety of the minister. Typical of the older understanding, Irish born and Princeton educated pastor Thomas Murphy (1823–1900), writing in 1877, says, "It should be laid down as our first principle that eminent piety is *the indispensable qualification* for the minister of the gospel."[15] He places piety before talents, learning, study, "favorable circumstances, or skill in working, or power in sermonizing." Without what he calls "high tone" or "eminent piety" or "elevated spirituality," then "nothing else will be of much account" in a given ministry.[16] "It is not possible for us to overestimate," he claims, "the importance of the deepest piety in those who are called to (the ministry's) sacred duties."[17] He devotes 53 pages to "The Pastor in the Closet," and 59 pages to "The Pastor in the Study," before he ever deals with public ministry. For Murphy, the foundation of public ministry is personal piety. "The public prayer of the pastor should be an echo of the deep earnestness which he has learned in the closet."[18] Again, "the one who is mighty in private with God will also be mighty in public."[19]

Similarly, Ebenezer Porter, one-time President of Andover Seminary (at the time a conservative seminary founded as an alternative to the too-liberal Yale), writing in 1834, claims that "the amount of usefulness in the ministry, depends in no small measure on the character of your public prayers." This is an extraordinary perspective in itself, given the tragic neglect of public prayer in evangelical churches today. One's "usefulness," or

---

15 My emphasis.
16 Thomas Murphy, *Pastoral Theology: The Pastor and the Various Duties of His Office* (1877; Audubon, New Jersey: Old Paths Publications, 1996), 38.
17 Ibid. 47.
18 Ibid. 214.
19 Ibid. 215.

what we might call one's "fruitfulness" or "success" depends, he says, not on one's skill as preacher or manager or counselor; not on one's intelligence, attractiveness, or disposition, but "on the character of (one's) public prayers." To this he adds, "if you would pray well in public, you must be a devout man."[20] For Porter, the foundation of pastoral success is found in devotion to God, and expressed in public prayer.

The Anglican Calvinist Charles Bridges, also writing in 1849, lists "spiritual character" as his first necessary qualification for Christian ministry, that is, that ministers should be "holy—in a peculiar sense men of God—men consecrated to God by a daily surrender of time and talents to his service ..."[21] Bridges spends 80 pages investigating the "causes of the want of success in the Christian ministry" that arise from the defects in the personal character of ministers.[22] Devotion to Christ, for Bridges, is central to fruitfulness in ministry.

J. W. Alexander, son of Archibald, Princeton Seminary professor and pastor, wrote in 1864 "of all people on earth, ministers most need the constant impressions derived from closet piety."[23] W. G. T. Shedd, writing in 1867, devotes 19 pages to the "Religious Character and Habits of the Clergyman," maintaining that "The foundation of influence in parochial life is the clergyman's

---

20 Ebenezer Porter, *Lectures on Homiletics & Preaching, and on Public Prayer; Together with Sermons and Letters* (New York: Flagg, Gould and Newman, 1834), 299,301.

21 Charles Bridges, *The Christian Ministry; With an Inquiry into the Cause of Its Inefficiency; With an Especial Reference to the Ministry of the Establishment* (London: Seeley, 1849), 26.

22 Ibid. 103–183.

23 James W. Alexander, *Thoughts on Preaching: Being Contributions to Homiletics* (1864; Edinburgh: The Banner of Truth Trust, 1975), III.

character, and the root of clerical character is piety."[24] R. L. Dabney, writing in 1870, says the same of preaching: "the prime qualification of the sacred orator is sincere, eminent piety."[25] Phillips Brooks, in his famous Yale lectures in 1877, identified "personal piety" as "that first of all the necessary qualities," which provide "the true conditions of a minister's success." Without this, he says, the preacher's work is "weary and unsatisfying and unprofitable work."[26] Further, "first among the elements of power which make success I must put the supreme importance of character, of personal uprightness and purity impressing themselves upon the men who witness them."[27] C. H. Spurgeon, writing in 1881 in a chapter entitled, "The Minister's Self-Watch," claims "Holiness in a minister is at once his chief necessity and his goodliest ornament."[28] Moreover, "we must cultivate the highest degree of godliness *because our work imperatively requires it.*"[29] Similar concerns can be seen in the other nineteenth century pastoral theologians such as: Lyman Beecher, William M. Taylor, William S. Plumer, John Brown, and William G. Blaikie.[30] We

---

24   Shedd, *Homiletics and Pastoral Theology*, 282.

25   Robert L. Dabney, *Sacred Rhetoric or Course of Lectures on Preaching* (1870; Edinburgh: The Banner of Trust Trust, 1979), 40.

26   Phillips Brooks, *Lectures on Preaching Delivered before the Divinity School of Yale College In January and February*, 1887 (New York: E.P. Dutton and Company, 1907), 37–39.

27   Ibid. 49.

28   C. H. Spurgeon, *Lectures to My Students*: A Selection from Addresses Delivered to the Students of the Pastors' College, Metropolitan Tabernacle (London: Passmore and Alabaster, 1881), I,14.

29   Ibid. I,12.

30   Henry Ward Beecher, *Yale Lectures on Preaching* (New York: Fords, Howard, and Hulbert, 1893), I, 37ff; William M. Taylor, *The Ministry of the Word* (1876; Harrisonburg, Virginia: Sprinkle Publications, 2003) 25–78; William S. Plumer, *Hints & Helps in Pastoral Theology* (1874; Harrisonburg, VA: Sprinkle Publications, 2003), 36–59; John Brown (ed.), *The Christian Pastor's Manual*

44 *Serving with Calvin*

cite this great cloud of witnesses with a sense of urgency, hoping that our contemporaries will give piety its due consideration.

Among twentieth century authors, by way of contrast, "piety" is a virtually unknown term, "godliness" an underappreciated necessity of ministry.[31] There would seem to be some fear in more recent times that too strong a connection between ministerial piety and fruitfulness in ministry might imply human self-sufficiency and a diminished role for the work of the Holy Spirit. Yet the Apostles, fully convinced of the necessity and priority of God's power in ministry (e.g. John 15:1–5; Romans 1:16; 2 Corinthians 2:14–3:6; 12:7–10), show no hesitancy in connecting piety and fruitfulness. The Apostle Paul's long lists of character qualities for church leaders are well known (1 Timothy 3; Titus 1). He urges Timothy, "discipline yourself for the purpose of godliness (*eusebeia*); for ... godliness is profitable for all things" (1 Timothy 4:7–8). Further,

> Pay close attention to yourself and to your teaching; persevere in these things; for as you do this you will ensure salvation both for yourself and for those who hear you. (1 Timothy 4:16)

Timothy's character and conduct ("yourself") are placed

(Ligonier, 1826, Pennsylvania: Soli Deo Gloria, 1991), with articles by Abraham Booth, "Pastoral Cautions," 66–104; John Erskine, "The Qualifications Necessary for Teachers of Christianity," and David Bostwich, "The Character and Duty of a Christian Preacher" in John Brown (ed.), *The Christian Pastor's Manual* (1826; Morgan, PA: Soli Deo Gloria Publications, 1991); cf. James M. Garretson, *Princeton and Preaching* (Edinburgh: The Banner of Truth Trust, 2005), 56–64; Blaikie, *The Work of the Ministry*, 180, 239–252.

31 Even D. Martyn Lloyd-Jones, *Preaching & Preachers* (Grand Rapids, Michigan: Zondervan, 1971), and John R Stott. *Between Two Worlds: The Art of Preaching in the Twentieth Century* (Grand Rapids, Michigan: William B. Eerdmans Publishing Company, 1982), are disappointing in this respect.

alongside of his "teaching" as items of parallel importance requiring careful scrutiny. Both are crucial for fruitful ministry. Character and conduct together in Christian leaders "ensure salvation," says the Apostle Paul. When the Apostle speaks of the ministry he conducts, he refers to "how devoutly and uprightly and blamelessly we behaved toward you believers" (1 Thessalonians 2:10, NASB). Apparently this was worth mentioning. Apparently this was a key ingredient in fruitful gospel ministry. Ministers are to live lives that are devout, upright, and blameless. He tells the Corinthians that "in holiness and godly sincerity, not in fleshly wisdom but in the grace of God, we have conducted ourselves in the world, and especially toward you" (2 Corinthians 1:12). Holy, godly, sincere, wise, gracious conduct is crucial in gospel ministry. Similarly the Apostle Peter directly relates Christian virtues such as "moral excellence "(*aretē*), "godliness" (*eusebeia*), and "love" (*agapē*) to fruitfulness (2 Peter 1:5–7):

> For if these qualities are yours and are increasing, they render you neither useless nor unfruitful in the true knowledge of our Lord Jesus Christ. (2 Peter 1:8)

Usefulness and fruitfulness in Christian service are directly related by the Apostle Peter to the possession and growth of Christian virtues.

The Apostles Peter and Paul were only saying what Jesus said before them: "apart from Me you can do nothing" (John 15:5). He is the True Vine and we are but branches. We have the responsibility to abide in Him if we are to have life and bear fruit (John 15:1–11). Dependent prayer is vital. "He is the best student in divinity that studies most upon his knees," William Gurnall (1617–1679) insists in his Puritan classic, *The Christian in Complete Armour*.[32] "How dare we pray in battle if we have never cried to the Lord while buckling on the harness," Spurgeon complains.[33] In the end managerial skill, entrepreneurial initiative, and market-awareness are at best icing on a cake that is baked in the prayer closet. At worst, they are a tragic diversion from the ordinary spiritual means that are the true keys to spiritual power and effectiveness. "My people's greatest need is my personal holiness," said the saintly Robert Murray M'Cheyne.[34]

Thankfully some voices are still being raised in support of piety over personality. Erroll Hulse contributed, "The Preacher and Piety" to *The Preacher & Preaching*.[35] David Eby affirms in connection with preaching, "Vigorous personal piety is indispensable. No ardent, active spirituality, no potent preaching."[36] J. I. Packer has reminded us the preacher "must speak as one who … knows the reality and power of which he speaks." The preacher, Packer maintains, "is called to be a living advertisement for the relevance and power of what he proclaims."[37] Perhaps the loudest voice has been that of David Wells, who right through his works has warned of the shifting

---

32 William Gurnall, *The Christian in Complete Armour: A Treatise of the Saints' War Against the Devil* (1662 and 1665, Edinburgh: The Banner of Truth Trust, 1964), Volume 1:172.

33 Spurgeon, *Lectures to My Students*, 45.

34 David Haslam, "Quotes from Robert Murray M'Cheyne," http://web.ukonline. co.uk/d.haslam/mccheyne/rmmquotes.htm.

35 Erroll Hulse, "The Preacher and Piety," in Samuel T. Logan, Jr., *The Preacher & Preaching Reviving the Art in the Twentieth Century* (Phillipsburg, New Jersey: Presbyterian & Reformed Publishing Company, 1986), 62–90.

36 David Eby, *Power Preaching for Church Growth: The Role of Preaching in Growing Churches* (Ross-shire, Great Britain: Christian Focus Publications, 1996), 80.

37 Packer, "Why Preach?" in Logan (ed), *Preacher & Preaching*, 16,17.

job descriptions of the clergy, from pastor/preachers to manager/ marketers.[38] The church is not selling a product it is presenting a Person. Consistency between the character of the One presented and the one presenting is indispensable if our message is to be credible. Alec Motyer states simply, "It is not the most able who are blessed in their ministry, but the most holy."[39]

We must continue to insist that faithful, effective and fruitful *public* worship is *supernatural* worship. It is *spiritual* worship. It is Holy Spirit inspired and animated. Such worship can never be duplicated by gregarious but superficial leaders, however charming they may be. It cannot be simulated through use of energizing music, stimulating visual media and talented but worldly speakers, though it may be counterfeited. We must also understand and be heard saying that traditional Reformed worship is not a formula that if implemented by the numbers, I's dotted and T's crossed, that guarantees success. Pious, devout, virtuous leadership is indispensable if worship is to be faithful, effective, and fruitful.

Well might we ask with the Apostle Paul, "Who is adequate for these things?" (2 Corinthians 2:16). We will never be up to the task in our own strength, virtue, or piety. "Our adequacy is from God," the Apostle Paul answers, and we with him (2 Corinthians 3:5). High as the standards are, we must reach them *in Christ*, however imperfectly. There is a difference between not fulfilling the New Testament standards and imperfectly fulfilling them.[40] We must insist that our leaders fulfill the requirements of piety, though they do so imperfectly. Robert Murray M'Cheyne's

---

38 e.g. David Wells, *God in the Wasteland: The Reality of Truth in a World of Fading Dreams* (Grand Rapids, Michigan: Wm. B. Eerdmans Publishing Co.), 72ff.

39 J. Alec Motyer, *Preaching? Simple Teaching on Simply Preaching* (Ross-shire, Scotland: Christian Focus Publications, 2013), 131.

40 See more on this theme, Chapter IV, "Preach the Whole Gospel."

48   *Serving with Calvin*

dictum will ever remain true: "A holy minister is an awful weapon in the hand of God."[41]

Humility

Third, those who lead worship must be *humble*. Recall John Chrysostom's (c. 347–407) answer when asked what were the three most important Christian virtues. First, he said, was humility. Second, he insisted, was humility. And third, he maintained, was, yes, humility. Every week a crowd gathers to see the minister lead a service and hear what he has to say. This can be heady stuff and the road to ruin for the weak. An exaggerated assessment of one's importance comes easily to ministers. An inflated sense of one's wisdom, and with that, one's indispensability, are occupational hazards. We confess surprise and dismay at the size or even the obtrusiveness of many clergy egos, a vice to which, we report to our compounded dismay, even the most traditional of Reformed ministers are not exempt. Vanity clearly is a major motivating factor for some church leaders in their drive for "success," however it may be defined. Making a name for oneself, so fundamental to worldly ambitions, is not absent from the clergy's private lists of priorities. The need for recognition, for worldly affirmation, for success, perhaps more than any other factors, contribute to the temptation to compromise the gospel and gospel ministry, to water it down or spruce it up.

---

41   Cited in Logan, *Preacher & Preaching*, 12, 13, 63. The whole citation is as follows: "In great measure, according to the purity and perfections of the instrument, will be the success. It is not great talents which God blesses so much as great likeness to Jesus. A holy minister is an awful weapon in the hand of God." The original source is Andrew A. Bonar, *Robert Murray M'Cheyne: Memoir and Remains* (London: Banner of Truth, 1966), 281.

For ministers to serve faithfully and fruitfully a fundamental death to self must take place (2 Corinthians 4:12). Jesus demanded self-denial and cross-bearing (Matthew 16:24–25). The apostles crucified the flesh and its lusts (Galatians 5:24). Jesus commended poverty of spirit and meekness as among the highest of virtues (Matthew 5:3, 5). The greatest of all, He said, must be the servant of all (Matthew 20:25–28). No one in recent times made more of the need to die to self than did William Still (1911–1997), over 50 years the pastor of the Gilcomston South Church of Scotland congregation in Aberdeen. "You will have to die," he told ministerial students over 50 years ago, "not only to your own sin, but to self in many of its most seemingly innocent and legitimate aspects, for only then can the death and resurrection power of Jesus Christ be communicated to men."[42] Failure in ministry comes, he says, from "not living in an instant, tensile experience of the death/ resurrection of Christ, dead to all but the mighty purpose of God."[43] "To minster fruitfully," he says, "you must minister as a dead man ... Every time you essay to minister there must be a new death. 'Deaths oft': 'I die daily': said Paul. This is the glorious agony of the man who is used of God amidst the opposition of the world, the church, and certainly the devil, that he is ever a dying man."[44] Ministers must die to ambition, die to success, die to ego, die to recognition, die to power and control. "The Word will never come through a living man," says Still, "he must be dead."[45] Faithfulness and eternal fruitfulness are directly related to humbly surrendering our aims and dreams to the greater cause of the glory of Christ.

---

42 William Still, *Work of the Pastor* (Aberdeen: Didasko Press, 1976), 21.
43 Ibid. 58.
44 Ibid. 78,79.
45 Ibid. 96.

Wisdom

Fourth, those who lead worship must be *wise*. Wisdom is a much neglected category of Christian discipleship. Yet the Bible gives it a great deal of emphasis, both directly (the Old Testament "Wisdom Books" of Proverbs, Ecclesiastes, Job, and various wisdom psalms) and more generally. Wisdom has much to say about how we order our worship.

Wisdom, according to the Bible, is *a correct understanding of the nature of things* (truth, people, places, events, nature).[46] The Puritan George Swinnock (1627–1673), in his classic work, "The Incomparableness of God," defines wisdom as "a right understanding of things, and the ordering ourselves and actions suitable to that understanding."[47] "The wise," says J. I. Packer, "are realists who adjust to the way things are."[48] Wisdom is understanding what to do, given the nature of things in creation, providence, and redemption. Wisdom is the correct application of truth to circumstances. It is gained both through Scripture (e.g. Psalm 19, 119) and through careful observation of the world. For example, Jesus expects that His disciples will have discerned the relative virtues of sand and rock as foundational material for buildings, so as to build on the latter and avoid the former. He expects they will have learned enough about the properties of wine and wineskins so as not to waste new wine in old wineskins (Matthew 7:24–27; 9:16–17). They will have learned these things

---

46 See Terry L. Johnson, *The Case for Traditional Protestantism* (Edinburgh: The Banner of Truth Trust, 2004), II, 30–46.

47 George Swinnock, "The Incomparableness of God in His Being, Attributes, Works, and Word," in *The Works of George Swinnock*, Vol. IV (1868; Edinburgh: The Banner of Truth Trust, 1992), 104.

48 J. I. Packer, "Theology and Wisdom," in J. I. Packer & Sven K. Soderlund (eds), *The Way of Wisdom: Essays in Honor of Bruce K. Waltke* (Grand Rapids: Zondervan Publishing House, 2000), 8.

(and so grasp the point of His teaching) not so much by reading Bible verses, but by observation of the nature of the world around them. This is the wisdom of the book of Proverbs. Wisdom there is not so much "by the book" but by shrewd observation. "I looked out of my window and saw," he says (Proverbs 7:6). The wise are those who "go to the ant" and observe (Proverbs 6:6–11). The wise will know how and when to tend their fig trees, their flocks, and till their land, not because of the commands of God in Scripture, but because they know how the created order works, they know the will of God as observed in the natural order of things (Proverbs 27:18, 23; 28:19). Conversely the unwise or foolish are those who harm themselves and others by foolishly ignoring what nature reveals. "Does not even nature teach you?" the Apostle Paul asks (1 Corinthians 11:14). The unwise exchange the natural (what corresponds to human nature as observed) for the unnatural (what is contrary to human nature as observed) (Romans 1:26). Wisdom, says D. E. Johnson, in his comments on Colossians 2:2–3, is "comprehensive insight into the nature of things, the meaning of life, the way to discern appropriate causes of action in various circumstances."[49]

Ephesians 5:15ff could serve as a case study in wisdom.

> Therefore be careful how you walk, not as unwise men, but as wise, making the most of your time, because the days are evil. So then do not be foolish, but understand what the will of the Lord is. And do not get drunk with wine, for that is dissipation, but be filled with the Spirit (Ephesians 5:15–18).

---

49 S. W. Johnson, *Him We Proclaim: Preaching Christ from All the Scriptures* (Phillipsburg, New Jersey: P&R Publishing, 2007), 84.

The Apostle Paul urges that believers "walk not as unwise men but as wise." Then he identifies specific areas in which we are to do so. The first has to do with the *stewardship of time*. We are to be "making the most of (our) time, because the days are evil." To obey this command we must understand both the priorities the Bible establishes and the nature of the moment. For example, at any given moment should one's available time be devoted to work, the family, leisure, or the church? To answer that question requires that we carefully discern an array of variables. If I don't concentrate on my work might I lose my job? Or, has the family been neglected? Or, is this a time properly devoted to leisure? Or, should gospel work receive priority attention at the moment? There are no formulas, no rule books, no works of casuistry that can answer these questions as they are raised at any given moment. Only wisdom can determine the priority.

Next the Apostle Paul counsels *moderation in the alcohol consumption*. "Do not be drunk with wine," he says. How do I fulfill that command? I must understand the characteristics of both myself and the alcoholic beverage I am consuming. Again, no book can calculate for me ahead of time the relationship between the beverage, my body weight, my immediate food consumption, and the other factors which may determine whether or not I cross the line that separates sobriety from drunkenness.

The Apostle Paul goes on to address husbands and wives (Ephesians 5:21ff). How is a wife to be "subject" to her husband and yet not be a doormat? How is a husband to lead and not be a tyrant? The answer is, good wifery and good husbandry requires that one be a good student of one's Bible, circumstances, *and one's spouse*. One must understand both what the Bible teaches about the mutual obligations of husbands and wives *and* the nature of one's spouse *and* the circumstances of any given occasion. "Live with your wives in an understanding way," the Apostle Peter counsels husbands (1 Peter 3:7). For one to be an understanding husband, one must be a keen student of Scripture and of one's wife, as well as the circumstances of the moment.

Where is the line that separates faith from presumption? Wise stewardship from uncharitable tight-fistedness? Modesty from immodesty? Love from undisciplined indulgence? Discipline from oppression? Hard work from idolatry of vocation? Leisure from sloth? All of these determinations lie between the lines of Scripture and can only be determined by wisdom. We can understand why the Apostle Paul's major prayers in the New Testament all concentrate on wisdom. The disciples of Christ need wisdom, knowledge, and enlightenment (Ephesians 1:17–21). They need knowledge and discernment if they are to "approve the things that are excellent" (Philippians 1:9–11). They need knowledge, wisdom, and understanding if they are to "walk in a manner worthy of the Lord, to please Him in all respects, bearing fruit in every good work" (Colossians 1:9–12).

We have extended our digression on wisdom because wisdom is vital if Reformed worship is to be properly implemented. Church leaders must correctly discern the variables. It is important to understand that nearly everything that we do in worship, as in life, must be governed by wisdom. God has given us the basic elements of worship. But then wisdom takes over. We are to preach, but which text and how long? We are to sing, but which song? We are to pray, but about what and at what length? Where is the line that separates the reverent from irreverent? The appropriate from the inappropriate? The suitable from the unsuitable? The Bible expects us to discern what is "proper" or "fitting" or "suitable" (*prepo* 1 Corinthians 11:13; Titus 2:1; 1 Timothy 2:10; Ephesians

5:3) or "respectable" (ESV) (*kosmiō*—1 Timothy 2:9) as well as what is "out of place" (NIV) or "not fitting" (NASV) (*anēken*— Ephesians 5:4). It expects us to pursue "whatever is honorable, is lovely, is excellent, and is worthy of praise" (Philippians 4:8), yet it never defines any of these terms or identifies where the line may be found that separates the proper, suitable and fitting, honorable, etc. from the improper, unsuitable, unfitting, and dishonorable, and so on. The questions of what to sing, what to preach, what text to read, what tone to set, and the time to allot to each element are all determined by wisdom. Wisdom, in almost every case, is found by rightly combining the Bible's teaching with the circumstances in which it is applied.

The breadth of wisdom's reach explains why the regulative principle of worship resolves few of the conflicts in the worship wars. "We preach, read Scripture, sing Scripture, pray, and administer the sacraments in our services," says one advocate of the new worship, "so what's the problem?" Nearly everyone across the Reformed spectrum claims allegiance to the regulative principle. The devil, one might say, is in the details. *Nearly every decision in worship* (beyond disputes over the elements) *is made between the lines of Scripture*, where wisdom must lead us to right conclusions.

Every church has its own history, time, place, affiliations, commitments, and mixture of people. Together these constitute a church culture. Typically church cultures change slowly. It would be foolish, if not arrogant, to ignore the culture of a church when attempting to implement even necessary change. When I first came to Independent Presbyterian Church in 1987 I received wise counsel not to change anything for five years, which counsel I followed, mostly. "You need to think of yourself as turning the Queen Mary," I was told. Move slowly. Expository preaching, longer Bible readings, Scripture-enriched prayers, psalm and hymn singing, more frequent observance of the Lord's Supper, and a more reverential tone are all crucial, but they may need to be introduced gradually, with great care, and with pastoral sensitivity. Don't change everything at once. Teach, educate, and inform. Don't overwhelm the congregation with what for them is new. Be wise about their capacity for novelty. Don't kill the patient, or more likely, don't drive him off.

Anyone tempted to see this counsel as compromise may wish to consult again the history of Reformed Protestantism. It's true that Zwingli began to preach *lectio continua* in January of 1519, barely a year after the beginning of Luther's reforms. Yet not until the publishing of *De canone missae* (*On the Canon of the Mass*) in August of 1523 did the mass begin to be reformed. Even then, vestments were retained, the use of the *Kyrie eleison, Gloria*, collects, *Sursum corda*, and *Sanctus* continued, as did the use of Latin and the essential structure of the liturgy and its ceremonies. Six years into the reform movement Reformed Protestants were still conducting their services in Latin! It was only because of pressure from underneath, from the discontented masses, that the "cleansing" of the churches was undertaken in the summer of 1524 as paintings and decorations were whitewashed, and relics, statutes, ornaments, and vestments were removed. Zwingli's critique of the mass, his *Commentary on True & False Religion*, was published in March of 1525, following which the mass was abolished and the reformed liturgy approved in April 1525. However, note this was seven and one-half years after the posting of the 95 theses and nearly six and one-half years since the reform of preaching in Zurich. *Progress was slow and pastorally calculated.*

The same caution was shown in the French-speaking world

as William Farel's *La Manière et fasson*, "the first manual of evangelical worship in the French language," was not published until 1525.[50] When the pace of reform was accelerated by Calvin and Farel in 1537, they were banished by the Genevan Town Council in 1538. Let the impatient beware. A similar story of slow change may be told in all the cities of the Reformation. Even Luther, who proposed a German Mass in 1519, and who, as we have noted, in *The Babylonian Captivity of the Church* (in 1520) saw the need "to alter almost the entire external form of the churches and introduce ... a totally different kind of ceremonies," was slow to act.[51] Alarmed by an iconoclastic riot in Wittenberg in early 1522, his *Formula Missae* was published in December 1523 bringing some reforms. However, like Zwingli's first effort, Latin was retained. His concern, as he stated in his preface, was for those who were weak in faith and the damage that might be done by "the fickle and fastidious spirits who rush in like unclean swine without faith or reason, and who delight only in novelty and tire of it as quickly, when it has worn off."[52] Prodded further by the introduction of German language liturgies in Strasbourg, Zurich, and Basal, Luther published his *Deutsche Messe* on October 29, 1525, eight years after the 95 Theses almost to the day. Even then, his reforms were cautious.

Those with an awareness of what is pastorally wise and politically achievable will realize that the reform of worship takes time, that change comes slowly, that customs become entrenched,

---

50   Bard Thompson, *Liturgies of the Western Church* (Philadelphia: Fortress Press, 1961), 186.

51   Martin Luther, "On the Babylonian Captivity of the Church," in James Atkinson (ed.) *Three Treatises* (Philadelphia: Fortress Press, 1970), 152, 153; See *Worshipping with Calvin*, Chapter 3.

52   Cited in Quill, "Liturgical Worship," in Pinson (ed.), *Perspectives on Worship*, 29; from *Luther's Works*, 53:19; Thompson, *Liturgies of the Western Church*, 106–107.

and that alteration is difficult and costly. Jesus taught his disciples "as they were able to hear it" (Mark 4:5). Implement historic Reformed worship as the people are able to receive it. Be content for services to evolve naturally, organically, and steadily into the priorities of Reformed ministry. If today's Christians are to worship with Calvin, it is vital that the church have pastoral leadership that is devout, humble, and wise.

✣ Chapter 3 ✣

Preparing the Services

Having established the commitment to a properly prepared, thoroughly examined, devout, humble, and wise pastoral leadership, consideration must now be given to guidelines for the services themselves. The minister will play a key role in establishing each of the items which follows. Sessions and boards of elders must approve of the principles governing and characteristics shaping the services. But pastoral leadership is the key to seeing that it is effectively done. We will divide our discussion into two somewhat overlapping categories. First, *general* considerations: what we mean and don't mean by ministry in public worship services; and, second, *specific* counsel: the characteristics of those services.

60   *Serving with Calvin*

General considerations

Public Services of Worship[1]

We begin, first, by focusing our comments on public worship services. We are not addressing the characteristics of private or informal gatherings, or church business meetings, or small group gatherings, or of family worship. We are urging of the Lord's Day assembly of Christ's disciples that we *first maintain the integrity of worship services as public services of worship*. We are saying two things.

1. They must be *worship* services. The many questions about what one should do or should not do in worship may easily be answered by asking the question, is it worship? The consideration is not do the people like it, does it make them feel good, or is it popular? Rather one should ask, *is a given activity a legitimate element of the church's public devotional life?* Does it give expression to the people's praise of God or demonstrate their submission to his will? If not, eliminate it. If so, there are still a few questions to ask of it, but one is well on the way to having a final answer. At the church I serve we have very different settings in which we worship. In the morning we meet in a nearly perfect example of Protestant architecture on a grand scale. Complete with a fourteen foot high solid mahogany "high pulpit," it is one of the most beautiful places of worship in North America. During the summer we travel a few miles down the road to a camp facility where we have an informal evening service in what looks like a camp lodge. A few years back we became so

---

1   The following pages have considerable material that has been reworked and altered from the form in which they originally appeared in *The Pastor's Public Ministry* (Greenville, SC: Reformed Academic Press, 2001), and in the *Westminster Theological Journal* before that.

3 — Preparing the Services

informal in that setting, with hymn requests, prayer requests, a "light and lively" atmosphere, that we judged that the services were close to losing their integrity as *worship* services. Today the services are still informal, in that we sit in removable chairs, we dress more casually, and I preach more dialogically. Yet with an opening prayer of praise that is lengthy and weighty, with the reading of the law and a confession of sin, with a distinct prayer of intercession, and a metrical psalm, the service is once again clearly a service of worship, with the "reverence and awe" that is to characterize our praise (Hebrews 12:28).

Perhaps one takes the view that the church's public gatherings are more than times of worship. Perhaps one is convinced that they ought also be times for "sharing," conducting some church business, transmitting information, etc. If so (though I don't grant the point), then still one ought to differentiate between worship per se and these other activities. For example, announcements can be given before the call to worship. If the congregation wants a "hymn sing," this also can be done before the service starts. Business meetings can be held after the benediction. These too are wisdom issues. Protect the integrity of the church's public devotional life by not allowing it to be undermined by distracting non-liturgical activity.

2. They are *public* worship services. By this we mean that the worship of the Christian assembly should clearly be public not private, and congregational not personal. There is no need to cater to the needs of individual devotion in public worship. Personal confession of sin and personal petitions can be taken care of in private, at home. The concerns of the public assembly are public. It is necessary in the nature of things, in a public service, for the individual to subordinate his immediate state of mind to the requirements of group expression. A person may not "feel" like

God is "Holy, Holy, Holy," but he praises him as such anyway. He may not feel like confessing his sin or confessing his faith that day. Yet he rightly joins in because these are public, congregational, collective exercises, expressing the faith and convictions of the community as a whole. Of course it ought to be the aim of every worshiper for his heart to match his mouth. But in the meantime he adopts the public language by faith. Without this step of faith, public worship becomes impossible, as each individual searches for language which more perfectly express the condition of his own heart. Public worship need not be "Ipod-ized." It need not collapse into an anarchy of individual expression. Our congregational hymns, psalms, creeds, and public prayers express *what we believe and aspire to be.*

So then, the *exercises* of public worship services are *public and congregational.* There is a tendency to add to public worship moments for silent and personal prayer, moments for personal confession, and moments for personal intercession which we see as being entirely unnecessary, even contrary to the nature of the service as a public service. If it is necessary to add such activities in order to encourage "personal participation," what are we to make of the rest of the service? Is the congregation not participating during the minister's prayers and preaching or during congregational responses such as songs and creeds?

Nothing we do should say or imply that worship only becomes authentic when participants withdraw into individual worship. Leaders should not be encouraged to close their eyes up front, ostentatiously, as though it were necessary to escape to solitude, one's own little world as it were, to experience true worship. Any act or gesture which tends to isolate oneself from the others is contrary to the nature of public, collective worship.

All congregational responses should be collective and in unison.

Idiosyncratic gestures and postures should be discouraged, as they tend to separate and/or draw attention. This one should not be raising his hands, or that one kneeling, or this other one standing, or that one with eyes open, or another with eyes closed. *All of the movements, gestures, and postures of public worship should be understood as public and congregational in nature.*

In addition, because the services are public, its *concerns* are public. Richard J. Mouw, past President of Fuller Theological Seminary complains about preachers who "seem convinced that I have come to church eager to be updated about their daily lives."[2] "Don't clutter each sermon with whom you saw, and what you watched and where you shopped," agrees William Brosend, professor of homiletics at the School of Theology, Sewanee: The University of the South.[3] The intimacy and informality that may be appropriate to private devotions or family worship are often unsuitable for services that are public. One may wear one's pajamas for personal devotions, or digress momentarily on "what's for supper," but such is not advised for the public. One may ask questions about the Bible of one's four-year-old during family worship, but such is unlikely to be edifying during public worship, however cute it may be. In a house church or small group setting it may be appropriate to take personal prayer requests, to confess particular sins, to pray personal petitions, to have personal testimonies. However, once a gathering increases in number beyond a half-dozen or so these matters must be handled in a more generalized way. Otherwise the congregation may easily become cliquish, or be perceived as such. Or it may get bogged

---

2   Richard J. Mouw, "Preaching Worth Pondering," *Fuller Focus* 5 (November 1996) 2–3.

3   William Brosend, "Enough About Me: There is no I in Preach," in *Christian Century*, Vol. 127, No. 4, February 23, 2010.

64   *Serving with Calvin*

down in matters of personal but not general relevance.[4] These too
are wisdom issues. Intercessions should be of a general nature, as
should the confession of sin, as should the confession of faith, or
else the congregation will quickly divide into the in-group whose
needs and experiences are known and publicly recognized, and all
the rest. There is an informality or familiarity that is inappropriate
for public gatherings. Maintain the measure of formality that is
suited to services that are public.

Ordinary means

*Second, the ministry we have in mind is an ordinary means
ministry.* How do the benefits of what Christ did long ago and
far away get to us today? We receive these benefits by the Holy
Spirit working through the word. Yes, God can work where
and when He wills, with means and apart from means. We
have heard of the mother of a Fuller Seminary professor who
was converted listening to Simon & Garfunkel's song, "Mrs.
Robinson" ("Jesus loves you more than you will know"). We
are not limiting the freedom of God when we urge focus on the
appointed means of grace. We only mean to urge that the church,
for its part, ought to concentrate on those means which God
has promised to bless. There are many well-meaning, loud but
distracting voices promising "success" for ministers who embrace
the new pattern, the new paradigm, the new program, heretofore
undiscovered in the history of the church! There will always be
another Yellow School Bus, hand-bell choir, or XYZ discipleship
program promising to revolutionize a given ministry. Rather
than expend energy and resources testing for novelties that God

---

4   "Great individuality in public prayer, dwelling on things appropriate to (the
     minister's) own condition, but not theirs, is an impertinence and a wrong," warns
     Blaikie (*Work of the Ministry*, 174).

might sovereignly bless, but to which no promise of blessing is attached, focus instead on the reading, preaching, singing, and praying of the word of God, and the administration of God's visible words, the sacraments of baptism and the Lord's Supper. To those inclined to see worship as spectacle or entertainment our answer is this: "If they do not hear Moses and the prophets, neither will they be convinced if someone should rise from the dead" (Luke 16:31). What could possibly be more spectacular than to raise the dead? Yet Jesus says even a resurrection has less efficacy than the simple proclamation of the gospel message, never mind light shows, pyrotechnics, skits, dance, and musical performances. Those who stage spectacles are wasting time and energy better spent proclaiming Moses and the Prophets, Jesus and the Apostles. Such a ministry is not likely to attract attention. Denomination publications and national magazines are not likely to devote feature stories to an "ordinary means" ministry. The media, even Christian media, is chronically devoted to the new, the novel the idiosyncratic, the unusual, and allergic to the tried, the true, the tested, and the traditional. This bias should not surprise or dissuade us. Commit the church and its ministry to the ordinary means of the word, sacraments, and prayer, and God will be pleased, and you will not be disappointed. "God's method of church growth," says Alec Motyer, "is preaching the word, watered by believing prayer."[5]

Frequency

Third, the services we have in mind are the morning and evening services of the Lord's Day. Worship is ministry. This has been a constant theme for us. The claims of contemporary churches

---

5   Motyer, *Preaching?*, 18.

notwithstanding, the church ministers to its community primarily at its Sunday services. We've noted that for all churches there is a dramatic drop off in participation once ministry moves away from the Lord's Day.[6] The vast majority of people are reached through gospel ministry, such as it is, on Sunday.

The second service, the evening service seems threatened with extinction in our day. Sunday evening attendance in the Christian Reformed Church (CRC) has plummeted from 56% of members in 1992 to 24% in 2007. Services have been cancelled; others have been replaced by an alternative such as small groups.[7] Given the CRC's heritage of Sunday evening worship, the numbers can only be worse for other evangelical churches. Yet the retention of this service is vital for a church convinced of the efficacy of "ordinary means" ministry. The ordinary means of grace must have sufficient context within which to operate if they are to realize their promised impact. A second service, 52 weeks a year, provides the church with a total of 104 opportunities to read, preach, sing, pray, and administer the word. Eliminate the evening service and that number is cut in half. Miss a Sunday a month or so, as is common today, even among the best of members in our highly mobile society, and the number drops to 40. This means, for example, that over the course of a year the congregation will hear 40 chapters of Scripture read instead of 104. They may sing 40 metrical psalms (one per service) instead of 104, and hear 40 expositions of Scripture rather than 104. Over a five-year period

---

6   For Warren participation plummets from 10,000 on Sundays to a committed group of 3,500 who agree to have daily quiet times, tithe, to be active in a small group. If 75% of these attend their small group each week, just over 2,600 of the 10,000 are involved in a weekly basis, a 74% decline. *Purpose Driven Church*, 132–134.

7   Matt Vande Bunte, "Sunday night services a fading tradition," *Christian Century*, October 19, 2010, Vol. 127, No 21, 14.

the difference is even more dramatic: 200 chapters read, psalms sung, and expositions heard versus 520; over 10 years, 400 versus 1040. Are believers sanctified by the truth (John 17:17)? Does faith come by hearing the word of Christ (Romans 10:17)? Do Reformed churches rely on the Holy Spirit working through the word? Then these differences in the quantity of Scripture read, preached, sung, prayed, and administered are crucial, and a second service is vital.

Furthermore, the evening or second service is standard Reformed practice. It "was established in the earliest stages of the Reformation in the 1520s and 1530s," says Scott Clark.[8] Its roots are found in the pattern of morning and evening daily sacrifices (Exodus 29:38–43; Ezra 3:3) and the prayers and praise that accompanied those sacrifices. The Chronicler records the singing of Psalms 105, 96, and 106 in connection with the offering of sacrifices (1 Chronicles 16:8–43; cf. 2 Chronicles 6:4–7; 23:13, 18; 29:20–28; 30:21) and the offering of prayers (1 Chronicles 29:11–22; 2 Chronicles 6:1–42; 30:16–20; Ezra 9:5–15). From Nehemiah it's clear that Scripture reading and exposition were also joined with prayer in the worship of Israel (Nehemiah 8:1–18; 9:3–38). The sacrifices of the temple were not to be duplicated in the synagogues of local communities, but the psalmody, prayer, Scripture reading, and exposition could be, and were, morning and evening. The devotional pattern of the temple became the devotional pattern of the synagogue and the prayer closet. Already in Scripture King David is found lifting up his hands (i.e. in prayer) "as the evening offering" was being presented (Psalm 141:1–2). References to morning prayer

---

8   R. Scott Clark, *Recovering the Reformed Confession: Our Theology, Piety, and Practice* (Phillipsburg, NJ: P&R Publishing, 2008), 294.

68   *Serving with Calvin*

are frequent in the psalms (e.g. Psalm 5:3; 59:16; 63:1; 88:13; 119:147). The people of God structured their devotional life after the pattern of the Temple. The synagogue continued this pattern, holding two services each Sabbath. The early church, in turn, followed the pattern of the synagogue. Pliny the Younger's letter to the emperor Trajan (c. 112) reports two services, and Tertullian (c. 160–c.215) defended as normative the practice of morning and evening prayer, as did Cyprian (c. 200–c.258). The medieval church expanded this pattern but never contracted it. "The practice of morning and evening services (matins and vespers) continued," says Clark, "through the medieval church and into the Reformation."[9]

The *Book of Common Prayer* (1549, 1559, 1662), the *Heidelberg Catechism* (1563), the Canons of Dort (1619), and Westminster *Directory* (1644) all call for two services each Lord's Day. The argument for twice daily worship from morning and evening sacrifices was standard among Reformed writers. Baxter, for example, citing the various Old Testament texts, concludes, "There is at least equal reason that gospel worship should be as frequent."[10] Twice-Sunday services was the practice among the Puritans of England and New England, the Presbyterians of Scotland, and among most English-speaking Protestants until recent times. "The entire Christian tradition, East and West,

---

9   Ibid. 338.
10 Richard Baxter, "A Christian Directory," in *The Practical Works of Richard Baxter*, Vol. 1 (1673; Ligonier, PA: Soli Deo Gloria Publications, 1990), 422. Granted this argument is made in the advocacy of family worship but the same principle applies to public worship on the Lord's Day. For those who resist his logic he admonishes: "Let them know that if they will open their eyes, and recover their appetites, and feel their sins, and observe their daily wants and dangers, and get a heart that loveth God, these reasons will then seem sufficient to convince them of so sweet, and profitable, and necessary a work" (422).

ancient and medieval, Roman and Protestant, has recognized the fundamental ... pattern of morning and evening service," says Clark.[11] The restoration of the second service is a vital plank in any program of church reform today.

Indispensable to the discipline of morning and evening worship on the Lord's Day is a strong doctrine of the Christian Sabbath. Though there has been some debate about Calvin's view, Scott Clark conclusively summarizes the biblical, theological, and historical data demonstrating both the antiquity of first-day of the week Christian Sabbatarianism and the uniformity of the Reformed tradition on the matter. Clark cites Richard Gaffin regarding the practice of Sabbath observance among the continental Reformed as well as Britain's Puritans: "Here we may speak of a Reformed consensus, or, as it may also be put, a consensus of generic Calvinism."[12] That consensus included observing the Lord's Day as an entire day devoted to worship and rest and excluding ordinary secular activity. Twice on Sunday worship has always been a part of that observance.

The evening service is likely to prove unsustainable without a strong doctrine of the Christian Sabbath. Sabbath and second service are "co-dependent," we might say. Without an evening service, the stretch of time from noon to midnight may prove too long and too tempting ordinarily to resist indulging "worldly

---

11 Ibid. 338,339; see also C. W. Dugmore, "Canonical Hours" in *New Westminster Dictionary of Liturgy*, ed. J. G. Davies, who connects the dots: "the prayers at dawn and at dusk ... derive, through the hours of prayer in the synagogue, from the hours of sacrifice in the Jerusalem Temple" (140).

12 Clark, *Recovering the Reformed Confession*, 320; c.f. Richard B. Gaffin, Jr., *Calvin and the Sabbath* (Ross-shire, UK: Christian Focus, 1998); and "Westminster and the Sabbath," in *The Westminster Confession into the 21st Century: Essays in Remembrance of the 350th Anniversary of the Westminster Assembly*, ed. J. Ligon Duncan, II (Ross-shire, UK: Christian Focus, 2004) 123–144.

employments and recreations," as the *Shorter Catechism* calls them. The evening service establishes a congenial rhythm of worship–rest–worship that is conducive of Sabbath observance. Remove the evening service and the temptation to run to the store, vacuum the family room, watch the ballgame, balance the checkbook, etc., may prove overwhelming.

Conversely, deny or even underemphasize the Christian Sabbath, specifically the identity of the whole day as the Lord's Day, as designed for worship, "holy rest," and works of necessity and mercy, and an important motivation to return Sunday evening may vanish. Saturday or mid-week evening gatherings can never replace Sunday as the time of Christian worship. After 2000 years of Apostolic example and church witness it remains normative, the popularity of alternative times notwithstanding (John 20:1, 19, 26; Acts 20:7; 1 Corinthians 16:2; Revelation 1:10). Similarly if the Lord's Day becomes the "Lord's Morning," or even the "Lord's Hour," if Sunday afternoon and evening are up for grabs among competing interests, secular and religious, an evening service will be very difficult to sustain. Anglican bishop J. C. Ryle (1816–1900) claimed, typically of previous generations, that the Sabbath was "the best safeguard" of the Christian religion's status in a given nation, and that "much of our spiritual prosperity depends, under God, on the manner in which we employ our Sundays." The Puritan tradition, of which we Reformed Protestants are the spiritual heirs, referred to the Sabbath as "the market day of the soul," the day given exclusively to our spiritual business.[13] "The two services are a way to frame the whole day as belonging to the Lord," argues Ron Rienstra,

---

13   J. C. Ryle, *Expository Thoughts on the Gospel of Luke*: Vol 1 (1856; Grand Rapids: Zondervan Publishing House, 1951), I:163.

of Western Theological Seminary and frequent contributor to *Reformed Worship* magazine.[14]

Ordinary means ministry in the context of simple, spiritual, scriptural worship is the great need of our day. But for it to succeed, that is, for sufficient ministry of the word to occur, it must have an adequate forum within which to function. Two distinctive services on Sunday provide that forum.

Specific characteristics

Let's move along to the details. What ought to characterize our public services? We recommend the following.

Catholicity

First, design the services with the whole people of God in mind. The early congregations of Christianity were diverse.[15] They were not segregated by age, taste, style, class, ethnicity, race, or culture. No attempts were made to appeal to a single demographic. No homogenous churches resulted as a result of an appeal to a single demographic. Indeed, the heterogeneity of the early church was a source of problems. There were tensions between Hellenistic Jews and Palestinian Jews (Acts 6:1–6). Jewish Christians at times excluded Gentile Christians from fellowship (Galatians 2:11–14), and Gentile Christians were tempted to despise Jewish Christians (Romans 11:11–21). Congregations consisted of wives and husbands, parents and children, slaves and masters (Ephesians 5:21–6:4; Colossians 3:18–25; Titus 2:9–10), young men and old men, young women and old women, widows and married

---

14 Matt Vande Bunte, "Sunday night services a fading tradition," *Christian Century*, October 19, 2010, Vol. 127, No. 21, 14.

15 See *Worshipping with Calvin*, Chapter 8.

(1 Timothy 5:1–16; Titus 2:2–8), rich and poor (1 Timothy 6:9–19; Galatians 2:15; James 2:1–9; 5:1–6).

This diversity was not only a source of problems, but it was also a source of strength. The church's unity in diversity was an important part of its witness to the world. Unity in diversity demonstrated visibly that Jesus had broken down "the barrier of the dividing wall" and had established "one new man," reconciling diverse groups (of which the Jewish-Gentile division was primary) into "one body" (Ephesians 2:13–22).

Consequently care should be taken to preserve the diversity of the communion of the saints by designing a common worship. The church should not favor the cultural preferences of one group over another. The worship service should employ not pop culture, not youth culture, not anglo-contemporary culture, not ethnic-contemporary culture, not cowboy culture, not hip-hop culture, not jazz culture, and not classical culture. Follow a hip-hop format and we will build a hip hop congregation. Those whom we privilege will be those whom we gather. Instead, when designing the church's public ministry employ catholic forms drawn from the church's own liturgical culture of format, order, music, lyrics, and prayers. The order of the service should be familiar, rooted in the Bible and history. Historic psalms and hymns should be sung. Traditional instrumentation should be used along with traditional hymn/lyric combinations. Standard vernacular speech should be used, not that of a subculture. Traditional decorum should be observed. The communion of all the saints can only be maintained if the church sticks to its historically rooted and time-tested liturgical culture. This catholic uniformity facilitates communal diversity. We should have no interest in tailoring our services to appeal to the youth, for example, because to do so is to alienate all the non-youth who might enter our doors. No one should enter our churches, look around, and conclude, "this is for someone else," be it cowboys, surfers, or rock-n-rollers.

Does this mean that there can never be any change? No, it means that all changes should take place organically and slowly and through common consensus. For example, ministers should not abruptly abandon traditional clergy garb for something more "hip" in order to appeal to youth, if so doing will prove unsettling to the older members. The church's time-tested liturgical culture, because it targets no single group, and belongs to no single group, belongs to all the groups, young and old, rich and poor, sophisticated and unsophisticated, red, yellow, black, and white. This preserves unity and harmony in the church, and preserves unity in a rich diversity in which "there is neither Jew nor Greek, there is neither slave nor free man, there is neither male nor female; for you are all one in Christ Jesus" (Galatians 3:28).

Excellence

Second, a spirit of excellence should pervade public services. It is not enough for a church to commit itself to historic Reformed worship and ministry. Reformed worship can be poorly done, and when it is it harms the cause. A church must be committed to doing Reformed worship *well.* Each element of worship should be expressed well. Transitions should be carefully considered. Music should be skillfully handled. It should be clear to anyone attending the worship services of Reformed Protestantism that the planners and leaders care a great deal about what happens and how it happens. Sometimes, we must admit, this seems not to have been the case. Too often sermons have been poorly organized, prayers haphazard and ill-conceived, and the music amateurish. Poor results are then blamed on faithfulness ("People don't want the pure word," etc.) when perhaps incompetence is

74   *Serving with Calvin*

the real reason. This should never be the case given our theological convictions. Sovereignty is not an excuse for sloppiness. Confidence in the power of the Holy Spirit, and gratitude for Christ, the builder of the church (Matthew 16:18) should not ever undermine our quest for excellence in all that we do (Philippians 4:8–9). Certainly excellence can be overdone. It can become "excellentism."[16] But God commends excellence (Exodus 23:19; Numbers 18:29–30), including skill in leading worship (Psalm 33:3; 1 Chronicles 15:22; 28:21; 2 Chronicles 34:12). Competence matters. Quality counts. Attention to detail contributes to the "success" of a service. Only unblemished lambs should be offered in sacrifice. God should get our best.

Order

Third, Reformed worship should be ordered by the logic of the gospel, by "gospel logic" i.e., a biblical, logical, and experiential order in our approach to God that is Christ-centered and gospel-driven. Too many services seem to have no aim, no goal, no flow, no organizing principle. One thing seems to follow another randomly, with no discernable reason for the order of events. This is disconcerting for worshippers, who struggle to make sense out of the service as a whole. Where is the service going?, they wonder. What is the arrangement of songs, prayers, readings, and exposition designed to do?[17]

Praise

The worship of God begins with the praise of God. We "enter His gates with thanksgiving, and His courts with praise" (Psalm

---

16   Reggie Kidd, *With One Voice: Discovering Christ's Song in Our Worship* (Grand Rapids: Baker House, 2005), 101–102.

17   See *Worshipping with Calvin*, Chapter 7, for an elaboration of this theme.

100:4). "Praise is the gateway to God's presence," as Hughes Old succinctly puts it.[18] "Let us come before His presence with thanksgiving, let us shout joyfully to Him with psalms" (Psalm 95:2). Worship begins with praise, both spoken in prayer and sung. "Come before Him with joyful singing" (Psalm 100:2). On this point Scripture, the historic liturgies, and recent aids to popular piety all agree. Jesus taught us to begin our prayers with praise: "Our Father, who art in heaven, hallowed be Thy name. Thy kingdom come, Thy will be done, on earth as it is in heaven." Jesus teaches us to praise God's name, stature, holiness, and work before we offer any petitions for ourselves. The psalms which are classified as hymns of praise, such as 8, 19, 29, 33, 46, 48, 65, 66, 93, 96–100, 104, 111, 113, 114, 117, 135, 136, and 145–150, and are believed to have been intended primarily for use in public worship (and often indicate such themselves), all begin with a call to worship. The historic Protestant liturgies all begin with a "Call to Worship" or invocation. Matthew Henry in *A Method for Prayer* identifies "the first part of prayer" as adoration and praise, and Isaac Watts in *A Guide to Prayer* identifies it as "invocation, or calling upon God," and the "second part" as adoration.[19] Today's popular aids to prayer such as the acrostic A-C-T-S, Adoration-Confession-Thanksgiving-Supplication, or the three P's, Praise-Pardon-Petition, likewise guide one to approach God with praise. Indeed, this is the pattern of conversion: we come to Christ only when we begin to understand God and what He requires of us. For these reasons we counsel

---

18   Hughes O. Old, "The Psalms as Christian Prayer. A Preface to the Liturgical Use of the Psalter" (Unpublished manuscript, 1978), 86.

19   Matthew Henry, *A Method for Prayer*, Ed. J. Ligon Duncan, III (1710; Greenville, South Carolina: Reformed Academic Press, 1994), 21; Isaac Watts, *A Guide to Prayer* (1715; Edinburgh: The Banner of Truth Trust, 2001), 10.

76   *Serving with Calvin*

that one begin worship with what might be called a "cycle of praise," beginning with a call to worship, prayer of praise, and a majestic psalm/hymn of praise. "A sense of awe and wonder should characterize and permeate (the opening) prayer," advises Donald Macleod (1917–1982), former President of Princeton Theological Seminary.[20] It is "a prayer of adoration in which due recognition is given to the glory of the one true and living God; to His majestic being as the one God in three persons, infinite, eternal, and unchangeable; and to the wonder of His redeeming grace," adds Rayburn.[21]

Similarly, the opening hymn should be "objective," continues Macleod. It should be about "the nature or attributes of God, the majesty of the Eternal (should be) unfolded before them."[22] It should "assist the congregation to focus upon some attribute of God's being," he continues.[23] "Praise to the Lord, the Almighty," "O Worship the King," and "A Mighty Fortress is Our God" provide good examples of what we mean. "The opening hymn," he says again, "recognizes God as God."[24]

Continuing the theme of praise, the "confession of faith" may be seen as an affirmation of God's glorious works in creation and

---

20   Donald Macleod, *Presbyterian Worship: Its Meaning and Method* (Richmond, VA: John Knox Press, 1965), 33,34.

21   Rayburn, *O Come, Let Us Worship*, 183.

22   Macleod, *Presbyterian Worship*, 22.

23   Ibid. 32.

24   Ibid. "The first hymn should be one of general praise, serving to inspire feelings of worship and adoration towards God" says W. G. T. Shedd, in *Homiletics and Pastoral Theology*, 270. It should be "emphatically a hymn of worship," says J. A. Broadus, *On the Preparation and Delivery of Sermons*, (1870; reprint, Nashville: Broadman Press, 1944), 365. "The first (psalm or hymn) is most suitably a direct invocation of God, to be sung as an act of homage, and an expression of longing desire and trust, of humility, faith, and love" (W. G. Blaikie, *Work of the Ministry*, 169).

redemption. The gloria patri and/or doxology cap off the cycle with a crescendo of praise. We do not see order as an absolute, nor do we see any item in the cycle as unalterable. But it is a sensible, logical beginning to worship, and frankly, we fail to see any better.

Cycle of Praise

Call to Worship
Invocation and Prayer of Praise
Psalm\Hymn of Praise
Confession of Faith
Gloria Patri\Doxology

Confession

The praise of God may then be followed by the confession of sin. Repeatedly in the Scripture a vision of the true God leads to fear and awe and a sense of one's finiteness, sin, and unworthiness. "When the people see who God is," Donald Macleod observes, "they are led to see what they are in themselves."[25] Moses, after viewing the "backsides" of God's glory, "made haste to bow low toward the earth and worship"(Exodus 34:8); Isaiah responds to the vision of the Lord of hosts upon his throne, surrounded by Seraphim repeating "Holy, Holy, Holy," by crying out, "Woe is me, for I am ruined! Because I am a man of unclean lips, and I live among a people of unclean lips; for my eyes have seen the King, the Lord of hosts" (Isaiah 6:5). Peter, after Jesus performs a miracle, becomes aware of the One with whom he is dealing and calls out, "Depart from me for I am a sinful man" (Luke 5:8). Seeing a vision of Christ on His throne in heaven, John writes, "And when I saw Him, I fell at His feet as a dead man"

---

25   Macleod, *Presbyterian Worship*, 23.

78   *Serving with Calvin*

(Revelation 1:17). A true knowledge of God leads to a knowledge of ourselves, and the new self-awareness is sobering. No one ever stated this more eloquently than Calvin:

> Again, it is certain that man never achieves a clear knowledge of himself unless he has first looked upon God's face, and then descends from contemplating him to scrutinize himself. For we always seem to ourselves righteous and upright and wise and holy— this pride is innate in all of us—unless by clear proofs we stand convinced of our own unrighteousness, foulness, folly, and impurity. Moreover, we are not convinced if we look merely to ourselves and not also to the Lord, who is the sole standard ... As a consequence, we must infer that man is never sufficiently touched and affected by the awareness of his lowly state until he has compared himself with God's majesty.[26]

We recommend that the cycle of praise be followed by a full cycle of confession. American Presbyterianism has not made widespread liturgical use of the Ten Commandments. This is not the case with the Dutch and other continental Reformed churches where their use in connection with the confession of sin dates back to the Reformation. The experience of using them on Reformation Sunday (with liturgies of Knox, Calvin, and Baxter) was so positive that our church began to use them on a weekly basis on Sunday nights. We highly commend their use in one of the Sunday services as a prelude to confession. This cycle gives a gravity and weightiness that is typically lacking in modern worship, providing an effective antidote to the trivialities of our

---

26 John Calvin, *Institutes of the Christian Religion—Vol. 1 & 2*, in John T. McNeill (ed.) The Library of Christian Classics, Volume XXI (Philadelphia: The Westminster Press, 1960), I.i.2, I.i.3, 37, 39.

day. Confession of sin also clears the way for God's blessing, removing from our hearts whatever idols or lusts are obstructing the grace of God (see Isaiah 59:2; Psalm 66:18). Confession includes an appeal to the cross and the atonement which Christ accomplished, and leads to the promises of the gospel which assure us of pardon. A cycle of confession might look like this:

CYCLE OF CONFESSION
Reading of the Law of God
Confession of Sin
Assurance of Pardon
Psalm\Hymn of Thanksgiving

Means of Grace

The service now moves into a cycle employing the means of grace. Those who have contemplated God have seen their true, corrupt selves because they have been illuminated by both the light of His glory and the dark backdrop of the law's condemnation. They have repented of their sin, trusted Christ, and now are ready to grow in their faith. When we know our *need* of grace we make use of the *means* of grace. This order flows from our daily experience with Christ as well as the logic of a public approach to God. To begin worship with the means of grace, say, with an intercessory shopping list, without first having paid homage to God and confessed our sins is inappropriately self- centered. However, having praised God and confessed our sins, we humbly turn to the Scriptures, read and preached, to prayer, and to the sacraments for the grace that is necessary to sustain the Christian life.[27] The

---

27 "The heart that knows grace longs to thank God for his mercy ... having thanked God for his grace, we naturally desire to see more grace in our lives and in the lives

natural movement from praise to proclamation, seen clearly in Psalm 96, reminds us that preaching is an element of worship no less than prayer and praise. The tri-fold command to "Sing to the LORD" in verses 1–2a becomes "*Proclaim* good tidings of His salvation from day to day. *Tell* of His glory among the nations, His wonderful deeds among all the peoples" (Psalm 96:2b–3). The Liturgical Revival Movement has at times disparaged preaching as an element of worship. Here there can be no doubt. Because "great is the LORD and greatly to be praised," He is to be praised both with song and preaching (Psalm 96:4).

CYCLE EMPLOYING THE MEANS OF GRACE
Prayer of Illumination
Reading of Scripture
Sermon
Prayers of Intercession
Sacraments

Thanksgiving & Benediction

The service then concludes with a response of thanksgiving and blessing. This includes the collection as an expression of gratitude for the gifts of God.

CYCLE OF THANKSGIVING AND BLESSING
Exhortation to Give or Prayer for Giving
Collection
Concluding hymn[28]

---

of others" (Bryan Chapell, *Christ-Centered Worship* (Grand Rapids, MI: Baker Publishing Co., 2009, 92).

28 The final hymn "should ... refer to the discourse ... being didactic and applicatory of the sermon" (Shedd, *Homiletics,* 270, 271). "The last (psalm or hymn) is selected to

Benediction

Again, let us underscore that neither the order nor the items under each cycle is absolute and unalterable. For example the collection can be justified at just about any point in the service: as an opening declaration of Christ's Lordship, as a response to forgiveness (as in our congregation), as a response to the sermon, or it may be dropped all together.[29] Sins may be confessed without the Law. Indeed the prayers of confession and intercession may be combined into one "great prayer," as in the American Presbyterian tradition. There is room for considerable variation. Yet this basic outline provides a worship service with the logic, order, and flow that is often missing in today's worship. It does so in a way that is consistent with scriptural example, with Christian experience, with the history of liturgy, with the popular aids to devotion, and the Reformed tradition.

Form and freedom

Fourth, maintain a healthy balance between form and freedom. The Reformed tradition has always sought to maintain *some form*, its Psalters providing orders of service with fixed forms (e.g. Lord's Prayer, Creed, some written prayers) and *some freedom* (e.g. free prayers and preaching, broad rubrics). It has not been happy with imposed liturgies, with obligatory books of prayers or homilies, or with acts of uniformity. Some are tempted by the trivialities of much of today's worship to follow the swing of the pendulum all the way back to Rome, Canterbury, or Antioch. We recommend that this temptation be resisted, that Reformed churches not go

---

follow up the discourse" (W. G. Blaikie, *Work of the Ministry,* 169).

29 For the argument that the "offering" is appropriate but not necessary, see Robert Godfrey, "The Offering," *The Outlook* 41 (Nov. 1991).

beyond a few fixed forms, that they not load up on responsive readings or even the ancient liturgical responses. The *sanctus*, the *sursum corda*, the *gloria*, the *kyrie eleison*, the invitatory, the salutation, the suffrages, and so on, date from the fourth century and after. Written liturgies were not a part of the life of the church in the early centuries. Most of them were removed by the Reformed churches in the 1520s. It is our view that over use of congregational responses tips the scales too far in the direction of the liturgical churches, and undermines a distinctive strength of Reformed worship, its freedom in the context of form. Historic Reformed worship suffers neither from the suffocating uniformity of a strict liturgy, nor from the liturgical chaos of the churches which use no order of service and permit no fixed forms.

Maintaining the balance between form and freedom is important, in no small measure because the efficacy of the church's public ministry depends upon the free functioning of the word gifts of Ephesians 4:7–13 (evangelists, pastors, teachers), which in turn depend upon spiritual gifts and graces. John Owen (1616–1683), that great champion of freedom in worship, argued repeatedly from this text that Christ has appointed the ministry to flourish not by "the prescription of a form of words" but by the imparting of spiritual capacities. "It is," he says, "by the communication of grace and spiritual gifts from heaven unto them by Christ Himself," that God provides for the right functioning of the public ministry. Through the communication of spiritual gifts and graces to ministers of the gospel, He provides for "the right discharge of the work of the ministry unto the edification of his body."[30] The spiritual gifts of preaching and prayer must not be diminished by a superabundance of written or set forms.

Baxter defended the use of set forms of prayer. Yet he also saw the danger that ministers "stifle (their) own gifts and grow negligent."[31] The "grand incommodity" as he puts it, of a set liturgy, is "that it usually occasioneth carelessness, deadness, formality, and heartless lip-labour in our prayers to God."[32] "When a minister knoweth beforehand that ... he hath no more to do but to read that which he seeth before him, he is apt to let his thoughts fly abroad, and his affections lie down." He counsels, as we do, a mixture of both free and set prayers as the method that "will best obviate the incommodities of both."[33] He cites the works of the Reformers Luther, Melanchthon, Bucer, Zwingli, Calvin, and Beza, and of English non-conformists such as Cartwright, Greenham, and Perkins for support. Some form tends to anchor the public service, providing weight and substance. The use of the Creed, the Lord's Prayer, the Ten Commandments, the occasional written prayer, may help obviate the incapacities of the minister and maintain the order and dignity of the service.

A generation later Isaac Watts (1715) urged careful attention to order even while he urged freedom in worship.

"Sinful sloth and indifference in religion have tempted some men to believe that God is not an interested and exact inquirer into outward things ... they imagine that for the substance and form of their sacrifice, anything will serve. And as though he were

---

30   John Owen, "Discourse Concerning Liturgies and their Imposition, in William H. Goold (ed.), *The Works of John Owen*, Volume XV (1850–53; Edinburgh: The Banner of Truth Trust, 1965), 10,11. On the value of some set forms when the gifts of the minister are lacking see Baxter, "Christian Directory," *Works*, Vol. 1, 679–80.

31   Baxter, "Christian Directory," *Works*, Vol. 1, 680.

32   Ibid. 682.

33   Ibid.

not a God of order, they address him often in confusion. Because the heart is the chief thing in divine worship, like some foolish Israelite, *they are unconcerned what beast they offer him*, so long as it has a heart."[34]

Two hundred years after Owen and Baxter, and nearly a hundred years after Watts, a committee of the Free Church of Scotland, made up of such luminaries as Douglas Bannerman (1841–1903), W. G. Blaikie (1820–99), A. B. Bruce (1831–99), John Laidlaw (1832–1906), and S. D. F. Salmond (1837–1905), published *A New Directory for the Public Worship of God*, a revision of the *Book of Common Order* (1560–64) and *The Westminster Directory* (1643–45). They expressed the same concerns voiced by Owen and Baxter, which we can characterize as typical of the Reformed church.[35] While incorporating the use of creeds and of specimen forms of prayer (e.g. confession, thanksgiving, praise, and intercession), they were zealous to maintain freedom amidst the new forms. "All of us hold strongly that the duty and privilege of *free prayer* in the public worship of God should be jealously guarded and maintained."[36] They sought to avoid "merely imitative movements in the direction of Anglican forms and usages."[37] Presbyterian worship from the

---

34 Watts, *Guide*, 174 (my emphasis). He says, further, citing one whom he calls "a great divine," "Though set forms made by others are as a crutch or help of our insufficiency, those which we compose ourselves are a fruit of our sufficiency. And that a man ought not to be so confined by any premeditated form as to neglect any special infusion, he should so prepare himself as if he expected no assistance, and he should so depend upon divine assistance as if he had made no preparation" (183).

35 For example, Samuel Miller, *Thoughts on Public Prayer* (1844; Harrisonburg, Virginia: Sprinkle Publications, 1985), 150–176.

36 D. Bannerman, *et. al.*, *A New Directory for Public Worship of God* (Edinburgh: Macriven & Wallace, 1898), vi.

37 Ibid.

time of the Reformation, they argued, has required its ministers to depend on the Holy Spirit's gifting and helps and that they "stir up the gift of God which is in (them)" (2 Timothy 1:6). Taking a page from Owen, and the whole Reformed tradition, these Free Church of Scotland reformers saw value in worship that requires that ministers "cultivate the power of leading the devotions of a congregation in such a way as really to meet and give expression to the spiritual wants and cravings of the earnest and living members of the Church." By and large, the Scottish church, they believed, had achieved "a decidedly high average attainment ... not only in preaching—but in the gift of edifying and acceptable public prayer."[38] The balance between form and freedom should be tilted in the direction of freedom, anchored, to be sure, by form, but tilted towards freedom.

Reverence

Fifth, establish an atmosphere of reverence. D. G. Hart considers reverence "perhaps the most important principle of Reformed worship."[39] Those who attend historic Reformed worship services ought to sense that they are meeting with God. Like the unbeliever who visited the early Corinthian assembly, he should overhear such convicting preaching (or "prophesy"), and observe such zealous devotion that "he is convicted by all, he is called to account by all; the secrets of his heart are disclosed; and so he will fall on his face and worship God, declaring that God is certainly among you" (1 Corinthians 14:25). Serious, soul-

---

38 Ibid. xiii.
39 D. J. Hart, *Recovering Mother Kirk: The Case for Liturgy in the Reformed Tradition* (Grand Rapids, Michigan: Baker Book House, 2003), 76; D. J. Hart & John R. Muether, *With Reverence and Awe: Returning to the Basics of Reformed Worship* (Phillipsburg, NJ: P&R Publishing Company, 2002), 121ff.

86   *Serving with Calvin*

searching proclamation is not, by the way, terribly seeker-friendly. Instead the visitor is "convicted," he is "called to account," and "the secrets of his heart are disclosed." That this might make him uncomfortable does not seem to cause concern for the Apostle Paul. Indeed, this would seem to be the intention. The result is conversion, leading to strong acts of devotion, whether literal or figurative. He will "fall on his face and worship God," presumably joining with the others in reverential posture. We should not fail to miss that it is clear even to the unbeliever who visits the Christian assembly that the people are dealing with God and God is dealing with them. Edmund Clowney called this "doxological evangelism," a fitting name for the impact reverent worship makes upon even the unbelieving.[40]

Beware of the light, superficial, frivolous atmosphere sought by many churches today, which can create quite the opposite impression. "Because it is God we approach," Plantinga and Rozeboom insist, "believers reject anything that looks like flippancy. Chatty prayers, jokes about God, and references to 'the Big Guy' demean both the giver and the receiver. The incarnation licenses boldness, not sauciness."[41] They cite John Wilson, editor of *Books & Culture*, who complains that because the "prevailing mood" of the typical Protestant worship service is "casual, comfortable, chatty, busy, humorous, pleasant, and at times even cute," it betrays the claim of a divine encounter in worship or a "sacred presence." This casual mood, he says, "is

---

40   Edmund Clowney, "Declare His Glory Among the Nations," message from Urbana 76, found at http://www.urbana.org/_artciles.cfm?RecordID=879.

41   Cornelius Plantinga, Jr. and Sue A. Rozeboom, *Discerning the Spirits: A Guide for Thinking about Christian Worship Today*, Calvin Institute of Christian Worship Liturgical Study Series (Grand Rapids, Michigan: Wm. B. Eerdmans Publishing Co., 2003), 134.

a sign not of sacred reality but of various congregational self-preoccupations."[42] The unbeliever, in such a setting, is unlikely to conclude that the assembly is dealing with Almighty God. He may note that the congregation is enjoying itself. He may agree that the "worship leader" is charming. The musicians, he may see, are entertaining. But meeting with God? Is the unbeliever perceiving, "God is certainly among you"? Rarely, if ever, we fear, is this obvious to visitors to our assemblies. Surely this ought not to be. After all, we are commanded to worship "with reverence and awe" (Hebrews 12:28). We take this to mean that reverence and awe are mandatory. Both the devotion of the congregation and the leadership of the minister ought to be convicting of divine realities. For this to happen, the minister must adopt a sober, serious tone.

It is essential that God be worshiped with a "dignity" which is "fitting for sound doctrine" (Titus 2:1), with both joy *and* "trembling" (Psalm 2:11), and with an outlook that is consistent with physical acts of devotion such as bowing and kneeling. "O come let us worship and *bow down*," says the psalmist, "Let us *kneel* before the Lord Our maker" (Psalm 95:5). Whether God is concerned with our posture in worship or not we'll leave to others to debate for now. However all should agree that He is concerned with our *attitude* in worship, and the attitude commanded is one which is consistent with physical prostration: humility, reverence, and devotion.

Some contemporary commentators have reacted pejoratively to concerns that traditionalists have voiced about the growing irreverence in worship today.[43] Thankfully, previous generations

---

42 Ibid. 137.

43 John M. Frame, *Worship in Spirit and Truth: A Refreshing Study of the Principle and Practice of Biblical Worship* (Phillipsburg, NJ: Presbyterian & Reformed

of writers, whose outlook can help us escape the limitations of "our time," show similar concerns. Scottish Presbyterian theologian Patrick Fairbairn (1805–1874) urged ministers to have an "attitude of profound reverence and holy earnestness."[44] While cautioning against an artificial or sanctimonious manner, he urged language "pervaded by a subdued, reverential, hallowed air."[45] All of the older authors urged ministers to spend much time on their knees prior to worship so that they would enter the pulpit in a proper frame of mind. "In the closet, alone with God, with the world shut out, is the proper place to get the mind and heart into the proper tone for conducting the public devotions," says Thomas Murphy (1823–1900).[46] The unction sought for the preaching should characterize "all the other parts of the service," as well.[47] Those leading worship services should avoid unduly drawing attention to themselves. They should not attempt to "warm-up the crowd," like a stage performer, by being too cute, clever, or charming. Murphy asks, "What is more unbecoming than irreverence or levity in the presence of Jehovah."[48] Samuel Miller warned that "all coarseness, levity, or vulgarity—everything that borders on the ludicrous, or the want of real dignity, ought to be shunned ...."[49] He spoke of the "gravity" of character and "solemn

---

Publishing, 1996), 82.

44 Patrick Fairbairn, *Pastoral Theology: A Treatise on the Office and Duties of the Christian Pastor* (1875; Audubon, New Jersey: Old Paths Publications, 1992), 314.

45 Ibid. 313.

46 Murphy, *Pastoral Theology*, 214.

47 Ibid. 215.

48 Murphy, *Pastoral Theology*, 208.

49 Samuel Miller, *Letters on Clerical Manners* (Philadelphia: Presbyterian Board of Publications, 1852), 245.

purpose" that ought to characterize his "every look, motion, and attitude in the pulpit."[50]

Avoid, as we have said, even being too personal, too revealing. The worship service is not about the preacher. What he has just experienced or is now feeling is irrelevant. Motyer is cautious about personal illustrations. "We don't want to put ourselves on centre stage; the pulpit is danger enough."[51] He is to lead the congregation to God, not to himself. For this reason, standing behind the pulpit or lectern, or at least standing still, is to be preferred to wandering around the platform or worse yet, up and down the aisles. We cannot point to chapter and verse to forbid this. However, we can appeal to wisdom. A wandering preacher does not get lost in the message. He does not become a little-noticed prop while God speaks to the people. No, too often, he is the message. Neil Postman, an astute non-Christian observer, has remarked regarding television preachers, whose patterns of ministry have tended to be mimicked by ministers in local churches, that the preacher is "tops" while God, he insists, "comes out as second banana."[52] No minister should allow his movements, his abilities, his eloquence, his personality to become the prominent feature of the service. Historic Reformed worship aims to maintain a God-centered, reverential tone and a God-centered focus throughout. The contemplation of God is to lead to joyful praise, and then to confession of sin, and then to a dependent looking to the means of grace, and finally to a thankful response. The minister must lead. Yet he must also quickly get out

---

50   Ibid. 251, 253.

51   Motyer, *Preaching?*, 115.

52   Neil Postman, *Amusing Ourselves to Death* (New York, NY: Penguin Group, 1985), 47.

of the way and let the Holy Spirit, working through the word, take over.

Pace

Sixth, establish a pace that is consistent with the urgency of the gospel. It is difficult to pinpoint precisely what we mean by "pace." However, we all know from experience of times when a service seemed to have been rushed, and of other times when it seemed to drag. Somewhere between these two extremes is a pace that is appropriate. Even though we cannot exactly identify what that pace is, or delineate principles by which to judge pace, we still know that finding the right pace is crucial if a congregation is to feel that a historic Reformed worship service is "alive," or that it "moves," or is "going somewhere." Let us suggest the following.

For those who are inclined to conduct services that feel like a race, remember that one is dealing with eternal things in worship. "Be not in haste to pass from one point of the service to another," cautions Miller.[53] Time for contemplation is needed if the people are to begin to "plumb the depths of the Almighty." When I first began my ministry in Savannah, an older member gently told me that I ought to shorten my sermon on communion Sunday because he felt the Lord's Supper was rushed. I promptly ignored his advice about my sermon (it was already down to 25 minutes) but took very seriously the problem of a hurried communion service. We needed to slow down. We cannot race if we are to observe the Supper properly. There is a noticeable tendency in evangelical circles, both in preaching and in worship, to mimic the rapidly changing images of television by darting from one thing to another. In preaching this means short "sound bites" of text,

---

53   Miller, *Clerical Manners*, 153.

3   *Preparing the Services*   91

story, illustration, a second story, exhortation, a third story, and finally back to the text. The other parts of the service take on an "and now, this!" quality. No time is left for deep thought. The pace won't allow it. It *does* allow for entertainment. But not for serious contemplation. If one is speeding, slow down. "All excessive haste damages the holy," cautions Abraham Kuyper. "Hast is completely unknown in the glory of heaven."[54]

On the other hand, Rick Warren warns, "Almost all churches need to pick up the pace of the service."[55] Those who are inclined to drag slowly through a service of worship are to be reminded that eternity is at stake. Because we are worshiping the true God through the only Mediator, there is an urgency about all that we do. Richard Baxter (1615–1691) famously "preached as if to never preach, as a dying man to dying men."[56] If what we believe is true, then we ought to be energetic about our praying, singing, preaching, and the transitions between each element. Every prayer pleads for grace. Every sermon urges souls to Christ. We have a finite amount of time. We have eternal truths to dispense. Every split second counts. Consequently the service ought to move briskly from one item to the next. It shouldn't be rushed. Yet it shouldn't drag either. The Rev. William Still wrote pointedly:

> Here's another thing: what another profession calls 'timing' is very important if we are to gain and hold people's attention, to proclaim the greatest news on earth. Some men have no sense of split second time which could make such a difference to their

---

54   Kuyper, *Our Worship*, 233.
55   Warren, *Purpose-Driven Church*, 255.
56   Richard Baxter, Thompson, *The Autobiography of Richard Baxter*, Everyman's Library, edited with Introduction, Appendices and Notes by J. M. Lloyd Thomas, 1696 (London: J.M. Dent & Sons Ltd., 1931), 26.

presentation of the truth. It appears that pious souls think long pauses between items in a service are reverent and appropriate, not realizing that an empty pause simply invites people's attention to wander—and with all the skills of the media today people have become much more critical of sloppy presentation. There is nothing so devastating to attention as the delay in commencing the service after the organ music has ended. Be on your toes, and determine to hold the attention of your congregation from the first moment to the last. You have the greatest news in the world to tell them. Begin as if you knew that, and wanted them to know it.[57]

This dual sense of infinite truth and finite opportunities ought to produce an urgency which animates and enlivens leadership in worship. We must make the most of each occasion. We must make the most of our time. Evaluate every element in the service and ask, "What took too much time and what needs more time?"[58] Not even a moment may be wasted. Every second must be put to maximum use if the worship of the Reformed church is to be as fruitful as it can be.

Economy
Seventh, conduct services with an economy of language. One observes a distressing amount of extraneous chatter even in otherwise fine worship services. This can particularly be the case at the beginning of the services. Five to ten minutes easily can be lost if care is not taken to limit announcements and stay on task. Restrict the number of announcements to three or four at the

---

57 William Still, *Congregational Record and Bible Readings,* Gilcomston South Church of Scotland, Aberdeen, February 1989.

58 Warren, *Purpose-Driven Church,* 255.

most, and only announce those matters that pertain to the whole congregation.

Transitions between items in the service also must be handled with care. Informal commentary should be avoided. Use an economy of language to move the congregation from item to item, saying just enough to enhance understanding of the elements without become a drag on the service. One should also avoid "bathetic" language, as Timothy Keller wisely counsels. "We should not talk overly about how we feel or about our experiences and convictions ... and we should not tell others how they are supposed to feel at the moment."[59] Watch the "justs" the "sos" and the "reallys." Refrain from indulging extraneous casual, idiosyncratic, or sentimental language.

Length

Eighth, limit the length of historic Reformed services from an hour to an hour and a quarter. Don't test the patience of the congregation week in and week out with long services. The same rule applies here as does to sermon length. Reformed worship will be unfamiliar, new, and even difficult for many. However, it will be more tolerable if it is acceptably short in duration. They will grow to love Reformed ministry and worship. However, it will always be wiser to leave them wishing for more than exhausted by what was too much.

Aesthetics

Ninth, maintain high aesthetic standards. Theological and moral relativism will never get out of the batter's box in the conservative

---

59 Keller, "Reforming Worship in the Global City," in D. A. Carson (ed.), *Worship by the Book* (Grand Rapids, Michigan: Zondervan, 2002), 224–225.

94   *Serving with Calvin*

Reformed churches. Ironically, aesthetic relativism is already rounding second base, and is well on its way to home. We say ironically, because ultimately truth, righteousness, and beauty are interrelated. Indeed they are perfectly integrated in God himself. Earthly beauty is ultimately a reflection of beauty as it is in God (e.g. Isaiah 4:2; Psalm 96:6, 9). The more one knows about the true God, the more one will know about true beauty. Moreover, both truth and righteousness have an aesthetic dimension. When the truth is clearly articulated, when its coherence is demonstrated, its implications elaborated, it is lovely to see. "How beautiful are the feet of those who bring glad tidings of good things" (Romans 10:15; Isaiah 52:7). Righteousness lived out in the lives of the saints, its order, its harmony, modesty, innocence and purity, is likewise beautiful to behold.

Ultimately we cannot separate truth, righteousness and beauty. The Bible expects that we are able to understand and identify what they are, though we may know them with varying degrees of clarity. The Apostle Paul can urge us to "let (our) mind(s) dwell on" whatever things are "true," "pure," and "lovely" (Philippians 4:8). What are these but the categories of truth, righteousness, and beauty? He assumes that we can identify such and concentrate our minds on them. The "beauty of God" is written on the hearts even of unbelievers, leaving them without excuse when they prefer the vulgar, the crude, and the ugly (Romans 1:18ff; 2:14–16).[60] A civilization rapidly fleeing from God will not only reject truth and righteousness, but will also reject beauty, the evidence of which can be seen in significant portions of the music, art, architecture, fashion and styles of recent decades. A church

---

60   Kenneth A. Myers, *All God's Children and Blue Suede Shoes* (Westchester, Il: Crossway Books, 1989), 75–87, 119–32.

that mimics the aesthetic judgments of a rebellious culture will find itself immersed in the vulgar, the crude, and the ugly.

Nowhere is this subject of aesthetics as volatile today as when applied to music. For many, musical preferences have taken on a deeply personal and almost sacred aura. Criticisms of a given musical form, if it happens to be in earshot of those who prefer it, is seen as a highly inappropriate personal assault, like criticism of one's religion. Personal artistic preferences are above evaluation in today's world. Aesthetic distinctions, whether of excellence or appropriateness, are almost entirely seen as matters of personal taste and style. Even Reformed pastors Mark Dever and Michael Lawrence affirm that the style of music used on Sundays is "incredibly unimportant."[61]

Consequently the two components of church song—words and tunes, are both almost universally assumed to be secondary issues. On the one hand, this consensus is not surprising given the environment of aesthetic relativism in which the church ministers. On the other hand, this indifference is ironic given the dominant role music plays in shaping the ministry of the church and the crucial role it plays among church-shoppers. Many ministers, who typically have the highest level of theological and pastoral training in a given congregation, turn music matters over to music directors and "worship teams" (contrary to our counsel above), his opinion being no more than one among many. He has learned to consider his aesthetic judgments mere personal style preferences to be denied in favor of popular alternatives. Rarely is the impact of a post-Christian culture's aesthetic taste upon Christian ministry and worship taken into consideration.

---

61 Michael Lawrence and Mark Dever, "Blended Worship" in J. Matthew Pinson, *Perspectives on Christian Worship: 5 Views* (Nashville, Tennessee: B & H Academic, 2009), 218.

96   *Serving with Calvin*

Instead the popular aesthetics of moment are allowed to shape the aesthetic judgments of the church.

This aesthetic indifference flies in the face of the common consent of humanity going back to the ancient Hebrews and Greeks, the Reformers, the Enlightenment and post-Enlightenment philosophers and scholars since. Recent books by Carson Holloway, *All Shook Up*, and Jeremy S. Begbie, *Resounding Truth*, demonstrate the utmost seriousness with which the philosophers from Plato, to Aristotle, to Rousseau, to Nietzsche have taken music. Holloway notes the "lack of seriousness" today "about music and a failure to come to grips with its power."[62] By way of contrast Plato gave the first place in education to music in his *Republic* because of the capacity (in Plato's words) of "rhythm and harmony" to "insinuate themselves into the inmost part of the soul" and "most vigorously lay hold of it."[63] Aristotle argued much the same, observing that "we are altered in soul when we listen to such things."[64] Essentially their argument was that good music has the capacity to order and discipline the soul, establishing in young people in particular the pattern of restraint and self-control. Control of one's passions and impulses makes a life lived for noble ends possible since it frees one from the disordered and random pursuit of immediate gratification. Bad music, however, has the opposite effect. It breaks down discipline and encourages the casting off of restraint, and the pursuit of immediate gratification,

---

62 Carson Holloway, *All Shook Up: Music, Passion, & Politics*, (Dallas: Spence Publishing Company, 2001), 6.

63 Ibid. 24; see also Plantinga and Rozeboom, *Discerning the Spirits*, 69–74; Jeremy S. Begbie, *Resounding Truth: Christian Wisdom in the World of Music* (Grand Rapids: Baker Academic, 2007), 77–184.

64 Ibid. 3.

resulting in a disordered and consequently self-centered and unworthy manner of living.

Calvin R. Stapert demonstrates the same aesthetic concerns among the church fathers. From Clement of Alexandria (c. 150–211/216) to Tertullian (AD 155–222) to Ambrose (c. 338–397) to Chrysostom (c. 347–407) to Augustine (354–430), the Fathers vigorously denounce the lascivious music of pagan Roman society and the base passions that it provokes.[65] Augustine, with all the Fathers, finds nothing in pagan music that is of use for Christians. Christians, he says, "should not turn to their [the pagans] theatrical trivialities to discover whether anything valuable for spiritual purposes is to be gathered from their harps and other instruments."[66] He even cautions of the power of *Christian* music to arouse feelings that might be mistaken for the work of the Holy Spirit.

Similarly, the Reformers, who knew the views of the Fathers, were very attuned to this power in music.[67] Building upon the thought of Augustine, Calvin recognizes that music is a "gift of God" whose aim is "recreating man and giving him pleasure." However he urges its "moderate" use lest it become the "occasion for our giving free reign to dissolution, or making ourselves effeminate in disordered heights," or "become the instrument of lasciviousness" and "shamelessness." Taking a cue from Plato (whom he names) Calvin observes,

There is scarcely in the world anything which is more capable

---

65 Calvin R. Stapert, *A New Song for an Old World: Musical Thought in the Early Church*, The Calvin Institute of Christian Worship Liturgical Studies (Grand Rapids: William B. Eerdmans, 2007), 42–148.

66 Ibid. 181; see *Confessions*, X, xxxiii.

67 The following quotes are all taken from his "Preface to the Psalter," 1543, found in Elsie Ann McKee (ed.), *John Calvin: Writings on Personal Piety*, The Classics of Western Spirituality (New York: Paulist Press, 2001), 91–97.

98   *Serving with Calvin*

of turning or moving morals this way and that, as Plato prudently considered it. And in fact we experience that it has a sacred and almost incredible power to arouse hearts in one way or another.[68]

Because of this "incredible power," its use ought to be carefully considered. He cites the precedent of the "ancient doctors of the Church" who denounced the "unseemly and obscene songs" to which their contemporaries were "addicted" as "mortal and Satanic poison for corrupting the world." He distinguishes words from tunes, arguing that when bad words are joined to appealing melodies, the song

> ... pierces the heart much more strongly and enters into it; just as through a funnel, wine is poured into a container, so also venom and corruption are distilled to the depths of the heart by the melody.[69]

Both the church fathers and Reformers would be astonished at the naiveté of today's church respecting musical form and its power for evil. Calvin's solution to this potential corruption is *words* that God Himself has selected, and *tunes* that are appropriate. Respecting the words, we cite him again,

> Now what St. Augustine says is true, that no one is able to sing things worthy of God unless he has received them from him. Wherefore, when we have looked thoroughly everywhere, and searched high and low, we shall find no better songs nor more appropriate to the purpose, than the psalms of David, which the Holy Spirit made and spoke through him. And furthermore,

---

68   Ibid. 95.
69   Ibid. 96.

when we sing them, we are certain that God puts the words in our mouths, as if He Himself were singing in us to exalt His glory.[70]

Regarding tunes,

> Care must always be taken that the song be neither light nor frivolous; but have gravity and majesty, as St. Augustine says. And thus, there is a great difference between music which one makes to entertain people at table and in their houses, and the psalms which are sung in the church in the presence of God and his angels.[71]

He characterizes the world's song as, "in part vain and frivolous, in part stupid and dull, in part foul and vile, and in consequence evil and harmful." Consequently, Reformed Christians should sing God's own words and use melodies that are capable of carrying the gravity and majesty "appropriate to the subject," and "suitable for singing in the church."[72] The church, in other words, is to have its own distinctive musical form, unlike that of the pagan world, characterized by "gravity and majesty."

This perspective, what we might call the "sacred music" perspective, has been the characteristic outlook of the church for most of its history. Most Christian traditions have distinguished between the music of the world and that of the church. Most, if not all, have distinguished between music that is appropriate for divine worship and that which is inappropriate, including in the twentieth century both Karl Barth and Dietrich Bonhoeffer, as well as evangelical Protestants prior to the 1960s.[73]

---

70 Ibid.
71 Ibid. 94.
72 Ibid. 97.
73 Begbie, *Resounding Truth*, 152–162.

Appropriateness, what is suitable or proper, or fitting, though left without precise definitions, are ethical categories to which the Apostles make appeals (e.g. Romans 13:13; Ephesians 5:3–4; Colossians 3:15; 1 Timothy 2:9–10). They must be discerned through wisdom, yet they exist. T. David Gordon writes appreciatively of those through the centuries who have "devoted themselves … to creat(ing) music suitable to that remarkable occasion in life when the creature meets the Creator, when the mortal meets the immortal, when, yes, the temporal meets the eternal, when times meets eternity."[74] Our distinctive encounter with the divine in worship has been understood to require a distinctive musical expression. It is doubtful that prior to the late nineteenth century the church ever sought to have music that sounded like that of the world. Its music was its own, its "sacred music." Nevertheless, this catholic consensus has not inhibited contemporary evangelicals from abandoning the "sacred music" category and aesthetics altogether.

Rick Warren, pastor of the mega Saddleback Church, claims that "Music is nothing more than an arrangement of notes and rhythms; it's the words that make a song spiritual. There is no such thing as 'Christian music,' only Christian lyrics."[75] "To put it mildly, this is an unfortunate way of putting things," says Begbie, regarding Warren's views.[76] Other Christian leaders have

---

74 Gordon, *Why Johnny Can't Sing Hymns*, 76–77.

75 Rick Warren, *The Purpose Driven Church*, 281. This statement is all the more remarkable because he also says he "made the mistake of underestimating the power of music" earlier in his ministry; he endorses Aristotle's view, "Music has the power to shape character;" and he concedes, "Music is the primary communicator of values to the younger generation" (279–280). Does he mean music or lyrics? Does he mean the lyrics combined with certain kinds of music? Is some kind of music a more powerful corrupting tool than others?

76 Begbie, *Resounding Truth*, 47.

Preparing the Services

appealed to Luther and his alleged use of "bar tunes" and the Wesleys' alleged use of popular music to reach the unchurched. "History takes a hit," is Lester Ruth's response, citing "poor history" and "gross simplification." For example, "bar," as in "bar music," refers not to a drinking establishment but to "technical German musical terminology" for "a kind of phrase structure in music."[77] T. David Gordon points out that, "There is no evidence at all that Luther ever said that worship had to be conducted in contemporary sounding idioms." The opposite is more likely. Like Calvin, Luther also believed in sacred music, that is, "music that is deliberately and self-consciously different from other forms of music." "Luther," Gordon continues, "did not argue that a prayer or hymn had to sound *contemporary*; he argued that it had to be *intelligible*."[78] Understanding a language is not the same thing as preferring a style. Regardless, Warren's view is widespread. Apparently even Presbyterian theologian William Edgar agrees: "No style is in itself incompatible with worship music."[79] The categories of appropriateness, suitability, and fitness seem to have disappeared, along with the lovely and beautiful.

It is doubtful whether the "notes on a page" view is actually believed by those who affirm it. For example, Warren distinguishes several types of songs used at Saddleback, for which the acronym IMPACT is used. Services there begin with music which Inspires Movement. They select a "bright upbeat number that makes you want to tap your foot, or at least smile."[80]

---

77 See Plantinga and Rozeboom, *Discerning the Spirits*, 32–33; Jones, *Singing & Making Music*, 171–178; Begbie, *Resounding Truth*, 104–105; Chapell repeats this myth (*Christ-Centered Worship*, 299).

78 Gordon, *Why Johnny Can't Sing Hymns*, 46.

79 William Edgar, *Truth in All its Glory: Commending the Reformed Faith* (Phillipsburg, NJ: P&R Publishing, 2004) 232–33.

80 Warren, *Purpose-Driven Church*, 256.

Apparently there is a type of music whose qualities ensure this response, music whose inherent properties universally produce these desired effects. Then music is selected which is conducive of Praise, that is "joyful songs *about* God." Next, music is selected which is conducive of Adoration, that is, "more meditative" songs in which "the pace is slowed."[81] He continues describing songs which enhance Commitment and Tying it all together: music for IMPACT. The irony is rich. Warren, and with him nearly all the aesthetic relativists, nearly all those making indiscriminate use of pop music, recognizes that there are certain kinds of music that are conducive of certain kinds of ends and other kinds that are not. The traditionalist is saying no more.

Abandoning the attempt to wed the words of Psalm 23 to the music of "Rudolph the Red Nosed Reindeer," Frank Burch Brown, of Christian Theological Seminary in Indianapolis, concludes "this music is not infinitely malleable or suited to all purposes."[82] There are styles of music that indeed are incompatible with the reverential tone sought in divine worship. Sousa's marches, hard rock, Hip-Hop, rap, John Cage's random compositions, and Schoenberg's atonal works are not suitable for worship. We would have to respectfully disagree with the musical relativists. Music has a God-given nature, man has a God-given nature, and human nature responds to one sort of music differently than it does to another. Some music is conducive of a martial spirit, some to unrestrained self-expression, some to the expression of grief, some to the expression of romantic and even erotic love, and some is particularly conducive to the expression of the full-range of emotions experienced in the context of reverential public worship.

---

81 Ibid.
82 Frank Burch Brown, "Worship Mismatch" in *Christian Century*, Vol. 126, No. 5, March 10, 2009.

"Not all kinds of good art and music are equally good for worship, let alone for every tradition or faith community," insists Frank Burch Brown.[83]

A narrow biblicist might object, "the Bible says nothing about this alleged power of music" or about the suitability of one kind of music over another. Augustine, Calvin, and the Christian tradition would respond that this is a matter of wisdom. As we've noted, the Bible says nothing about the relative properties of rocks, sand, and buildings, yet Jesus expects us to be wise about the nature of things and build accordingly (Matthew 7:24–27). The Bible says nothing about the relative properties of wine and wineskins, yet Jesus expects that we should be shrewd enough observers of the nature of things to know not to put new wine into old wineskins (Matthew 9:16–17). The essence of biblical wisdom is this understanding of the nature of things whether one is a farmer (Proverbs 10:5–6, 12:11), shepherd (Proverbs 27:23), an orchardist (Proverbs 27:18), a man walking down the street (Proverbs 7:6–23), or an attendant of the King (Proverbs 23:1–2; 25:6–7). The wise will carefully discern the nature of people, things, and circumstances and bring their lives into conformity with the realities discovered. Consequently a wise person will pay attention to the relative properties of music and human nature and draw correct conclusions about its power to sanctify or corrupt. Begbie, for example, speaks of a "sonic order" that is "embedded" in material reality. It includes physical entities that make sound (the instruments), sound waves that have their own integrity, and a physical body which receives the sound, all in

---

83 Quoted in Plantinga and Rozeboom, *Discerning the Spirits*, 52,53, from Brown, *Good Taste, Bad Taste, and Christian Taste: Aesthetics in Religious Life* (New York: Oxford University Press, 2000), 250–51.

relation to time.[84] It operates according to givens that are built into the world. "Music is embedded in a sonic order."[85] There are given acoustical laws. Again, "music is embedded in given, ordered, acoustical phenomena."[86] Christian music, he insists, will recognize "the importance of a courteous honoring of this environment as embodied creatures, and specifically of sonic order, and seeing artistic freedom as a responsive, responsible relation to given constraints."[87]

It has not been wise of evangelicals to ignore aesthetic issues.[88] Regrettably those who have raised concerns often have been branded as elitists, legalists, narrow-minded fundamentalists, and ignored.[89] Among the commonly noted properties of music that must be taken into account as the church makes aesthetic judgments, one might summarize as follows:

1. *Music has the power to move and express the emotions.* Even as David was able to soothe Saul's troubled spirit with his harp (1 Samuel 16:23), so there is music that saddens, that gladdens, that arouses a martial spirit, that inflames erotic desire, that prepares one for sleep, and so on. Music may both arouse the whole range

---

84 Begbie, *Resounding Truth*, 42.

85 Ibid. 57.

86 Ibid. 306.

87 Ibid.

88 Secular observers have not failed to deal with these issues. In addition to Holloway, Allan Bloom, *The Closing of the American Mind* (New York: Simon & Schuster, 1987); Robert Pattison, *The Triumph of Vulgarity: Rock Music in the Mirror of Romanticism* (New York: Oxford University Press, 1987).

89 Among the others who have raised concerns are: John Blanchard, Peter Anderson, Derek Cleave, *Pop Goes the Gospel: Rock in the Church* (Darlington, England: Evangelical Press, 1989); Calvin Johansson, *Discipling Music Ministry: Twenty-First Century Directions* (Peabody, MA: Hendricksen, 1992); John Makujina, *Measuring the Music: Another Look at the Contemporary Christian Music Debate* (Salem, Ohio: Schmul Publishing Co., 2000); Myers, *All God's Children and Blue Suede Shoes.*

of human emotions and provide a vehicle for expressing them when they are already present. Moreover, "not all that moves us is of God."[90] Both dictators and, regrettably, churches, have used music to manipulate emotions, to "whip up crowds into mindless enthusiasm," as Begbie puts it.[91] The responsible use of music requires discernment and intensity.

2. *Music has the power to stimulate the memory.* As anyone who learned the "A-B-C" song or the "Books of the Bible" song knows, music is a great aid to the memory. This is why the lyrics of songs cannot be disregarded. What we sing we rehearse in the mind and lodge in the memory.

3. *Music has the power to discipline or corrupt the soul.* This is the argument of the philosophers and theologians and other careful observers of the sonic order. "Though the links between music and morality are often hard to trace," says Begbie, "they are certainly there."[92] Good music, that which consists of ennobling lyrics and moderate tunes, has the potential to discipline the soul and restrain the passions, making edification possible. Bad music, that which consists of unworthy lyrics and tunes, is likely to inflame the passions, break down restraint and corrupt the soul.

Traditionally, right words (God's own) with appropriate tunes have been seen as a powerful tool of sanctification. This is the primary virtue of the psalms. They carry all the sanctifying power of God's word, but driven more deeply still into the soul by the music. God commands us to sing. However, it is critical that words and music be critically evaluated and kept in proper proportion. The church is responsible to use the very finest suitable prose, poetry, and music in the worship of God.

---

90 Plantinga and Rozeboom, *Discerning the Spirits*, 74.
91 Begbie, *Resounding Truth*, 306.
92 Begbie, Ibid. 24.

The church's sung praise should be drawn primarily from the church's own cultural heritage of language and song, its "sacred music." The older music "has a privileged position," maintains D. T. Williams, author and Professor of English and Director of Arts & Sciences at Toccoa Falls College, "because it has already been sifted by time."[93] We urge churches not to settle for the blemished lambs of contemporary street language, cheap lyrics, and frothy music. Do not be persuaded by those who think that meaningful communication can only occur as the church adopts the idiosyncratic language and music of America's subcultures, as though, for example, proper English cannot be understood and traditional hymns cannot be appreciated by anyone but old white people. Rather than unifying the church, alleged requirements of "contemporaneity" and "accessibility" are dividing and potentially atomizing the church. As we have seen, if I can only "relate" to *my* preferred forms of language and music, and if I otherwise am turned off by *your* preferred form, then I *must* have my own worship service, and you must have yours (see chapter 6 for the development of this thought).

Better, it would seem, to find the highest common denominator and seek to draw the diversity of subcultures together on the basis of the church's treasury of excellent but accessible language and music. Among the greatest gifts of God to the church in the twentieth century is our rich heritage in lyrics and song. We'll have more to say about this in chapter 5, "Singing."

Beyond music, the church would be wise to be informed by the whole Christian tradition as it evaluates art, architecture, fashion, and style. It cannot afford to mindlessly ape popular culture.

---

93 D. T. Williams, "Durable Music," in *Touchstone: A Journal of Mere Christianity*, Volume 22, Number 6, July/August 2009, 21.

The Christian tradition, in all its splendid variety, has produced not only the world's most beautiful music, but also its art fills the world's museums and its architecture attracts worldwide admiration. The Christian tradition has demonstrated a profound and enduring aesthetic sense. Our buildings, our interior design, our graphic design, our sense of the appropriate and suitable, ought to reflect that historic sense.

Simplicity

Tenth, and last, keep it simple. Hughes Old and John Leith have been champions of simplicity in their writings, as was Calvin before them.[94] Speaking of the processional psalms, Dr. Old writes,

It is doubtful if the New Testament Church ever used these psalms as processional psalms any more than the synagogue did. The synagogue showed little interest in trying to reproduce this kind of Temple ritual. Processions, entrance rites, as well as incense, vestments, musical instruments and the whole elaborate sacrificial system, were never received into the liturgical usage of the synagogue. In this the church followed the lead of the synagogue. The primitive Church was much more apt to find in these psalms an expression of the Christian hope of entering the heavenly Jerusalem. When Christians gathered for worship they had a sense of entering into the heavenly Jerusalem (Revelation

---

94 "Simplicity is a recurring theme in all of Calvin's writings, and it was a characteristic of his practice ... He was the enemy of the ostentatious, the pompous, the contrived, the needlessly complicated. His style was plain and direct." John H. Leith, *Introduction to the Reformed Tradition*, Revised Edition (Atlanta, GA: John Knox Press, 1981), 84.

1:10) and if they sang these psalms when they met together it was that which they had in mind.[95]

We have regarded 1 Corinthians 1 & 2 as our case study in simplicity.[96] The Apostle Paul preached in a plain style, not in "cleverness of speech," not with "superiority of speech or of wisdom," but in "weakness and in fear and in much trembling." His message and preaching "were not in persuasive words of wisdom, but in demonstration of the Spirit and of power" (1 Corinthians 1:17; 2:1–4). His reason for doing so is telling: "that your faith should not rest on the wisdom of men, but on the power of God" (1 Corinthians 2:5). A plain style ("the foolishness of preaching"—1 Corinthians 1:21) is suited to a plain gospel ("Christ crucified"—1 Corinthians 1:23; 2:2). No doubt the classically educated Apostle was a student of the rhetorical arts. However, like Augustine after him, he refused to employ them lest his *method* obscure his *message*. "The apostles had as little flourish in their tongues, as edge upon their swords," says Stephen Charnock (1628–1680) in his monumental Puritan classic, *The Existence and Attributes of God*. He contrasts those who proselytize either through force of arms, or with human reason and eloquence, with the methods of the early church. Commenting on 1 Corinthians 2:4 he continues, "their presence was mean, and their discourses without varnish; their doctrine was plain, a 'crucified Christ;' a doctrine unlaced, ungarnished, untoothsome to the world."[97]

The principle of simplicity may be generalized. What is true of preaching is true of each element of worship (reading, praying,

---

95 Old, "Psalms as Christian Prayer," 112–113.
96 See *Worshipping with Calvin*, Chapter 9.
97 Stephen Charnock, *The Existence and Attributes of God* (1853; Grand Rapids, MI: Baker Books, 1996), 71.

singing, administering the sacraments) and of the service as a whole. Simplicity is exactly what we find in the glimpses the New Testament gives us of the early church's assemblies: the Apostles teaching, the fellowship, the breaking of bread, and the prayers (Acts 2:42; cf. 4:23–31).

We should have no interest in creating or borrowing elaborate rituals or ceremonies. Our worship is essentially spiritual and, as a consequence, simple. Jesus was saying this when, in that most profound of New Testament statements on worship, He declared that right worship is not that which is offered in Jerusalem or Samaria but that which is in spirit and truth (John 4:20–24). If it is no longer necessary to worship God in Jerusalem, then in one stroke the whole Old Testament system of worship comes tumbling down. Jerusalem was important only because it contained the temple. In the temple were found the priest, the altars, the sacrifices, the incense, the lambs, and so on (Hebrews 9:2–5). Jesus swept it all away. New Testament worship does not depend on buildings, holy items, rituals of approach, obligatory gestures and postures, and holy days. There is no New Testament book of Leviticus. New Testament worship is spiritual and simple. We ought to keep it such, with simple services of prayer, singing, preaching, and the sacraments. Don't allow the liturgical pendulum to swing from today's trivialities to the other extremes to be found at home in Rome or on the Canterbury trail.[98] Maintain the liturgical balance that is a hallmark of Reformed worship. Anchor the service with perhaps a few fixed forms (but

---

98 Regrettably, Scott Hahn, *Rome, Sweet Home* (San Francisco: Ignatius Press, 1993) and Robert Webber, *Evangelicals on the Canterbury Trail* (Wilton, Connecticut: Morehouse-Barlow, 1985) have found a receptive audience among conservative Protestants fed up with the superficiality of evangelical worship. Geneva is a better home than either Rome or Canterbury or Antioch.

not too many), and leave room for praying and preaching that flows from the prepared heart. This is the strength of historic Reformed worship: ordered, reverent, substantial worship, combined with passionate praying and preaching.

Moreover, because Reformed worship is simple, those who lead it will have to work at it, both to keep it simple and to do it well. Worship "deserves special attention from the clergy of a simple ritual," says Shedd.

The impressiveness and effectiveness of non-liturgical worship must depend mainly upon the taste and judgment of the individual clergyman. He has no fixed and imposing forms by which to be guided, inevitably, in the conduct of public worship. He therefore specially needs a judicious discipline in this direction—a liturgical culture obtained in the general manner that has been indicated. The clergyman, then, carries his rule with him. He has an unwritten liturgy in his own cultivated and pure taste, which he is at perfect liberty to vary, with times and circumstances. One who has acquired this true liturgical sense and feeling will render the services of the sanctuary impressive by their appropriateness, by their symmetry, and by that unity which we have seen to be the inmost essence of beauty. Without drawing away the attention of the congregation from more important matters, as a formal and splendid ritual is apt to do, such a minister will throw a sacred and spiritual atmosphere over the entire services of the sanctuary, more impressive than even the dim religious light of the cathedral.[99]

---

99 Shedd, *Homiletics*, 275.

Having given these eleven general guidelines for effective and faithful worship leadership, can specific guidelines be given for each worship element? What is needed, we hear, are "how-to's" for reading, preaching, praying, singing, and administering the word. We will attempt to provide these guidelines in the following pages.

112

❧ Chapter 4 ❧

Administering the Elements—1

We are now prepared to make recommendations with respect to each of the elements of historic Reformed worship and how they ought to be handled. Much of the detail that follows cannot be mandated. Rather what we recommend is what we deem to be wise, in light of all that we have seen from Scripture, theology, and history, both in this work, and in *Worshipping with Calvin* before it. We remind those leading the services that their ministries will be assessed primarily on the basis of how they lead the church's public assembly, especially how they preach. The Lord's Day services are the one time of the week in which they regularly will minister to the whole congregation. They may meet with individuals periodically for counsel or fellowship. There may be regular, even weekly gatherings with small groups of members. However, the whole congregation, not merely a part of the congregation, meets weekly, not merely periodically, under the leadership of those who conduct the Lord's Day services. Members' experience of the value of their pastors' ministry primarily will take place in the public assembly.

Preparation for leading these services should receive the lion's share of the minister's attention. We say this not merely for the sake of the pastor's "success," or so that he'll be highly evaluated by his people, but because the Lord's Day services are his opportunity to minister to all his people, not merely his favorites, or a select few. He should not squander the opportunity.

Reading Scripture[1]

C. H. Spurgeon, who ordinarily preached on single verses, lamented the decline of the expository sermon in his day. "The present plan of preaching from short texts, together with the great neglect of commenting publicly upon the word is very unsatisfactory," he maintained. "We cannot expect to deliver much of the teaching of Holy Scripture by picking out verse by verse, and holding these up at random."[2] His solution to the problem was the expository reading.

Nowadays since expository preaching is not so common as it ought to be, there is more necessity for our commenting during the time of our reading the Scriptures. Since topical preaching, hortatory preaching, experimental preaching, and so on—all exceedingly useful in their way—have almost pushed proper expository preaching out of place, there is the more need that we should, when we read passages of Holy Writ, habitually give running comments upon them.[3]

---

1 See *Worshipping with Calvin*, Chapter 5, "Read the Word," for background.
2 C. H. Spurgeon, *Commenting and Commentaries*, New Updated Edition (1876; Grand Rapids: Kregel Publications, 1988), 25.
3 Ibid. 26.

4   *Administering the Elements—1*

How do we go about recovering the public reading of Scripture, specifically *lectio continua* Scripture reading in our churches? The Apostle Paul instructed Timothy to "give attention to the public reading of Scripture" (1 Timothy 4:13). Substantial portions of Scripture should be read in the assemblies of God's people because this is what God required of them in Bible times, what was practiced by the Patristic church and throughout most of their history, Reformed churches, and above all, because the reading of Scripture edifies the people of God. Our recommendations will fall into two categories: *what* to read, and then *how* to read.

What to read[4]

1. *Read a portion of each Testament in each service,* as advised by the Westminster *Directory for the Public Worship of God.* The first reading might be the text to be preached. The second reading might be an additional *lectio continua* text. By "portion" we mean read *roughly* a chapter. Some chapters are long and need to be divided. Others are short and may be read in combination with part or all of an adjoining chapter. In other words, the reading should be of *suitable* length. But the basic guideline should be a chapter per Testament per service.

2. *Read the Testament not being preached.* This guideline is proposed as a way of maintaining biblical balance. If the Gospel of Matthew is being preached in the morning service, the second reading would be an Old Testament book. If the books of Samuel and Kings are being preached in the evening, then read a gospel,

---

4   Some of the following previously appeared in T. L. Johnson, "The Ebb & Flow of *Lectio Continua* Bible Reading in the English-Speaking Reformed Church, 1539–2000," in Robert L. Penny (ed.), *The Hope Fulfilled: Essays in Honor of O. Palmer Robertson* (Phillipsburg, New Jersey: P&R Publishing, 2008), 290–316.

Acts, or an epistle alongside of the Samuel/Kings text being preached.

3. *Start with books of the Bible that are accessible to the congregation.* It would probably prove unwise to begin the implementation of a program of *lectio continua* readings in the book of Leviticus. It can be done, but it is not recommended. Start with the Gospels, Acts, Psalms, Epistles, Proverbs, or an Old Testament narrative.

4. *Consistent with this, skip over (with descriptive, summarizing comments) exceptionally remote or difficult texts.* Passages such as Exodus 25–31 (describing the details of the Tabernacle and its furnishings, Joshua 15–21 (outlining the distribution of the Promised Land to the 12 Tribes), 1 Chronicles 1–9 (genealogies), Nehemiah 3 (describing the placement of workers on the walls of Jerusalem), Nehemiah 7:7–73 (census of the restored exiles), ordinarily are best handled with a summary comment while transitioning to the next text to be read.

5. *Vary scriptural types.* It would probably be unwise to plow through one Minor Prophet after another, or read straight through Old Testament historical narrative from Genesis to Nehemiah. Instead, vary the diet. Move from gospel to Old Testament historical narrative to epistle to Old Testament poetry to Acts to Old Testament wisdom and so on.

6. *Limit the intrusions of the church calendar.* The church calendar of holy days and a selective lectionary (*lectio selecta*) go hand-in-hand. The point of the readings of the traditional lectionary is to explain the calendar. Basically a church must decide if its life is to be based upon the annual church calendar, its holy days, and its corresponding *lectio selecta* readings, or based upon the weekly Sabbath and *lectio continua* sequential readings and preaching. By my count, from the *Book of Common Prayer*

(1977), there are 17 named Sundays (e.g. Sundays of Advent, Lent, Palm, Easter, Pentecost, Trinity; Sundays after Epiphany, Ascension), 29 Holy Days (on specific dates, sometimes falling on Sundays), and 118 days of commemoration (also on specific dates, sometimes falling on Sundays). The church calendar is essentially a fasting schedule. It assumes a neo-Platonic ascetic philosophy whereby one becomes worthy of divine benefits through self-deprivation and self-dedication. The discipline of the church calendar has little in common with a Reformed spirituality. Our particular concern at this point is that the themes of the church calendar (or for that matter the themes of the secular calendar of Father's Day, Memorial Day, Labor Day, etc.) will overtake the content of the Sunday services if not consciously resisted. The practice of Reformed Protestantism for most of its history has been to observe something like the "Five Evangelical Feast Days" (Christmas, Good Friday, Easter, Ascension, and Pentecost: central events of the gospel). Sometimes we've done less than this (e.g. Puritans and the Scots), but rarely have we acknowledged the church calendar beyond them. This limitation helps to facilitate systematic Bible reading, a significant accomplishment. "After several years of using the *lectio continua* the congregation will discover itself to have learned an amazing amount of Scripture," notes Hughes Old.[5]

How to read

1. *Provide brief introductions to books and chapters.* By "brief" we mean normally a few sentences lasting 15–30 seconds. A few

---

5   Hughes Old, *Worship: That is Reformed According to Scripture* (1984; Louisville: Westminster John Knox Press, 2004), 172. See Ligon Duncan on "Reading the Bible in Corporate Worship" in Philip G. Ryken, et. al. (ed.), *Give Praise to God: A Vision for Reforming Worship* (Phillipsburg, NJ: P&R Publishing, 2003), 140–148.

comments setting the stage for the text to be read or anticipating a difficulty in the text can do much to enhance the spiritual profitability of the reading.[6] Spurgeon advises, "Two or three sentences will often reveal the drift of a whole chapter; the key of a great difficulty may be presented to the hearer in half a score words, and thus the public reading may be made abundantly profitable."[7] Care must be taken not to say too much. "Very little time in the service can be afforded for reading the lessons; do not rob the prayer and the sermon for the sake of commenting," Spurgeon counsels.[8]

2. *Read slowly, clearly and with nuance.* When J. C. Ryle was converted through the reading of Scripture in the context of worship the text was Ephesians 2:8, described by J. I. Packer as *skillfully* read in church "with significant pauses, thus achieving great emphasis."[9] The public reading of Scripture is "a real art," says Abraham Kuyper, "that no one possesses naturally."[10] Those who read should prepare through study of the designated passage and practice readings. Scripture may be read with more or less skill. Our concern is that care be taken to read the Scripture well. The reading should not be rushed. Neither should the reading drag. The text to be read should be studied carefully enough that it can be read with comprehension and nuance, enhancing the

---

6 Examples of these can be found at www.ipcsav.org (Our Worship, Worship Aids for Ministers, Liturgical Introductions to Scripture).

7 Spurgeon, *Commenting and Commentaries*, 26.

8 Ibid. 31.

9 J. I. Packer, *Faithfulness and Holiness: The Witness of J. C. Ryle* (Wheaton, IL: Crossway Books, 2002), 27.

10 Kuyper, *Our Worship* 105. He continues, "All accent must be avoided. The words must be pronounced clearly. The stress and pitch must be in the proper place. The reading must be calm and dignified, but without affectation or theatrical flair. The bearing of the reader should be quiet and serious" (105; cf. 164).

understanding of the congregation. There is a direct relationship between the skill with which Scripture is read and the value of that reading for the listeners. The best readers, says Spurgeon, "bring out the meaning by their correct emphasis and tone."[11] Edification, after all, is the goal at which we are aiming.

3. *Provide perspective*—Sometimes reading chapter after chapter of Old Testament prophetic passages can seem tedious as fiery denunciation follows upon fiery condemnation, page after page after page. Then, in the midst of these extended texts will come a thunderbolt of devotional inspiration. Reading extended portions of Scripture should be likened to listening to a symphony rather than the latest top-40 tune. The latter provides immediate gratification, the former requires perseverance. Yet the symphony rewards patience with a much deeper level of aesthetic pleasure. Think of Beethoven's Ninth Symphony, its third and fourth movements leading into the "Ode to Joy." It meanders. Years ago a member of my youth group commented, "It's going nowhere." "Ah, but it is," I answered. It builds to a magnificent crescendo. But part of what makes the crescendo so magnificent is the seeming aimlessness that precedes it. One cannot skip the third and early fourth movements and move directly to the Ode to Joy without diminishing the impact of the crescendo.

For those of a different cultural milieu, we can cite the example of Led Zeppelin's "Stairway to Heaven," always at the top of the lists of the greatest rock and roll songs ever written, which does much the same thing. In fact, it defies the genre by meandering for many times the normally acceptable length for pop music. Yet as it wanders, it builds to its famous crescendo that leaves listeners amazed if not exhausted.

---

11   Spurgeon, *Commenting and Commentaries*, 33.

120   *Serving with Calvin*

If a congregation reads through the Prophet Jeremiah, pages of prophetic condemnation will of necessity be endured. However, these severe passages build to devotional crescendos. For example, chapter 8 builds to the stirring questions of verse 22,

> Is there no balm in Gilead? Is there no physician there? Why then has not the health of the daughter of my people been restored? (Jeremiah 8:22)

Chapter 9 builds to this profound word,

> Thus says the Lord, "Let not a wise man boast of his wisdom, and let not the mighty man boast of his might, let not a rich man boast of his riches; but let him who boasts boast of this, that he understands and knows Me, that I am the Lord who exercises lovingkindness, justice, and righteousness on earth; for I delight in these things," declares the Lord. (Jeremiah 9:23–24)

And so on it goes. Shape the expectations of the congregation by reminding them that they are listening to a great scriptural symphony, not an instantly gratifying pop tune. The texts build to climatic insights. Devotional inspiration comes in bolts of illumination.

Preaching[12]

There are a number of superb books available on the preaching ministry, upon none of which can we improve. Our favorites are William Still's *Work of the Pastor*, Spurgeon's *Lectures to My Students*, John Stott's *Between Two Worlds*, and Lloyd-Jones'

---

12   See *Worshipping with Calvin*, Chapter 5, "Preach the Word," for background.

Preaching and Preachers. We cannot commend them too highly. Among more recent works, John Carrick's *The Imperative of Preaching* is superb,[13] and Dennis E. Johnson's, *Him We Proclaim*, is perhaps the most comprehensive exegetical analysis of what the Bible says about preaching yet written, particularly regarding what it means to preach Christ, navigating the various controversies in the process. J. A. Motyer's, *Preaching? Simple Teaching on Simply Preaching* is simply extraordinary. What we would like to do is offer a few suggestions based on over 25 years of ordained ministry. Our suggestions also reflect our work with pastoral interns over nearly as many years and our concern for what we perceive to be gaps in their seminary training. The following is a summary of how a Reformed preaching ministry might look.

What to preach

We begin, first, with what to preach. What content or subject matter should fill our sermons? Our first six points are actually one central point: preach the word. Don't preach around it. Don't preach about it. Don't use it as a resource for topics. Preach the Bible itself, all of it, word by word, phrase by phrase, paragraph by paragraph, chapter by chapter, book by book.

Motyer argues powerfully for Scripture-driven, content-driven, understanding-addressed preaching. He begins with Jesus' interaction with the disciples on the Emmaus Road in Luke 24, arguing that considerable "biblical psychology" might be gleaned from Luke's account. He notes insightfully that the disciples were "barred from seeing Jesus until they had first seen Him in the Scriptures" (Luke 24:16, 25–27, 31–32). [14] Only when He had

---

13   John Carrick, *The Imperative of Preaching: A Theology of Sacred Rhetoric* (Edinburgh: The Banner of Truth Trust, 2002).

14   Motyer, *Preaching?*, 16.

"explained" (NASB) or "interpreted (*diermēneuō*) to them in all the Scriptures the things concerning himself," did they come to understand. He "opened" the Scriptures to them with the effect that their "hearts burn(ed) within (them)" (Luke 24:16, 25–27, 31–32). Motyer urges, "The significance of these events is clear: we can neither know the risen Lord, nor know how and what to preach about Him to the world *except through the Scriptures*."[15] Luke tells us that then "their eyes were opened," "they rose" went to Jerusalem, and "told what had happened" (Luke 24:31, 33, 35). This leads Motyer to conclude, "The instructed mind is the foundation of the work of God in us. It is when the mind embraces with clarity what the Bible teaches that the heart is warmed, the will mobilized, the life redirected and the tongue loosed."[16] Teaching and preaching God's word is the key to it all.

Motyer argues convincingly that it is the Word of God that makes the church "a distinctive company in the world." It is what makes the church what it is. "The Word of God is the constitutive reality at the heart of the Church."[17] This is true beginning with the word of warning to Noah (Hebrews 11:7), the call of Abraham (Genesis 12:1; 17:1), and the nation of Israel, "whose distinctiveness was that they possessed the Word of God" (Deuteronomy 4:8).[18]

Motyer suggests that "the Growing Church" would be a more suitable title for the "Acts of the Apostles." He finds 37 references to the growth of the church in its 28 chapters. Of the 37, 24 link growth to the preaching of the Word of God. Once the growth of the church is actually called the growth of the word, "as if," says

---

15   Ibid. my emphasis.
16   Ibid. 28.
17   Ibid. 18.
18   Ibid. 19.

Motyer, "they were so closely related that they could be identified one with the other."[19] Pentecost, with its particular gift of the "tongues," a gift of "intelligible communication" (Acts 2:6, 11), establishes the "special focus" of that day, says Motyer. The Holy Spirit "came with the particular purpose of making the church a speaking church (John 15:26–27)."[20] Peter cites Joel 2:28–32 in which the outpouring of the Spirit is "for the particular purpose of creating 'prophets'" (Acts 2:17).[21] 2 Timothy is particularly important in this discussion because it "sits on the significant dividing line between the apostolic and the post-apostolic church (2 Timothy 4:6–8), and in it Paul offers Timothy (and us) a prospectus for the days ahead."[22] We find there not the anticipation of apostolic succession of office, not ongoing fresh revelations of divine truth, but a church that is to guard the truth already given (2 Timothy 1:13) and preach it (2 Timothy 3:15–4:5).

The Apostle Paul identifies himself as not only an apostle, but also as a "preacher" and a "teacher" (2 Timothy 1:11). A preacher is a *kerux*, a herald, a town crier, the "essential mark" of which, says Motyer, "is not noise but faithfulness to a message given by a superior authority."[23] A teacher (*didaskalos*) is concerned with conveying a body of truth. Its cognates are used in connection with "admonishing" (*noutheteō*), counseling (Colossians 3:16) and to "urge" or "exhort" (*parakaleō*) (1 Timothy 6:2). The Apostle "taught publicly from house to house" (Acts 20:19–20). The succession that he envisioned was that of "faithful men" who

---

19 Ibid.
20 Ibid. 21.
21 Ibid.
22 Ibid.
23 Ibid. 24.

would be able (*hikanos,* competent) to teach (*didaskō*) others (2 Timothy 2:2).

When we minister the word we, like Jesus, are to address the understanding. When Jesus preached the Sermon on the Mount, "he opened his mouth and *taught* them" (Matthew 5:1–2). When He concluded, the people were astonished, "for he *taught* them as one having authority" (Matthew 7:28–29). When Jesus completed the seven parables of Matthew 13 He asked, "have you *understood* all these things?" (13:51). Motyer comments, "He did not ask, 'Did you enjoy the parables?'—a question addressed to the emotions of the heart; nor did He ask 'What do you purpose to do by way of response?'—a question addressed to the will; but 'Have you understood?'—a question to the mind" (cf. 13:19,23).[24]

Motyer points out from Ephesians 4:17–24 that the difference between the converted and unconverted is that of the former, "The mind has been addressed; the truth grasped," whereas the latter "walk in the futility of their mind" and "their understanding (is) darkened."[25] The proclamation of the word of God to the understanding of our hearers is the key to gospel ministry. The word gifts of Ephesians 4:11ff are the key to the health of the whole body, the effective working of each part, and its productive growth. "What we need in our pulpits," says Motyer, "is didactic and applicatory exposition."[26] "The great work of a minister is to teach others," Gurnall insists.[27] This leads us to urge the following.

1. Preach the lectio continua
That is, preach expositorily and sequentially. A sermon in historic

---

24 Ibid. 26.
25 Ibid. 27.
26 Ibid. 101.
27 William Gurnall, *Existence and Attributes,* II:167,

Reformed worship should be an exposition of a text of Scripture. Ideally, Reformed churches should commit to preaching verse-by-verse through whole books of the Bible. As we have noted (see *Worshipping with Calvin*, Chapter 3), the Reformation can be said to have started for the Reformed churches when in January 1519 Zwingli abandoned the lectionary and began to preach through the book of Matthew. The shift from the *lectio selecta* preaching in favor of the *lectio continua* was an early mark of the Reformed churches and according to Hughes Old, "unquestionably one of the most clear restorations of the form of worship of the early Church."[28] Not only Zwingli, but Luther, Bucer, Oecolampadius, Calvin, the Scottish Reformers, and the Puritans of England and New England were all committed to expository, sequential preaching. We can say as well that it has been the commitment of the church in virtually every era of health and vitality throughout its long history. We've cited already Spurgeon's lament on the decline of sequential preaching in the Victorian era (see the beginning of this chapter).

We are sorry to report that there seems to be a waning commitment to expository preaching among Reformed ministers, and particularly among recent seminary graduates. Years ago one of the fathers of the Presbyterian Church of America, Dr. James Baird (1928–), himself a committed expositor, noted that fewer PCA ministers were preaching expositorily, and even fewer sequentially. I was surprised when he said it, and wasn't sure that he had it quite right. Now I am certain that he did. Why is this happening? One intern told me that he was afraid he would not find anything interesting in "the next text," and might be

---

28 Hughes O. Old, *The Patristic Roots of Reformed Worship* (Zurich: Theologischer Verlag, 1970), 195.

thought boring by the people. A healthy fear of boring the people is not necessarily a bad thing to carry with one throughout one's ministry. It may help keep one sharp. But what was he saying about God's self-revelation in Scripture? Boring? I'm sure that he really didn't want to be saying that, but I am also sure that he was merely expressing what many others fear deep down inside: the Bible alone is dull.

I insisted he begin preaching through the book of Philippians. Half way through his preparation for the first sermon he came to me full of anxiety that he would have nothing to say about the first four verses. I smiled and urged him to press on. The day of the sermon he came back to me brimming with enthusiasm saying that he had twice as much to say as he could in the allotted time and would only make it to the second verse. This experience repeated itself several times, and on each occasion he emerged more enthusiastic than the previous. Today he is a zealous and capable expository preacher, pastoring one of the premier churches of the Presbyterian Church in America.

Sequential expository preaching disciplines the preacher to preach the "whole counsel of God" (Acts 20:27). The Apostle Paul did not "shrink" (*hypostellō*, to hold back or conceal) from declaring the gospel and "the whole counsel of God" (Acts 20:20, 27). He didn't trim his sails. He proclaimed, says Motyer, "the Word of God, pure, direct, undiluted, nothing added, nothing subtracted, nothing adjusted."[29] The temptation to ride one's hobby-horse week after week is enormous. Preachers have their favorite themes. Expository preaching, says Lloyd-Jones, "will preserve and guarantee variety and variation in your preaching."[30]

---

29 Motyer, *Preaching?*, 102.
30 Lloyd-Jones, *Preaching & Preachers*, 75.

Preachers also have their hated themes, or at least, the themes they'd rather avoid. Stott cites P. T. Forsyth: "We need to be defended from (the preacher's) subjectivity, his excursions, his monotony, his limitations."[31] Verse-by-verse preaching forces the Bible's agenda in its biblical proportions upon the preacher. It forces him to dismount his favorite pony and ride every God-given theme he encounters, whether he likes it or not. Since the context of the preacher's sermons is dictated by the passages he is encountering, the effect is to deflect blame from him when he preaches on "touchy" subjects.

As a young, newly installed minister at the historic, downtown Independent Presbyterian Church of Savannah, systematically preaching through the gospel of Mark, it wasn't long until I encountered Mark 10 and Jesus' teaching on divorce. The message was predictably controversial. Those tempted to accuse me of attacking them regarding their wrongful divorces could see the obvious: I merely had preached the next text. Why had I preached on the subject of divorce? Because chapter 10 followed chapter 9 of Mark, which had followed chapters 8, 7, 6, and so on. My ministry had no other agenda than to preach the next verse.[32]

The central conviction motivating our advocacy of expository preaching is that Christ is found in "all the Scriptures" (Luke 24:27). The whole Christ is found in the whole Bible, as William Still would say, and we only become whole people when we feed on the whole Christ.[33] Our responsibility is to preach "all Scripture," since "all Scripture" is "inspired by God," and consequently is "profitable for teaching, reproof, correction,

---

31   Stott, *Between Two Worlds*, 316.
32   Stott in *Between Two Worlds* tells a similar story from Matthew 5:31–32, after 25 years of pastoral ministry (315–316).
33   Still, *Work of the Pastor*, 6ff.

128   *Serving with Calvin*

training in righteousness, that the man of God may be adequate, equipped for every good work" (2 Timothy 3:16–17). We may take the word "all" to mean that there are no exceptions. It is *all* "profitable." *All* Scripture equips us for "*every* good work." We may not deprive our congregations of any of it. Is Scripture not able to give us "the wisdom that leads to salvation through faith which is in Christ Jesus" (2 Timothy 3:15)? If so it is the duty of Reformed churches to preach the whole word, on each occasion explaining why God included those verses in the canon and the profit He wishes for us to derive from them. A sermon, as Old concludes from Nehemiah 8:8, "is not just a lecture on some religious subject, it is rather an explanation of a passage of Scripture."[34]

The media has had a negative impact on preaching, in that it has raised the expectation that the preacher must be "exciting" or "entertaining." As we have mentioned, too much preaching has come to resemble the sound-bites, or more accurately, the rapidly moving images of television. Story follows illustration follows anecdote follows joke follows story follows illustration, etc. Scripture takes a back seat to "relevance" and the preacher's ego. The Apostle Paul repudiates this kind of spruced-up oration, preferring "the foolishness of preaching," even if such were despised by rhetoric-conscious Greek audiences (1 Corinthians 1:21). We've looked carefully at the Apostle Paul's commitment to simple, straight-forward, plain-style preaching (1 Corinthians 2:1–5).[35] The Apostle's conviction is that the gospel, or "the word of the cross" is the power of God (Romans 1:16; 1 Corinthians 1:18). He is not concerned to decorate his message with "superiority of

---

34 Old, *Worship*, 60.
35 See *Worshipping with Calvin*, Chapters 8, 9, and 12); Chapter 3, "Simplicity," in this work.

speech or of wisdom." He doesn't mind preaching "in weakness and in fear and in much trembling." Indeed, he is convinced that this is the way that he must preach. If he were to dress up either his "message" (content) or "preaching" (form) in "persuasive words of wisdom" then his hearers might place their faith in him, in "the wisdom of men" rather than on "the power of God."

Insofar as there is a crisis in preaching, it is a crisis of confidence in the converting and sanctifying power of the word of God. Do today's Evangelical and Protestant churches believe that God saves sinners through His word? Do church boards believe that the gospel is "the power of God for salvation" (Romans 1:16)? Do evangelicals believe that God is "well pleased ... to save those who believe" through "the foolishness of preaching" (1 Corinthians 1:21)? Do Reformed Christians believe that "the Spirit of God maketh the reading , but especially the preaching, of the Word, an effectual means of convincing and converting sinners, and of building them up in holiness and comfort, through faith, unto salvation?" (*Shorter Catechism* Q #89). Then preach it; all of it.[36]

2. Preach topically as prudence dictates

The *lectio continua* should be the primary form of preaching for Reformed Protestants. It should be the foundation of our public

---

36 Some hesitancy about expository preaching has been expressed in recent years in some surprising places (e.g. Iain H. Murray, "'Expository Preaching'—Time for Caution," *The Banner of Truth Magazine*, Issue 557 (February 2010, 9–13). Also J. R. DeWitt, "A Few Thoughts On Preaching," *The Banner of Truth Trust Magazine*, Issue 588 (October 2012). While their concerns are well taken, the point seems that expository preaching can be, and has been poorly done. We may concede the point. Every type of preaching can be poorly done, and has been. Expository preaching has no lock on incompetence. The question is, all things being equal, what type of preaching ought to be the norm? What ought we to encourage?

ministry. It should be the norm. However, by saying this we are not invoking the law of the Medes and the Persians. The church has liberty to depart from the norm as it deems necessary. It may be that for one reason or another a *lectio continua* series has become long, and feels tedious. Or it may be that there is a topical issue (e.g. stewardship, family life, ethical issues) that needs to be addressed by a single sermon or a series of sermons. Or it may be that a current issue begs to be addressed. As the Holy Spirit leads and wisdom requires, the *lectio continua* may be set aside for a season in order to preach topically. These may take various forms, each with a long legacy.

catechetical—we have in English translation today the *Mystagogical Catechism* of Cyril of Jerusalem (*ca.* 315–386), Augustine's *Enchiridion* (421), Bullinger's *Decades* (1549–51), Thomas Watson's *A Body of Divinity* (1692), and many other collections of catechetical sermons. Churches in the Dutch Reformed tradition long have committed Sunday evening preaching to the exposition of the Heidelberg Catechism.

seasonal—sermons devoted to calendar events such as Christmas, Easter, Thanksgiving, and New Year have been faithfully and fruitfully preached. With all the world celebrating Christmas, there is no need for the Reformed church to ignore it.

eucharistic—for example, the collections of Calvin, Robert Bruce, Thomas Doolittle, Thomas Watson, Jonathan Edwards, and Spurgeon are all now in print, among others.

thematic—there may be times when sermons on the attributes of God, the fall and its consequences, the atonement, the *ordo salutis*, faith and repentance, the Christian life, marriage and family, and so on, are needed.

periodic—burning issues of the day, such as the outbreak of war, a natural disaster, national controversies cry for a word from the Lord.

The *lectio continua* need not be slavishly followed, just normally, and faithfully. Over the long haul, the *lectio continua* will cover all the topics: *all* the topics. Eventually, the preacher will get to them, naturally, and in the course of his regular preaching. However, there are times when it is prudent not to wait, say five years, to deal with a subject begging to be addressed.

3. Preach grammatical-historical-redemptive sermons

Proper Bible interpretation is grammatical-historical. That is, it gives careful attention to the intention of the author as revealed by the words that he used and the historical setting in which he used them. This has been understood at least since the Reformation and stands in contrast to an allegorical method of interpretation, so prevalent from late antiquity to the late Middle Ages. Proper preaching is also redemptive-historical, that is, it pays close attention to the place in which the text lies in the unfolding of redemptive history.[37] The canon of Scripture determines the meaning of texts within that canon. Where does the passage in view fit in the whole scheme of redemption? In light of its historical and biblical meaning, what does it mean for us today?

Preaching sermons that are grammatically, historically, and redemptively faithful typically means consulting several modern exegetical commentaries. It is vital that authorial intent be identified and understood. What did the biblical author mean for his audience to understand? Answering that question of necessity immerses the preacher in scholarly historical, grammatical, and

---

37 Johnson, *Him We Proclaim*, 151ff.

theological study. This cannot be short-changed. In order to escape the biases of our time, older exegetical commentaries should be read as well. One's preparation then can be rounded off by reading those works that excel at application. For example, one may consult Puritan era works such as Matthew Henry's *Bible Commentary*, or modern sermonic commentaries authored by leading preachers of recent times. Foundational for all our preaching is a grammatical-historical-redemptive understanding of the text in question. We shall have more to say about this as we proceed.

4. Preach the text

"Exposition," says Motyer, is "drawing out from the Word of God what the Holy Spirit has deposited there without addition, subtraction or modification."[38] Whether one's sermon is *lectio continua* or topical, it should be an exposition of a text, not merely a discourse on a subject found in the text. The preacher's text, says Abraham Kuyper, must "not be the hook on which he hangs some interesting ideas ..."[39] It is not enough to find a doctrine or topic in the text and preach that doctrine or topic, even if they are preached with great competence. The preacher must first show, more than that, convince his listeners, that *this* text teaches *that* doctrine. He must prove it to his audience. The congregation is not interested in his opinions and theories. There is no spiritual power in his stories and illustrations per se. Stories and illustrations are only profitable insofar as they illuminate the listeners' understanding of the text. The preacher's job is to show the people what the passage meant *then*, what it means *now*, and

---

38   Motyer, *Preaching?*, 101.
39   Kuyper, *Worship*, 189.

urge them to believe and do what God requires in that particular text. Read the sermons of Reformed preachers, from Calvin to the Puritans to the Princeton men to Lloyd-Jones to James M. Boice for good models. Their sermons are exegetically-based expositions of texts of Scripture.

Again, my interns have helped me to see the problem of failing to deal adequately with a text. They would read the passage, describe what it means, and then spend the next twenty-nine minutes talking about their subjects without again referring to their texts. Their preaching was an example of what William Gurnall described as "good truths but bad expositions."[40] Preaching that neglects to make frequent reference to the text is not nearly so effective as that which demonstrates clearly that the subject at hand is actually there in the passage before them. John MacArthur, pastor of the Grace Community Church of Sun Valley, California, is something of a genius at doing this. He is constantly forcing his listeners to look at the text and deal with what it says. He reads it and comments. He reads it again with more emphasis. He tells them what it says. Then he tells them what it doesn't say. He asks them questions about what it says. His use of the interrogative is especially effective.[41] "God so loved the world that He what?" he asks. "Who will not perish? 'Whosoever believeth.' Who does that include? Does that include me? Yes. You? Yes. That rich man? That poor man? That white man? That black man? Yes. 'Whosoever believeth,' it says. Even a thief? Yes. A murderer? A philanderer? A pimp? 'Whosoever!'" Explain, emphasize, elaborate upon, illustrate the text! The preacher must not wander off and tell his people everything he knows about

---

40 Gurnall, *Christian in Complete Armour*, II:187.
41 See Carrick, *Imperatives of Preaching*, 56–81, on the use of the interrogative in preaching.

the subject, and every story he knows remotely related to the subject. Teach them the text. Keep leading them back to the text. The preacher must show that the truth he preaches is "a truth contained in or grounded on that text," says the Westminster *Directory for the Public Worship of God* (1645), "that the hearers may discern how God teacheth it *from thence.*"[42] This is classic, traditional, historic Reformed and Protestant preaching.

B. B. Warfield, in his sermon, "The Prodigal Son," complains of the many commentators who put content into the parable that Jesus did not. He cites the example of speculating on the father's emotional state in the absence of the prodigal, of his longing for his return, his frequent glances down the road, and so forth. Yet Warfield points out, the parable tells us none of this. "And it would not have omitted to tell us so, if this state of mind on the father's part entered into the essence of its teaching. The fact is that this commentator is rewriting the parable."[43] Warfield explains further the error of the commentator:

He is not expounding the parable we have, but composing another parable, a different parable with lessons. Our Lord, with His exquisitely nice adjustment of every detail of this parable to his purpose, we may be sure, has omitted nothing needed for the most poignant conveyance of the meaning He intended it to convey. That the expositor feels it necessary to insert all this merely proves that he is bent on making the parable teach something foreign to it as it stands.[44]

---

42 Thompson, *Liturgies of the Western Church*, 364, my emphasis.

43 B. B. Warfield, "The Prodigal Son," in *The Saviour of the World: Sermons Preached in the Chapel of Princeton Theological Seminary* (New York: Hodder and Stoughton, 1913), 12.

44 Ibid.

We err, he says, "when we refuse to be led by the text and begin to twist it like a nose of wax to the teaching of our own lessons."[45] "The only safe course," he insists, "is strictly to confine ourselves to the lesson the parable was framed to teach."[46] These are wise words for interpreters of every era.

Ordinarily we should *allow the passage to provide the main point, structure, and application of the sermon.* "Every text has a main theme," an "overriding thrust," Stott maintains. He cites Charles Simeon (1759–1836) and J. H. Jowett (1863–1923), among others, for similar sentiments.[47] Alec Motyer would have us ask the question, "what is the central truth, the one great revelation round which this word, verse, passage, chapter, book revolves?" Our preparation should aim at identifying that central truth, and "all else must be subordinated to making it plain."[48] Every unit of a thought has a central message. Every text has a point. It serves a purpose. There is a reason why it is there, as opposed to not being there. John said that the whole world couldn't contain all that might have been written about Jesus (John 21:25). Consequently, a purposeful editorial Hand was at work including and excluding information according to God's purposes for the church. Answer the question as to why a text is there, and one has the application. "This passage is here so that we might believe or do what?"

Stott refers to the "golden rule" of sermon outlines: "each text must be allowed to supply its own structure."[49] He warns against artificially imposing an outline on the text. Once the central point

---

45   Ibid. 13.
46   Ibid.
47   Stott, *Between Two Worlds*, 224–226.
48   Motyer, *Preaching?*, 33.
49   Stott, *Between Two Worlds*, 229.

of the passage is found, discern how each subordinate thought serves that central point. These sub-points provide the outline for the sermon. This outline will be a structure not imposed artificially from the outside, but one which arises naturally from the passage. The text provides the main point. The text provides the outline. The text provides the application. Indeed the main point is the application, and the sub-points, the points of the outline, are the sub-applications. These sub-applications are but elaborations upon the main point. For example, one might argue that the main point of 2 Peter 3:10–13 is "holy conduct and godliness."

> *But the day of the Lord will come like a thief, in which the heavens will pass away with a roar and the elements will be destroyed with intense heat, and the earth and its works will be burned up. Since all these things are to be destroyed in this way, what sort of people ought you to be in holy conduct and godliness, looking for and hastening the coming of the day of God, on account of which the heavens will be destroyed by burning, and the elements will melt with intense heat! But according to His promise we are looking for new heavens and a new earth, in which righteousness dwells.*

The Apostle Paul teaches that Christians should lead holy lives because ...

i. Judgment ("the day of the Lord") will be *sudden* and *unexpected* ("like a thief"—v 10a).

ii. Judgment will be *comprehensive* and *fierce* ("the earth and its works will be burned up"—v 10b; "heavens will be destroyed ...;" etc.).

iii.The *result* of judgment day will be a "new heavens and a new earth" characterized by righteousness (v 13).

iv. Consequently, "Since all these things are to be destroyed in this way" we ought to live holy lives ("what sort of people ought you to be"), that is, "in holy conduct and godliness" (v 11).

Both outline and application are arising from the text. The preacher will preach: we should live holy lives because judgment will be sudden and unexpected, because judgment will be comprehensive and fierce, because judgment will usher in a righteous realm which we, as redeemed people, will want to be in conformity with. The indicatives of judgment lead to the imperatives of holy living. Much elaboration is in order as application is made to believer, to unbeliever, to the young, to the old as they are urged to prepare for the day of the Lord by believing in Jesus "who delivers us from the wrath to come" and live devout lives (1 Thessalonians 1:10).

Note that this is not a passage that anchors holy living in the highest motivations: love, gratitude, or zeal to please the Father. The preacher may wish to mention this. Fear is not the highest motivation for the Christian life, but it is a legitimate one. Every sermon need not say everything that can be said on a given subject. This sermon will emphasize what the Apostle Peter chose to emphasize. The structure of the sermon, the content, and the application arise from the text itself.

I recall as a seminary student preparing to preach and struggling to make applications. My problem was that I was trying to manufacture application out of thin air. Application is not difficult. It is always there in the text, sometimes explicitly, as in the epistles, and sometimes implicitly, as in historical narrative, but it is always there. For example, how does one apply Philippians 4:6–7?

Be anxious for nothing, but in everything by prayer and supplication with thanksgiving let your requests be made known to God. And the peace of God, which surpasses all comprehension, shall guard your hearts and your minds in Christ Jesus.

Assuming that the preacher has already provided the background and meaning of the text, he might help his listeners to understand why they worry. He must help them to identify the anxiety about which the text speaks, and its sources. Then he might direct them to prayer as the solution, explaining how the various elements of prayer address the problem of anxiety, all in Christ Jesus. Isn't that the Apostle Paul's point? Isn't he telling them not to be anxious but instead to pray, and that the result will be peace in Christ? Since it is his point, shouldn't it be the point of good exposition? Sinclair Ferguson says, "We short-change our hearers by failing to show how the application of Scripture arises from and is usually given with the very passage we are expounding."[50]

In keeping with this, *avoid preaching formulas.* History has seen its schools of preaching come and go. There are a number of advocates of one or another method today. A sermon always begins like this, they say, then it does this, and finally it ends like this. Some will assume that one must always start with an attention grabbing opening statement, develop the body of the sermon, provide an illustration, a human interest story, a poem for aesthetic effect, and then always, always, always end on a positive note. Frankly, formulaic preaching is predictable and boring. Ironically, this typically American formula, even the "Great American School of Preaching," has more in common

---

50   Sinclair Ferguson, "Evangelical Exemplar," *Tabletalk*, February 1999.

4   *Administering the Elements—1*   139

with medieval oratorical gimmicks than with the preaching of the Reformers.[51] While we appreciate the intent to always leave people on a positive note, our question is: where does one find this in the Bible? The Bible itself presents its contents with remarkable variety. There is no cookie cutter. "Don't always preach a 'three-pointer,'" Motyer warns.[52] Beware of "forced and artificial alliteration," he cautions. "Alliteration is often a good servant, always a bad master."[53] There is no formula. Sometimes Scripture crushes us. Sometimes it comforts us. The preacher's job is to preach the text. The text determines both the form and content of the message. This means that no single sermon method will work, except the non-method of letting the text speak for itself, with its emphasis becoming the preachers' own.

Certainly one always preaches in the context of the whole Bible and gospel message. The threat of judgment is proclaimed in light of the gospel call to repentance and promise of salvation. However, the preacher should take care not to blunt the edge of his text. The message of the passage being preached should not die the death of a thousand qualifications. The people need to hear the warnings of the Bible unfiltered. The threats, "Whatsoever a man soweth that shall he also reap," "Those who practice such things shall not enter the kingdom of God," "Depart from Me I never knew you," need to fall on the ears of God's people without the preacher explaining them away as always applying to someone else (Galatians 6:7; 5:21; Matthew 7:21ff). The Apostles did

---

51   See Hughes O. Old, *The Reading & Preaching of Scriptures in the Worship of the Christian Church*, Volume 6: The Modern Age (Grand Rapids: William B. Eerdmans, 2007).

52   Motyer, *Preaching?*, 97.

53   Ibid. 93; Motyer continues: "How tiresome alliteration is if every sermon is presented that way!" (92). It is "using the Scriptures as if they were a word game" (92), easily becomes "forced and artificial" (93).

not hesitate to address such warnings to the people of God and neither should today's preachers. They did not hesitate to connect God's blessings to the conditions of faithfulness and obedience, and neither should we (e.g. Matthew 7:7–8; 1 John 1:6–10; James 4:1–3, 7–10; Ephesians 6:1–3, etc.). Likewise every gracious promise need not be "balanced" by a reminder of the need of faithfulness and obedience. A preacher should not feel obligated to drag in James 2 every time he preaches on John 3:16 or Ephesians 2:8–9. Let the text speak! Don't nullify either the promises of God or warnings by superimposing on the text a framework that is foreign to it.

REFORMED PREACHING?

What would we make of a minister who preached a *lectio continua* series of 159 sermons on Job and in 61 of those sermons (38%) failed to mention the name of Christ at all? What if only 17% of those 159 sermons brought the sermon to a Christological conclusion? Many times he preached successive sermons without any focus on Christ. Surely we would say he failed as a preacher, wouldn't we? Every sermon should be about Christ, focus on Christ, and call us to Christ.

What if the preacher's name was John Calvin?

Ah, some would say, just as we suspected. Calvin was so wrapped up in the twisted logic of predestination and the decrees of God that he forgot Christ and the simple gospel. The problem with this line of criticism is that some leading theologians have seen Christology *as the center of Calvin's theology*, if not Christology, then union with Christ. From the middle of the nineteenth century to the middle of the twentieth century, it was popular among Calvin scholars to attempt to find a "central dogma," or controlling theme of Calvin's thought. The person and work of Christ so permeates Calvin's writing that some of these scholars identified this as the dominant motif in Calvin's thought. Hardly can it be claimed that he failed in his writings to give the Lord Jesus Christ His due.

G. Sunjin Pak, who succeeded David C. Steinmetz, perhaps the leading Reformation scholar of our day, as the Amos Ragan Kearns Professor of the History of Christianity at the Divinity School of Duke University, has written an academic book entitled, *The Judaizing Calvin*.[54] It seems that sixteenth-century Lutherans thought that Calvin wasn't sufficiently Christ-centered in his interpretation of the Messianic psalms (e.g. Psalms 2, 8, 16, 22, 45, 72, 110, and 118). After Calvin's death, Lutheran theologian Aegidus Hunnius (1550–1603) attacked Calvin's exegesis of these Psalms in his 1593 treatise *Calvinus Judazans*, "The Judaizing Calvin."

What was the difference between Lutheran and Calvinist preaching? Just this: faithfulness to authorial intent. Calvin always first seeks to answer "what did the author mean by what he said?" Calvin is determined to interpret and apply the text that is before him according to the intended meaning of the author. Consequently, he avoided the Lutheran flights of fancy where Christ was made to emerge from every text, however far fetched it might seem. Here is Derek Thomas' assessment of Calvin's method in his book *Calvin's Teaching on Job*:

---

54   G. Sujin Pak, *The Judaizing Calvin: Sixteenth-Century Debates over the Messianic Psalms* (Oxford: University Press, 2010).

The Reformer consistently prioritizes grammatico-historical considerations as he approaches the text of Scripture. His concern throughout is to adhere rigidly to the text before him, applying what he finds to the needs of folk who hear him as he deems it relevant.[55]

Similarly G. S. Pak suggests that for Calvin, "The original historical context, and the grammatical reading of the text" played a decisive role in his exegesis.[56] This meant that Calvin interpreted the Psalms first in terms of the experience of the psalmist: his conflicts and sorrows, his victories and joys as a type of the Christian believer. He does interpret the Psalms Christologically, David as a type of Christ, but only secondarily. Calvin so honored the original historical context that "he made the Christological content of these texts secondary to their reading concerning David."[57] "Calvin's typological readings," says Pak, "are mostly in reference to David as *a type of the pious member of God's church.*"[58] Further, Calvin "employs these Psalms to promote his program for the cultivation of Protestant piety *through the example of David.*"[59] Calvin certainly would hold that Christ is the central figure of redemptive history and that indeed Christ is the content of all Scripture. However, he would deny that he fails to maintain the centrality of Christ when he illustrates the principles of Christian life from the examples of the Old Testament saints. His teaching is still Christ-centered, because Christ is central to

---

55 Derek Thomas, *Calvin's Teaching on Job: Proclaiming the Incomprehensible God* (Geanies House, Ross-shire, Scotland: Christian Focus Publications, 2004). 334.
56 Pak, *Judaizing Calvin*, 8, also pp 135–36.
57 Ibid. 10.
58 Ibid. 130, my emphasis.
59 Ibid. 127, my emphasis.

the life of the believer as foreshadowed in the life of the psalmist. Indeed, Calvin says, "every doctrine of the law, every command, every promise, always points to Christ. We are, therefore, to apply all its parts to him." And again: "We must read Scripture with the intention of finding Christ therein. If we turn aside from this end, however much trouble we take, however much time we devote to our study, we shall never attain the knowledge of the truth."[60]

However, Christ-centered, for Calvin, does not mean that Old Testament characters must always be interpreted as types of Christ. They may also be interpreted as types of the Christian believer, who looks to the examples of Abraham, David, Elijah, and others in the fight of faith (e.g. Romans 4; James 5:17–18; Hebrews 11).

Another factor is highlighted by Leroy Nixon in his selective collection of Calvin's *Sermons from Job*. Calvin's preaching and teaching was theocentric and Trinitarian rather than merely Christological. Nixon refers to its "utter theocentricity." "Whereas preaching for Luther found its purpose in pointing to Christ, for Calvin it was realized in showing forth more comprehensively the Triune Redeemer God. Calvin seldom mentions one of the persons of the Trinity separately without setting Him in dynamic relationship to the Godhead."[61] Moreover Nixon claims,

> To treat (the members of the Godhead) independently was for him to hazard idolatry ... He seems convinced that to be Spirit-centered is the first step toward a fatal subjectivism, and that

---

60 Both cited by Thomas, *Calvin's Teaching on Job*, 310.
61 Leroy Nixon, translator, John Calvin's *Sermons from Job* (Grand Rapids, Michigan: William B. Eerdmans Publishing Co., 1952), xxviii; see also David L. Puckett, *John Calvin's Exegesis of the Old Testament*, Columbia series in Reformed Theology (Louisville, Kentucky: Westminster John Knox Press, 1995).

144 *Serving with Calvin*

Christocentrism may yield the first small inch to humanism. God Himself, in all His glorious fullness, is both the root and the flower for every sermonic stem."[62]

All of this is food for thought for us today. There can be a kind of gospel legalism that ignores that the Bible deals with many themes, not just redemption. Some of the preaching of the extreme elements of the "redemptive-historical" school has begun to resemble medieval allegorical preaching, so contrived and contrary to the biblical author's intent has it become. This is the very sort of thing to which Calvin's preaching was a refreshing corrective. We say this without meaning to endorse everything about Calvin's sermons. Still, the great man has served as the prototype of Reformed preaching for over 475 years. He would have us know that the Bible teaches us about God, providence, wisdom, and life. It teaches us about the Father and the Holy Spirit, as well as about Christ. It teaches us theology and anthropology as well as soteriology. It is, after all, a relatively modern and new-orthodox idea that we cannot speak of God without doing so in and through Christ. Reformed ministers may wish to adjust what they have recently come to understand as "Christ-centered" preaching, and get more in line with how that has been classically understood. Motyer cautions preachers not to force an evangelistic message into passages in which it is not "inherent," warning that to do so "would be a misuse of our stewardship."[63] "Our task," he says, "is to be faithful to the Scriptures," while "results are the work and business of the Holy Spirit."[64] Motyer tells the story of a minister preaching on

---

62 Ibid. xxix.
63 Motyer, *Preaching?*, 144.
64 Ibid. 142.

Psalm 95 whose message did not include an "evangelistic gospel." The thrust of his message was to call to obedience to God's word, as indeed is the focus of the psalm. Surprisingly a man was converted. The encouraging and reassuring truth, says Motyer, "is that Christ *is* in all the Scriptures, and in that basic sense, every preaching of Scripture is a preaching of Christ."[65] "We want to preach Christ," says D. E. Johnson, "but we also want to preach each biblical text with integrity."[66]

5. Preach Christocentrically

The preacher should preach the text, allow the text to determine the main point, structure, and application of the sermon, and avoid formulas. Yet his preaching should also be Christ-centered. In light of what we've just said, how is this so? Because each verse is located in the context of a unit of thought; each unit of thought (or pericope) is located in the context of a chapter; each chapter is located in the context of a book; each book is located in the context of the whole Bible; and the whole Bible is about Christ. For example, if we were preaching through Ecclesiastes, we might preach the message of futility in the opening chapters in light of the conclusion of 12:13—"fear God and keep His commandments." We would interpret 12:13 in light of the placement of Ecclesiastes in the Bible as a whole. We fear God and obey by coming to Christ, who in Himself is hidden all the treasures of wisdom and knowledge (Colossians 2:3). Yes the world and its commodities and experiences are futile and empty. Jesus alone is the "bread of life" (John 6:35). He alone fills the

---

65 Ibid. 143.
66 Johnson, *Him We Proclaim,* 128.

empty soul. Ecclesiastes must be preached in light of its context in the whole Bible.

Spurgeon said that wherever he preached he made a bee-line for the cross. It is not only possible (in light of the foregoing) but necessary to preach Christ in every sermon.[67] As we have seen, the Bible is all about the fall and redemption, sin and restoration, Paradise Lost and Paradise Regained. Every text of Scripture is somehow related to that overarching theme. Granted, sometimes the relation of a given text to the central theme may seem remote. Nonetheless, it remains true. The Law & Prophets, History & Wisdom, Poetry & Gospel, Acts & Epistles are all rooted in the theme of redemption. That is to say, they are all, ultimately, about Jesus Christ, the one to whom the story of redemption points and in whom its promise is fulfilled.

Regarding the Old Testament, there is a sense in which Israel's offices, institutions, and even its history point to Christ and are fulfilled in Christ. The *monarchy* points to great David's greater Son, that son of David in whom the promises of an eternal kingdom are fulfilled (2 Samuel 7:1ff; Matthew 1:1–2:12). The *prophetic* office is fulfilled in the great prophet like Moses who would succeed Moses (Deuteronomy 18:15; Acts 7:37; Hebrews 1:1–3). Even Jonah's three days in the fish foreshadowed the work of Christ (Matthew 12:46). The *priestly* office is fulfilled in Christ or Great High Priest (Hebrews 4:14–16; 5:1–10; 6:13–10:25). The kings, prophets, and priests all point to Christ, who in His three-fold office fulfills their redemptive functions. The sacrifices point to the lamb of God who takes away the sin of the world (John 1:29). Jesus said the temple's meaning was realized in His body (John 2:19–22).

---

67 See *Worshipping with Calvin*, Chapter 7.

The messianic typology of the Old Testament is clearly demonstrated in Matthew's gospel. Did Israel sojourn in Egypt? So did Jesus, and "out of Egypt did I call my son" (Matthew 2:18; Hosea 11:1). Did Israel wander in the wilderness for 40 *years*? So did Jesus, for 40 *days* (Matthew 4:1–11). Was Israel baptized "in the cloud and in the sea" (1 Corinthians 10:2)? So was Jesus baptized in the Jordan (Matthew 3:13–17). Jesus fulfills the predictive prophesy as well, of birth in Bethlehem (Matthew 2:6; Micah 5:2), of the prophetic forerunner who makes His way ready (Matthew 3:1–3; Isaiah 40:3), of ministry emerging from Galilee (Matthew 4:15–16; Isaiah 9:1–2), of Moses-like law-giving from the mountain (Matthew 5:7; Exodus 19:18–Leviticus 27:34). Israel, its history, institutions, and leaders all are fulfilled in Christ. All the Messianic promises are fulfilled in Him (Matthew 11:1–6; Isaiah 35:5ff; 61:1). He is the suffering servant of the Lord (Matthew 12:18–21; Isaiah 42:1–21). We could go on and on and on (e.g. Matthew 13:14–15; Isaiah 6:10; Matthew 13:35; Psalm 78:2; Matthew 21:5; Isaiah 62:11; Zechariah 9:9; Matthew 21:9; Psalm 118:26ff; Matthew 21:42; Psalm 118:22; and especially Matthew 22:44; Psalm 110; etc.). "The New is in the Old concealed," said Augustine (AD 354–430), "the Old is in the New revealed."[68] J. A. Motyer, alluding to the preceding quotation from Augustine, summarizes our point: "The Old Testament is Jesus predicted; the Gospels are Jesus revealed; Acts is Jesus preached; the Epistles, Jesus explained; and the Revelation, Jesus expected. He is the climax as well as the substance and centre of the whole. In him all God's promises are yes and amen (2 Corinthians 1:20)."[69]

This is how it is possible for the same Apostles who preach "the

---

68 Augustine, cited in Johnson, *Him We Proclaim*, 130.
69 Motyer, *Looking to the Rock*, 22.

148   *Serving with Calvin*

whole counsel of God" (Acts 20:27) also claim to preach "nothing but Jesus Christ and Him crucified" (1 Corinthians 2:1–2; cf. 1:22–24; 2 Corinthians 4:4–5). This is not hyperbole because the "whole counsel" is finally and ultimately about the redemption of a lost humanity through the crucified Christ.[70] Chapell, who devotes 26 pages to this theme, puts it this way:

> Christ-centered preaching rightly understood does not seek to discover where Christ is mentioned in every text but to disclose where every text stands in relation to Christ.[71]

His words caution preachers from forcing Christ into texts in which He is not found. We repeat: some so-called "Christ-centered" preaching has become ahistorical and contrived in its attempts to find Christ in its passages. Still, the "whole counsel of God" is properly preached only when "all the Scriptures" are interpreted in light of their relation to the cross of Christ (Luke 24:27). "Moses ... wrote of me," Jesus said (John 5:46). "All the prophets ... announced these days," the Apostle Peter agrees (Acts 3:24). The revelation of "Christ-crucified" is that decisive event which illuminates the meaning of all that went before it. Only in the light of the cross do we fully understand the meaning of God's pre-incarnational revelation. Consequently the Christian preacher faithfully preaches his text when he does so from the perspective of its placement in unfolding of redemptive history, and explicitly, in its relation to Christ-crucified. Some examples may be in order.

---

70   D. E. Johnson's chapter 7, "Theological Foundations of Apostolic Preaching" in *Him We Proclaim* is a brilliant exposition of how Christ is the theme of the Old Testament (198–238).

71   Bryan Chapell, *Christ-Centered Preaching: Redeeming the Expository Sermon* (Grand Rapids: Baker Books, 1994), 279.

The gospel is about the cross and atonement, repentance, forgiveness, reconciliation with God, justification, and adoption (Romans 3:21ff; 1 John 1:7–2:2). That should be clear enough. The gospel is also about post-conversion themes, if we may call them that, of sanctification, assurance, pain and suffering, marriage and family, humility and service. The Apostles treat practical spiritual and moral themes as *applications* of the gospel. When the Apostle Paul exhorts the Corinthians to practice sexual purity, he plants the cross right in the middle of his argument: "You were bought with a price; therefore glorify God in your body" (1 Corinthians 6:20). When he instructs husbands and wives, he invokes the sacrificial love of Christ for the church and the church's submission to Christ (Ephesians 5:21ff). When he underscores the eternal safety of the believer, he does so with the cross.

He who did not spare His own Son, but delivered Him up for us all, how will He not also with Him freely give us all things? (Romans 8:32)

Humility and service? We are urged to learn from the "attitude which was in Christ Jesus," who was "obedient to the point of death, even death on a cross" (Philippians 2:6–8). Persecution and suffering? We are to "follow in His steps," who "while reviled He did not revile in return" and "while suffering, He uttered no threats," but "bore our sins in His body on the cross" (1 Peter 2:21–24). Care for the needy? "We know love by this," says the Apostle John, "that He laid down His life for us; and we ought to lay down our lives for the brethren" (1 John 3:16–17). Love for fellow believers? "Beloved if God so loved us (in sending His Son to be the propitiation for our sins) so also ought we to love one another" (1 John 4:11). Finally, everything comes back to the cross. "The love of Christ constrains us," or "controls us" (NASB,

ESV), inspiring our obedience and service (2 Corinthians 5:14ff). We love because we were first loved; our love arises out of Christ's love for us and is a response to it, motivating us to keep Christ's commandments (1 John 4:19; John 14:15, 21).

At the same time we wish to warn against a Christo-legalism. We have already cautioned against formulas in preaching. Well intended advocates of "Christ-centered" preaching have spawned disciples who demand a certain pattern of words. When they don't hear that pattern, not infrequently they have claimed that the gospel was not being preached. Preachers of this school have been guilty of the most strained attempts to find Christ in texts in which He was not to be found in any immediate sense, leading to the allegorical interpretations and flights of fancy that would make a medieval theologian blush. D. E. Johnson warns of redemptive-historical preaching that draws "forced and unconvincing lines of contact between Old Testament texts and Christ."[72] He questions, "Do all redemptive-historical sermons sound essentially alike?"[73] Again we urge, let the text speak. Let us go where the text takes us.

One of our "unchurched" visitors (who later professed faith in Christ and joined the church) once asked, "Why are we always talking about what Paul says. Who is he?" Thereafter I began to notice how frequently preachers (like myself) speak of what Paul says, and Paul tells us, and Paul teaches, and Paul this and Paul that. Sometimes we throw in a James or a Peter. It is wiser to refer to Paul (and Peter) in a more Christ-centered way. He's not just Paul. He's the Apostle Paul. He's Christ's Apostle. "Here's what the Apostle of Christ says," or even, "Here's what Christ says

---

72 D. E. Johnson, *Him We Proclaim*, 52; cf. 128.
73 Ibid. 52.

through His Apostle." Similarly, Jeremiah is not just Jeremiah. He's the prophet Jeremiah. He's God's spokesman. "God tells us through His prophet ...," we might say. Our choice of words should constantly remind our listeners that all the treasures of God's wisdom and knowledge are found in Christ (Colossians 2:3; Ephesians 1:3; 2 Peter 1:3).

PREACH THE WHOLE GOSPEL

What we mean by preach the "whole gospel" is that we preach what Christ has accomplished *outside* of us at the cross, *and* what He accomplishes *inside* of us by the Spirit; the announcement of redemption *and* the call to repentance and faith; the objective facts and the subjective experience of salvation; justification *and* sanctification; the indicative *and* the imperative; salvation from the *guilt* of sin and the *power* of sin; the "second use" of the commandments (driving us to Christ) *and* the "third use" (as a guide to Christian living). We sense the necessity of making this point (and plan to elaborate at length) because of what we see as an alarming tendency today to allow the indicative to swallow up the imperative, to lose sanctification in justification, to focus on the forensic and neglect the renovative, to allow the second use to supplant the third use of the Law. The Bible is packed with ethical content. If one is committed to *lectio continua* preaching, it is inevitable that one's preaching will lay heavy emphasis upon the principles of Christian living, as well as the way of salvation.

INDICATIVE AND IMPERATIVE

A number of voices in recent years have been reminding us urgently that all gospel imperatives must be rooted in gospel indicatives. The commands of Christ, the demands of Christian discipleship must be built upon the foundation of what Christ has accomplished for us on the cross. Their point is well taken. We have demonstrated this to be the case. The Apostle Paul structures his presentation of the gospel in Romans, Galatians, Ephesians, and Colossians in this way of indicatives followed by imperatives.[74] We can also see the indicative/imperative structure paragraph by paragraph in Hebrews, 1 and 2 Peter, and also in Philippians, where Philippians 2:5–11 and 3:4–10 provide the hub around which most of the exhortations of Philippians 1–4 revolve. "The indicative has the priority," said Richard B. Gaffin, Jr., of Westminster Theological Seminary in Philadelphia, "the indicative is foundational."[75]

However, some commentators today have created the impression that one is only Christ-centered in one's preaching when proclaiming the "indicatives" of what Christ has done. By their definitions, only the announcement of what Christ accomplished on the cross qualifies as gospel preaching. Imperatives, as they classify them, are law not gospel. While this may be grammatically correct, and may even have some historical precedence in the Reformed tradition,[76] the radical distinction

---

74   The mainly doctrinal Romans 1–11 is followed by the mainly applicatory Romans 12–16; the doctrines of Galatians 1–5:12 are followed by practical exhortations of Galatians 5:13–6:18; the soaring theology of Ephesians 1–3 is followed by the practical wisdom of Ephesians 4–6; similarly Colossians 1–2 is followed by Colossians 3–4. We note as well, that even in these books this is not the whole story. If we may use Romans as an example, practical exhortations are sprinkled throughout the doctrinal section calling upon believers to rejoice, to not let sin reign, to mortify sin, to walk according to the Spirit, etc. (e.g. Romans 3:8, 5:1–11; 6:1–23; 7:14–25; 8:12–17).

75   Cited in Carrick, *Imperative of Preaching*, 28, from Dr. Gaffin's class lectures.

76   See R. Scott Clark; "Letter and Spirit: Law and Gospel in Reformed Preaching" in R. Scott Clark (ed.), *Covenant, Justification, and Pastoral Ministry* (Phillipsburg, New Jersey; P. & R. Publishing, 2007), 331–363. We are not entirely opposed to a narrow definition of the gospel, though we don't believe it stands up to biblical scrutiny. Jesus is said to preach the "gospel" when he announces the arrival of the

between law and grace overlooks the value of Jesus' instruction as good news, as Gospel. It overlooks what has been called the "grace of law."[77] God's commandments are not "burdensome" (1 John 5:2). "There is love in every command," says Thomas Watson.[78] God's instruction restores the soul. It rejoices the heart and makes wise the simple. It is more to be desired than gold and sweeter than honey (Psalm 19:8, 10). *Commandments* are more than *condemnation.* God's law, *torah,* is fatherly wisdom that imparts the discernment by which one is both delivered from evil and its destructive consequences and directed in the path of blessing (Proverbs 1–9; especially 1:8, 3:1, 4:2, 6:20, 23; 7:2).[79] Sinners "die for lack of instruction" (Proverbs 5:23). The word of God learned, studied and meditated upon keeps one from sin (Psalm 119:11). It is a lamp to our feet and light to our path (Psalm 119:105).

We insist that we are no less Christ-centered when we focus on *Christ's imperatives* than when we focus on *Christ's indicatives.* We are no less Christ-centered when we proclaim Christ's liberating

---

Kingdom of God and calls upon his hearers to "repent and believe in the gospel" (Mark 1:14–15; cf. Matthew 4:17). The same is said of John the Baptist (Luke 3:3, 18), Peter (Acts 2:38) and Paul (Acts 26:20). As long as everyone understands how language is being used it is permissible to use terminology in idiosyncratic ways. However, it is wise to do so only if one is careful to secure the connections between "gospel" and "response to the gospel," and "fruit of the gospel." No one should ever be accused of failing to preach the "gospel" because they are calling listeners to respond by repentance and faith, nor should that call be classified as "law." No one should be accused of not preaching the "gospel" when insisting on the fruit of the gospel in godly character and behavior, not when Jesus says, "you shall know them by their fruits" (Matthew 7:20; Luke 6:43–45). Our fear is that when the definition of the gospel is limited as described above, those connections are lost, leaving a truncated and false gospel behind.

77 See Ernest Kevan, *The Grace of Law: A Study in Puritan Theology* (London: The Carey Kingsway Press Limited, 1964).

78 Thomas Watson, *The Ten Commandments* (1959; London: The Banner of Truth Trust, 1970), p 6.

79 See Motyer, *Looking to the Rock*, 74–76.

teaching than when we proclaim His liberating *atonement*. What strange times we live in today, when it is said that preaching Christ's commands is not Christ-centered preaching! Sometimes we need to know not just want Christ has *done*, but what Christ has *taught*. Sometimes we need not another reminder of what Christ accomplished for our *justification* but His instruction for our *sanctification*. When we provide that instruction, we are not abandoning the gospel, but rather fulfilling its implications.

Proclaiming our deliverance from the *power* of sin is no less gospel, no less Christ-centered than preaching deliverance from sin's *penalty*. We remind ourselves that Christ is our Savior from both the *guilt* for sin and its *corruption*. "*The same gospel of grace that reconciles alienated rebels*," says D. E. Johnson, "continues to direct and drive their growth as reconciled children of God."[80] Moreover, teaching, catechesis, and moral instruction are an important means by which we are freed from sin's grip. The truth, Jesus said, makes us free (John 8:32). Truth brings light into the confusion and error of darkness. Jesus is "the light of life" (John 8:12). It is true that the "law" has no power to transform sinners, "weak as it (is)" (Romans 8:3). It has "no power of enablement," as John Murray put it.[81] Yet we shouldn't allow the weaknesses of the law in the hearts of the unregenerate obscure our understanding of the power of biblical teaching, instruction, and commands in the lives of the saints, regenerated and indwelt by the Holy Spirit. Through the imperatives the people of God are both warned away from troubling sin and instructed in the paths of peace. By meditating upon the law day and night, the man of God becomes

---

80   D. E. Johnson, *Him We Proclaim*, 43 (my emphasis).
81   John Murray, *Principles of Conduct* (London: The Tyndale Press, 1957), 185.

like a tree planted by streams of water, *bearing fruit* in its season (Psalm 1).

Some voices we hear today come perilously close to denying that not merely the law but the word of God is an effectual instrument for our sanctification. Jesus said we are sanctified by the truth of God's word (John 17:17). Does He only refer to the "gospel" truth, or also to the commands, ideals (virtues), examples, warnings and exhortations? The Apostle Peter says we grow by the pure milk of the word (1 Peter 2:1–2). Is that only the "gracious" word, the word of acceptance, or also the moral word, the ethical instructions of Jesus, the prophets, and the apostles? Is it not the whole word, law and gospel, that is "living and active and sharper than any two-edged sword" (Hebrews 4:12)? Is it not the whole word, the "living and abiding" word, that has converting and sanctifying power (1 Peter 1:23)?

It may be a problem that gospel imperatives can become isolated from gospel indicatives. When the imperatives stand alone, severed from Christ the True Vine, apart from when we can do nothing (John 15:1–5), they can become a kind of legalism, functionally defining the relationship between the believer to Christ solely in terms of commands. Redemptive-historical preachers in particular oppose *moralistic* and *exemplaristic* preaching. They warn against Christian sermons that would be acceptable in a synagogue because the preacher has failed to root his imperatives or ideals in Christ. However, the greater threat in an antinomian age is for indicatives to *swallow up* imperatives, and for the imperatives to disappear. We see a troubling trend in today's pulpit. The extreme elements of what has been called the "contemporary grace movement" have effectively intimidated ministers from preaching the commands and demands of Christ, lest they be accused of not preaching the gospel. The long-term impact of a diminished focus on obedience and holiness is sobering to contemplate. We can expect growing problems with carnality and worldliness to result if the current generation of preachers will not proclaim unambiguously what Jesus expects of His disciples: what He teaches that they *must* do and what He warns that they *must not* do. Indeed, we've heard sermons that we never thought we'd hear Reformed ministers preach. These ministers seem to understand the front end of the formula. They preach indicatives. The back end, however, has dropped out of their preaching. We insist that *imperatives do follow indicatives*, and *must*, if we are to proclaim the whole gospel. "The indicative always moves on to the imperative; the indicative and the imperative are inseparable in the theology of the New Testament," argues Carrick.[82] Further, he claims, there is "a fundamental incompleteness and insufficiency about the indicative mood considered in and of itself. The *indicative* mood must be complemented and supplemented by the *imperative* mood."[83]

BIBLICAL ETHICS

D. E. Johnson demonstrates from Colossians 1:27–2:7 that *content* of apostolic preaching is Christ ("Him we proclaim") but the *goal* (*teleios*) or purpose of that preaching is sanctification. They proclaim Christ "that we may present everyone mature in Christ" (Colossians 1:28). The goal is "transformation of the most radical and comprehensive sort."[84] Listen to this testimony by a pastor in

---

82 Carrick, *Imperative of Preaching*, 28; he goes on to cite Dr. Gaffin further: "imperative and indicative are given together; and the imperative is a consequence or attestation *apart from which the indicative does not exist*"(my emphasis).

83 Ibid. 29.

84 Johnson, *Him We Proclaim*, 64.

the Savannah area regarding the relevance of the Bible. Not only has the Bible given him the knowledge of salvation, but has shown him how to

"build a marriage ...
raise my kids ...
building lasting friendships ...
handle my money ...
treat my body ...
harness my appetites ...
reconcile relationships that have been bruised."

He continues, "This book has comforted me in sorrow ... strengthened me in times of weakness ...rebuked me when I've rebelled and affirmed me when I've obeyed. The Bible has given me perspective on my past, wisdom for the present, and hope for the future."

Surely, this is the testimony of believers all through the centuries. We knew nothing about how to be good spouses and parents until we were instructed by Scripture. The Bible's teaching transformed our marriages and families. We were ignorant in our duties as neighbors, citizens, employees/employers and church members. We had to be taught by God's commands about acceptable and unacceptable behavior. We had to be taught the distinction between good and evil, truth and error, right and wrong. A vision had to be cast for money and our stewardship of it, for our bodies and the control of our appetites, for relationships and how to maintain them. We also had to be urged to embrace that vision. Our whole lives were transformed not just by the cross *per se*, but also by regeneration and the indwelling of the Holy

Spirit, and in particular by the directions given by the God of the cross through biblical law/teaching.

For what other reason did Jesus spend so much time teaching? Why the Sermon on the Mount (Matthew 5–7) and the Sermon on the Plain (Luke 6), each of which is packed with ethical content? So much is this the case that the old-line dispensationalists finally just gave up and relegated the entire ethical dimension of Jesus' ministry to a future kingdom age where it wouldn't trouble their understanding of the gospel any longer. Did Jesus not intend to shape attitudes and behavior by teaching us about the attitudes and behaviors about which He approves and disapproves? Does the sermon only have "second use" implications and not "third use" as well (see further below)? *Teaching Christ's commandments is a central element of the Christian mission* (Matthew 28:20).

When we turn to the epistles, we find most of them are aimed as much at correcting bad behavior by churches and individuals as teaching correct doctrine. We've already looked at the indicative-imperative structure of Romans, Galatians, Ephesians, Philippians, Colossians, Hebrews and 1 and 2 Peter. Now we observe further that the foundational indicatives in these epistles lead not to ever more indicatives, but to imperatives. Beyond these epistles, we ask, what are we to make of 1 and 2 Corinthians, 1 & 2 Thessalonians, 1 & 2 Timothy, Titus, Philemon, James, (of which Carrick notes "an unparalleled prevalence of the imperative mood"), 1–3 John, Revelation 1–3, all of which consist predominantly of imperatives? "It is no exaggeration to say that the New Testament *teems* with what have been called 'imperatives of sanctification,'" says Carrick.[85]

---

85 Carrick, *Imperatives of Preaching*, 86.

DIRECTIONS, VIRTUES, EXAMPLES, WARNINGS

Why do we find throughout the epistles extensive *"household codes"* as they have been called, detailing the responsibility of parents, children, husbands, wives, masters, and slaves in the epistles? (e.g. Ephesians 5:21–6:9; Colossians 3:18–4:1; Titus 2:1–10; 1 Peter 2:13–3:7). Why is extensive instruction given regarding speech (Ephesians 5:1–4; Colossians 3:8–9, 4:4–6; 2 Timothy 1:16–18; James 1:19, 26, 3:1–12); diet (Colossians 2:16–23; 1 Timothy 4:1–5); sexual conduct (1 Corinthians 5–7; Ephesians 5:5–20; Colossians 3:5–7; 1 Thessalonians 4:1–8; 2 Timothy 1:22; 1 Peter 2:11–12; 4:1–5); gender roles (1 Corinthians 11:1–16; 14:34–38; 1 Timothy 2:9–17; 5:1–16; Titus 2:1–10); stewardship of wealth (2 Corinthians 8–9; 1 Timothy 6:6–10, 17–19; James 5:1–6; 1 John 3:17); and work (Colossians 3:22–25; 1 Thessalonians 4:11; 2 Thessalonians 3:6–12; 1 Timothy 5:8)? Is it just so that we might say, "I can't do any of this. I fail every day. However, isn't it wonderful that Jesus has kept these commands on my behalf?" Do these commands only have a "second use" function and not a "third use"? Were they not given so that we may conform our lives to them?

Why must it be spelled out that we are to *love one another*, (e.g. John 13:34–35; 15:12, 17; Ephesians 5:2; 1 Thessalonians 4:9; Hebrews 13; 1 Peter 1:22; 1 John 2:7ff, 3:11, 23, 4:7; 2 John 5), love our neighbors (Matthew 22:39–40; Galatians 5:14; Romans 13:8–10) and love our enemies (Matthew 8:43–44; Luke 6:27ff)? Why the extensive list of "one another's," urging us to bear one another's burdens, be kind to one another, forgive one another, encourage one another and so on? (Romans 12:9–10; 14:3–9, 19; 15:5, 7, 14; 1 Corinthians 12:25; Galatians 5:13; 6:2; Ephesians 4:2, 32; 5:21; Colossians 3:13, 16; 1 Thessalonians 4:18; Hebrews 10:24; James

5:16; 1 Peter 4:9; 5:5; 1 John 1:7). Is it not because apart from such urgings our love will fall short of its full Christian implications?

Why the multiple *lists of virtues*, such as the fruit of tribulation in Romans 5, the fruit of the Spirit in Galatians 5:22–23; the ideals for contemplation in Philippians 4:8–9; the characteristics of love in 1 Corinthians 13, the qualities of faith in 2 Peter 1, the qualifications for officers in 1 Timothy 3 and Titus 1, the "put offs" and "put ons" of Ephesians 4 and Colossians 3, and of course, the beatitudes in Matthew 5 and Luke 6. Is it not the intention of the Holy Spirit that by teaching these virtues that the people of God will admire them, learn to strive for them, and come to be characterized by them?

Why are the many *godly examples* put forward for us to imitate? Jesus' suffering on the cross is more than an atoning sacrifice, it is also a pattern of behavior for His people. We are urged to follow Jesus' example in regarding others as more important than ourselves, in looking out for the interests of others not just our own (Philippians 2:1–4; 5ff). His "attitude" is to be our own. He is our "example." We are to "follow in His steps," in quietly suffering unjustly (1 Peter 2:21). We are to live selflessly and sacrificially, loving as He did (1 John 3:16; 4:10–11). We are to "fix our eyes on Jesus," on His example of joyful endurance, "that we might not grow weary and lose heart" (Hebrews 12:1–3). Are we less Christ-centered when we preach the *example* of Christ than when we preach the *atonement* of Christ?

Bible characters also provide examples to follow, positive and negative. James points to the Old Testament prophets and Job as examples of patient suffering, and to Elijah as a man of prayer (James 5:10–12, 18). Jesus cited Abraham's rejoicing as a proper response to His ministry (John 8:56), and David as a guide in Sabbath observance (Mark 2:25). We are urged to imitate the

4   *Administering the Elements—1*   161

apostles (1 Corinthians 4:16; 11:1). Timothy was charged to be an example to other believers, "in speech, conduct, love, faith and purity" (1 Timothy 4:12) as was Titus (Titus 2:8). Elders are charged to be examples to the flock (1 Peter 5:3). We are urged to be "imitators of those who through faith and patience inherit the promises" (Hebrews 6:12). Their faith, their patience, and their diligence (6:11) are models for our own. Hebrews 11 presents 15 model believers to which the writer points us, plus "the prophets," who are examples of laying aside encumbrances and entangling sin and running the race with endurance (Hebrews 11:1–12:2). Why does Jesus urge us to "remember Lot's wife"? (Luke 17:32). Are we not to learn from her bad example? Do the Apostles not draw warnings from the past infidelities of the people of God (e.g. 1 Corinthians 10:1–14; Hebrews 3, 4)? D. E. Johnson asks if this handling of Old Testament characters does not "imply that such ancient examples, positive and negative, are ethically instructive for us, who inhabit a more privileged epoch of redemptive history?"[86] Too often advocates of an extreme school of redemptive-historical preaching have dismissed all appeals to biblical examples as "moralistic" or "exemplaristic." They have established a false dichotomy between Christ-centered proclamation and supposedly man-centered application. "*Christocentricity* must not be permitted to degenerate into *Christomonism*," Carrick maintains. Further, "the *indicatives of history* do not and must not exclude *the imperatives of ethics*."[87] Old Testament characters not only serve as types of Christ. They were also believers in Christ, and as such properly serve as

---

86   Johnson, *Him We Proclaim*, 53.
87   Carrick, *Imperatives of Preaching*, 130.

examples for Christians today, for good and ill. They were, after all, servants *of Christ.*

NEWNESS OF LIFE

The message of one ministry was summed up from the pulpit, "I'm messed up, you're messed up, we're all messed up. But thankfully we worship a perfect God." That's fine as far as it goes. However, as a summary of the gospel it doesn't go far enough. Surely *someone* in that congregation is experiencing liberation not only from the *penalty* but also the *power* of sin. Surely *someone* is making progress in sanctification. Hopefully the pastor, who, along with the officers, is to be an example to the flock (1 Peter 5:1–5), is growing in Christ-likeness. Hopefully there are elders who are "above reproach" (1 Timothy 3:3). Hopefully there are members who are manifesting the fruit of the Spirit (Galatians 5:22–24). Surely some who once were "messed up" have been raised up in newness of life and sin no longer masters them (Romans 6:1–14). Surely there are those in the congregation who are born again and have become new creations in Christ, the old passing away and all things becoming new (John 3:1ff; 2 Corinthians 5:17).

The *imperatives* of Christian living are commanded, *directions* for households are given, the ideal *virtues* are listed, the *examples* of faithful discipleship are presented not merely for the purpose of convincing us that achieving them is impossible. It is not conceivable that they are presented on page after page of the New Testament only for the sake of our justification and not for the purpose of our sanctification. They function not only in a "second use" capacity but also in a "third use." The imperatives, the household codes, the virtues, and the exemplary lives are presented not merely so that we may "preach the gospel to ourselves," that is, remind ourselves once more of the ground of our justification, but *so that we may live holy lives*. Ethical instructions are not a futile exercise because Christians are able to live holy lives. The experience of believers is not limited to Romans 3–5, but enters into Christ's victory of Romans 6, the struggle of Romans 7, the warfare and triumph of Romans 8, the confidence of Romans 9–11 and the consecration and service of Romans 12–16. We have been raised up in "newness of life" (Romans 6:4). "Sin shall not be master over (us)" and therefore we are exhorted to "not let sin reign in (our) mortal bodies" (Romans 6:12, 14). We who were dead in sins have been made alive in Christ. We have been re-created in Christ Jesus "for good works" (Ephesians 2:1–10). There has been a "radical breach with the power and love of sin," as John Murray put it, and so there is real potential for believers to live holy lives.[88] Faithful stewardship of the gospel requires that these themes be preached, that Christians might lead holy lives.

We include in the above the preaching of the Bible's *warnings*. It only makes sense to warn believers of the consequences of carnality if those warnings are a means by which we are helped to avoid and/or overcome carnality. Why the warnings of 1 Corinthians 6:9–10 and Galatians 5:19–21, that those who practice the evils listed "shall not inherit the Kingdom of God" (Galatians 5:21). Why the severe warnings of Hebrews 6 and 10? Why Jesus' frightening "Lord, Lord" warning of Matthew 7:22 to those who are workers of "lawlessness." Are these warnings given only to remind us of the ground of our justification or to remind us of the necessity of good works, obedience, and holiness

---

88   John Murray, *Redemption Accomplished and Applied*, (Grand Rapids, MI: Wm. B. Eerdmans Publishing Co., 1955), 143.

flowing from justification, and by so doing urging us to pursue "the holiness without which no one will see the Lord." (Hebrews 12:14)?

The Lord's law, testimony, precepts, commandments, fear, and judgments are a means by which His servants are warned and kept back from sin (Psalm 19:7–13). Since the Lord "disciplines us for our good, that we may share in His holiness," we should understand that His warnings of His discipline do the same. Since the Lord's discipline trains us and "yields the peaceful fruit of righteousness," His warnings of His discipline may have the same salutary effect (Hebrews 12:10–11). It is not necessary that we actually be the object of the Lord's afflictions before we change. It may be that in the Lord's mercy the warnings prove to be enough. When we preach these warnings, we are not to be accused of preaching "law" and of not preaching the gospel. It is not only by the "gospel," narrowly defined, that lives are transformed, but also by exhortations, warnings and promises of reward. If the latter items are not useful in changing us, then why does God bother to communicate them? Since He does, are we not obligated to relay the message?

SECOND AND THIRD USE TOGETHER

The Sermon on the Mount sets a very high ethical bar, indeed an unachievably high ethical bar. No one can love their enemies as Jesus requires, or "be perfect as my Father in heaven is perfect" (Matthew 5:43–48). One correctly might use Jesus' "law" in its second use, as a schoolmaster to drive condemned sinners, sinners who fall short of the ethics of Jesus, to Christ for justification.

Would one have then exhausted the meaning of the Sermon on the Mount? Not at all. One would not have even identified its "first and primary use" (as Calvin said of the so-called "third use") which is its role as teacher. The "second use" of the Sermon on the Mount must not be allowed to supplant the "third use," which is to instruct the disciples of Jesus on how they are to live; the beatitudes to which they are to aspire (Matthew 5:3–16); the Scriptures which they are to teach and keep, not merely externally like Pharisees, but from the heart (Matthew 5:17–48); the spiritual disciplines that they are to practice (prayer, tithing, fasting) and how they are to go about practicing them (Matthew 6:1–18); the tension between the things of this world and trusting God and how to resolve it (Matthew 6:19–34); and so on. It is a mistake to respond to the ethics of Jesus with admiration, focus entirely on the impossibility of their realization, and revert to their use in our justification ("Christ has fulfilled this law for us") and not go on to honor those commands as ideals to which believers are to aspire, as norms to which their lives are to conform. It is well and good to use the Bible's commands to stimulate the contemplation of our justification. However, it is invalid to stop there and not also teach the role of those commands in shaping our lives, that is, our sanctification. "Although good behavior is an inevitable consequence of the good news, it is not 'automatic' in the sense that it does not need to be taught," Stott maintains.[89]

Indeed, the Holy Spirit uses the imperatives, the Christian ideals, and exemplary believers, and warnings, as well as the indicatives, to transform the people of God. They all play a positive role in our sanctification, inspiring and restraining us. We must preach them all, following the apostolic patterns as well as the apostolic proportions, or we will neglect a substantial part of what Jesus and the apostles intended to communicate to the church.

---

89 Stott, *Between Two Worlds*, 158.

APOSTOLIC INSTRUCTIONS TO THEIR SUCCESSORS

Not only can we learn about the full content of our preaching by reviewing the actual teaching of the gospels and epistles, but by looking specifically at the apostolic instruction to their successors, particularly as found in the Pastoral Epistles. The inspired Scriptures are profitable, says the Apostle Paul for "teaching" (2 Timothy 3:16). He doesn't define the content, but perhaps it is best understood as the "salvation" of the preceding verse (2 Timothy 3:15). However, the four remaining descriptive terms all have ethical connotations: "reproof, correction, training in righteousness" as well as "equipped for every good work." (2 Timothy 3:16–17). I suspect the pejorative term "moralistic" might be attached by some to the preaching commended by the Apostle Paul. Negatively and positively he commends *behavior-altering preaching* of the "do this" and "don't do that" variety.

A few sentences later in 2 Timothy he repeats himself as he explains what he means to "preach the word" (2 Timothy 4:2). "Reprove," he says again, then adds an even stronger word, "rebuke," and finally, "exhort" (more on this in a moment). He writes out of concern for a time when professing believers will get carried away with their own "desires" (2 Timothy 4:3). His concerns are ethical. He wants preaching that confronts and corrects wayward passions, and does so by positive instruction and by reproof, rebuke, and exhortation. The result he wants is righteous conduct and stiffened resolve against wayward desires. "The goal of our instruction," the Apostle Paul tells Timothy in the first pastoral epistle, "is love from a pure heart and a good conscience and a sincere faith" (1 Timothy 1:5). The goal is love. The goal is right behavior. The goal is worthy conduct.

We may look further in 1 Timothy at how, having identified this goal, he goes on to give instruction in public prayer (2:1–8), regarding the dress and adornment of women and their exclusion from a public teaching role (2:9–15), and officer qualifications (3:1–13). I write, he says, "so that you may know how one ought to *conduct* himself in the household of God" (3:15). He doesn't neglect the indicatives of Christ (e.g. 1:12–16; 2:5–6; 3:16) but they are not his emphasis, not in the Pastoral Epistles or in significant portions of the New Testament epistles. His stress is upon behavior. "Teach and preach these principles," he says (1 Timothy 6:2). His "sound words" are "those of our Lord Jesus Christ," that is "teaching that accords with godliness" (1 Timothy 6:3, ESV). Godly behavior is the goal of the principles that the Apostle Paul taught.

Don't misunderstand. We are not disputing that imperatives should be rooted in indicatives. They should be. Always. What we are saying is that the indicatives must not be interpreted so as to nullify the imperatives, which we fear is happening with distressing regularly. We are also saying that sometimes the indicatives are so well established that they are assumed rather than redundantly repeated. We see this in the Pastoral epistles, in 1 & 2 Thessalonians, James, and 1–3 John (see "exhortation" ahead). What we are saying is that doctrinal truth requires practical, ethical responses and that is the task of the preacher to draw out those responses. We are to supply the apostolic "therefore" even when the apostles themselves don't.

THEOLOGICAL LINKS

Our preaching must not obscure the inseparable links that Scripture establishes between justification and sanctification, faith and works, grace and law. The elements of the *ordo salutis* are a "golden chain" of unbroken links (Romans 8:28–30). Those justified and adopted will be sanctified, will persevere, and will be glorified. Truth faith will result in good works (James 2:14–26). Grace will result in conformity to the law of God (Romans 3:31; 8:4, 13:8). So certain are these links that Jesus can say of prophets, professing believers, and of our own hearts, "You will know them by their fruits" (Matthew 7:16–20; Luke 6:43–45; James 3:11–12). Jesus urges us to reason backward from the behavioral and attitudinal fruits of our lives to the internal and spiritual reality that lies behind the fruits, whether good or bad. Ministers must preach these links and their implications.

Avoiding preaching the imperatives may lead to the old dispensational errors that spawned the "Lordship Controversy" of the 1980s. John MacArthur published *The Gospel According to Jesus*,[90] daring to criticize the notion that one could accept Jesus as Savior and not as Lord. The counter-attacks went so far as to deny repentance was necessary for salvation. "Faith alone" saves, they argued, faith being defined as no more than assent to being saved. Christ could be received as Savior now and Lord later, or not at all. This was how the "carnal Christian" was inserted into the *ordo*, linked to justification above it, and glorification below it, without any intervening links. Sanctification and perseverance were simply bypassed. Scores of people responded to evangelistic offers that couldn't be refused, to guaranteed deliverance from the fires of hell, without commitment, without repentance, without surrender. They became Christians, it was said, but remained permanently "carnal." We trust that the Reformed pulpit will not end up in this theological and ethical morass. However, this is where things trend when the inseparable links of the *ordo* are

---

90 John MacArthur, Jr. *The Gospel According to Jesus* (Grand Rapids, MI: Zondervan, 1988)

broken, and justification, or faith, or grace are allowed to stand alone without sanctification, good works or obedience.

Passivity in sanctification

Sever the links of the *ordo* and things will also trend toward a passive approach to sanctification. The same allergic reactions to law and works that sever them from grace and faith spill over into allergic reactions towards requirements of all sorts. Those who flee from duty, obedience, and sacrifice find solace in a theology that teaches effortless sanctification. "Jesus is everything, I am nothing, therefore, *I do nothing*" seems to be the formula. Consider this from a popular Presbyterian preacher: "When we stop narcissistically focusing on our need to get better, *that is what it means to get better*. When we stop obsessing over our need to improve, *that is what it means to improve*." Can "let go, and let God" be far behind? Mortification and vivification, are central actions of sanctification, requiring efforts suitable to athletic, military, and laboring metaphors (e.g. Romans 8:12ff; 1 Corinthians 9:24–27; Ephesians 4:17–6:20; Colossians 3:1–4, 6; 2 Timothy 2:1–26; etc.). True, we shouldn't be "narcissistically focusing" or "obsessing" over anything, ever. However, it is not possible to "put off" and "put on" without *significant focus* on "our need to get better" and "our need to improve." Imperatives, lists of virtues, godly examples, warnings and exhortations play a positive role in doing so.

Complacency

The severing of justification from sanctification, faith from works, grace from law, and effort from growth, has even been appropriated to defend mediocrity and failure. The gurus of lopsided grace assure us, "We are free to be weak ... free to lose

... free to be no one ... free to be ordinary ... free to fail," because Jesus is the opposite of all of the above. This means freedom from the pressure to have a model marriage, model children, to be the one "logging on hours of private prayer each day," and from the "heavy-duty pressure to be spiritual giants." One preacher assures us he is freed "to identify my own idols in front of my people." He admits,

"I'll say things like, 'I hate to admit this, but part of my motivation for preparing the sermon that I am preaching today is because I want you to think I'm a good preacher. It accentuates my sense of worth.' Is that embarrassing to admit? Absolutely! But it's incredibly liberating. I don't have to feel like I have to always be on, that I always have to be performing well, that every sermon's got to be a homerun, that I've got to be modeling perfect piety before all of our people. The pressure's off."

Preachers never should pretend or imply perfection. However, Jesus' strength is never an excuse for our weakness, but rather the basis of our strength. Is it not "when we are weak" that "we are *strong* (2 Corinthians 12:10)? In Christ *we* are strong. Jesus' victory is not an excuse for our defeat but rather the foundation of our victory. Are we not more than conquerors in Christ? Does He not give us the victory (Romans 8:37; 1 Corinthians 15:57)? Jesus' success is not an *excuse for our failure*, but the *ground of our success*. Can we not do "all things through Him who strengthens me"? (Philippians 4:13) Doesn't grace motivate us to "*work* out our salvation" rather than *slouch* in our depravity (Ephesians 2:10)? Are we not "strong in the Lord and the strength of His might" (Ephesians 6:10)? "I toil," says the Apostle, "struggling with all his energy that *he powerfully works within me*" (Colossians 1:29, ESV, emphasis added). Doesn't the grace of Christ inspire and enable us, like it did to the Apostle Paul, to *"labor even more than all of them"* (1 Corinthians 15:10)?

Where do we find models of passivity among the early Christians? The Apostle Peter? The Apostle Paul? Do we encounter in them contentment respecting personal holiness and ministry? Do we find benign neglect? Complacency? "I toil," we just heard the Apostle Paul say (Colossians 1:29, ESV). "I press on," says the Apostle (Philippians 3:12–14). "I buffet my body and make it my slave," he says, employing a boxing metaphor. Is this law? Is this legalism? Why does he push himself so? He answers in words that must be accommodated by our understanding of grace: "lest possibly, after I have preached to others, I myself should be disqualified" (1 Corinthians 9:27). The Apostles reveal a consistent "divine discontent" with their progress in sanctification and ministry. That discontent should be preached. Their activism and energy should be commended to believers today.

"Grace," as some are describing it, "gospel" as some are defining it, at times sounds more like license: license for mediocrity, license for passivity, license for failure, license for sloth, and ironically, license for ambition. At worst, it appears to be merely one form of narcissism (slavery to the opinions of others) replacing another (slavery to self). The doctrines of grace should not be turned into licentiousness (Jude 4). Neither should they be turned into personal therapy.

The grace of God both brings salvation and instructs us "to deny ungodliness and worldly desires and live sensibly, righteously and godly in the present age" (Titus 2:11–12). *Grace,* not law, teaches us to deny worldly desires and live righteously. *Jesus* teaches us self-denial and cross-bearing (Matthew 16:24–25). All this must be preached from the Reformed pulpit.

IMPERFECT OBEDIENCE

When examining officers according to the qualification of 1 Timothy 3 and Titus 1, our session realized that a particular candidate had several "problems" in relation to those criteria. One elder's response was, "well, none of us fulfills the qualifications—we all fall short." The implication of his comment was, "Let's put aside the qualifications and choose officers without regard, or at least without careful regard for the requirements." We hear much the same from preachers today regarding all of the Bible's ethical teaching. "We can't do these things. We all fail. The Bible's moral standards are too high. The duties and disciplines of the Christian are too arduous. So let's just relax about the various standards with gratitude that Christ has fulfilled them on our behalf." In other words, the need for practical holiness is dropped.

Our response in the context of officer exams was, "there is a difference between *imperfectly fulfilling* the requirements of office and *not fulfilling* them at all." We understand that only Christ perfectly fulfills the requirements of Christian ethics and ministry. The Apostles knew that only Christ perfectly fulfills these requirements when they recorded their ideals. Yet they wrote them, not so that we would give thanks that Christ fulfills them, thereby allowing us to disregard them, but so that they might be realized in the lives of church officers and members, though imperfectly. We *recognize* the difference between imperfectly fulfilling the ethical ideals of the Bible and not fulfilling them at all, we can *speak meaningfully* of that difference, and *make distinctions* based upon that difference. The *Westminster Confession of Faith* says the good works of Christians are accepted by God in Christ not because they are "wholly unblamable and unreprovable in God's sight." They are not. Never. Ever. Yet, "looking upon them is His Son, (He) is pleased to accept and reward that which is sincere, although accompanied with many weaknesses and imperfections" (XVI.6.). The Reformed faith has distinguished between perfect obedience and *evangelical* obedience, that obedience, though flawed, that is accepted in the evangel, in Christ.[91] So also is the case with the lists of virtues. We are meant to aspire to them and see them realized in our character and walk, though imperfectly.

PASTORAL SPECTRUM

The whole gospel, indicative and imperative, justification and sanctification, freedom from penalty and power, second use and third use, is important if for no other reason than because of the diversity of the people of God. Each time the minister enters the pulpit he addresses a spectrum of people. Some are of tender conscience, "bruised reeds" and "smoking flax," who are weighed down with feelings of guilt and are easily discouraged (Matthew 12:20). They need reassurance of the love of God in Christ. They need reminding of the forgiveness of their sins and of their reconciliation with God. They need grace.

However, they are not the only type of person to whom we speak. We also address the counterfeit believers who are self-deceived, who need to be exposed. Jesus warned directly those who say "Lord, Lord," that is, the nominal believer, as also did James, who sought to awaken those who "delude themselves" (James 1:22; Luke 6:46; Matthew 7:21–23). Nominal believers need warning. Unbelievers need what the Puritans need "law-work" as well as the gospel, since "through the law comes the knowledge of sin," the prerequisite for repentance (Romans 3:20). Some listeners have temporarily slipped into a drowsy spiritual

---

91   e.g. Watson, *The Ten Commandments*, 80.

condition, or have backslidden, and need to be exhorted. "Flee youthful lusts and pursue righteousness," the Apostle Paul urges (2 Timothy 2:22; 1 Timothy 6; 1 Corinthians 6:18). "Pray without ceasing," he commends (1 Thessalonians 5:17). "Abstain from every form of evil," he insists (1 Thessalonians 5:22). Preach the Bible. Preach the whole counsel of God. The whole people of God, because of their diversity of circumstances, need the whole Christ of the whole gospel. The whole people of God need the whole light of gospel truth, both to save their souls, and to deliver them from the horror, confusion, and hurt that comes from life lived in the darkness that life is apart from God's commandments.

GREAT COMMISSION

Finally, we insist on the preaching of the whole gospel because that is what Jesus commanded His disciples to do. The "Great Commission" is well known:

> *And Jesus came and said to them, "All authority in heaven and on earth has been given to me. Go therefore and make disciples of all nations, baptizing them in the name of the Father and of the Son and of the Holy Spirit, teaching them to observe all that I have commanded you. And behold, I am with you always, to the end of the age." (Matthew 28:18–20)*

What is the goal of our outreach, our evangelism and mission? It is not merely "converts," so-called. Our aim is disciples, defined as those who follow Jesus obediently into baptism and are taught "to observe all that I commanded you." What does Jesus want His disciples, that is, all true believers, to be taught? He wants them to be taught to obey. Jesus might have laid the emphasis in a different place in this His final instruction to the church. He might have placed emphasis on "teaching them that I love them." That would have a wonderful parting exhortation. "Teaching them to depend on the Holy Spirit" or "teaching them that the Christian life is all of grace" or "teaching them that they are accepted *no matter what*." No, the teaching that Jesus underscores, that He returns to in His parting shot, that must never be neglected and must always be taught is to *observe His commandments*.[92] "Obedience," says Thomas Watson, "carries in it the life-blood of religion."[93] This ethical emphasis must be characteristic of the Reformed pulpit if we are to preach the whole gospel. "To teach the standards of moral conduct which adorn the gospel," Stott maintains, "is neither legalism nor pharisaism but *plain apostolic Christianity*."[94]

6. Preach simple content

Moving along to our next point, we urge that pastors preach assuming pervasive ignorance of the Bible. Charles Colson gives the wonderful example of the message, "and if not," sent by British soldiers trapped at Dunkirk in May 1940. This was not a secret code but a citation of the Bible from Daniel (the occasion of Shadrach, Meshach, and Abednego, and the fiery furnace) by which the troops signaled their resolve to remain faithful to their soldierly tasks whether rescued or not (Daniel 3:18). "The oblique message was immediately understood by the British people," says

---

92 We are reminded of R. T. France's comments on the Great Commission in his excellent Tyndale commentary: "There is a thus a strongly ethical emphasis in this summary of Christian mission and discipleship, as there has been in Jesus' teaching throughout this Gospel. To 'make disciples' is not complete unless it leads them to a life of observing Jesus' commandments." R. T. France, *Matthew*, Tyndale New Testament Commentaries (Grand Rapids: Eerdmans Publishing Co., 1989), 415.

93 Watson, Ten Commandments, 1.

94 Stott, *Between Two Worlds*, 158 (my emphasis).

176   *Serving with Calvin*

Colson. Today, he says, the same message would be greeted with "raised eyebrows and blank stares."[95]

Young preachers tend to preach as though their audience were bringing to the table far more knowledge than is typically the case. Seminarians and recent graduates are pumped full of knowledge and seem to forget that relatively few know what they now know. This is especially true of those who are more theologically or philosophically oriented. I have heard discussions of "world-view" and hermeneutics that have been aimed way over the heads of most in the congregation. The young preacher was excited about what he knew, but no one else knew what he was talking about. Several times I have heard my interns launch into a critique of contemporary evangelicalism among people who know nothing of the personalities and issues involved. Lacking that background, their criticisms were irrelevant, if not incomprehensible, and oppressively negative. Others will speak of Paul and the Judaizers, Jesus and the Pharisees, Philippi, the temple, and so on, and assume everyone knows what they are talking about.

A few years back I preached through Galatians. At one point I had been talking about Judaizers for weeks, and was ready to launch into my sermon about the Judaizers this and Judaizers that when I saw a couple in the front row whom I knew to be visitors. On the spot, I decided to talk for half a minute or so about salvation by faith in Christ apart from works. I then described who the various parties involved were before finally jumping into the middle of the Apostle Paul's argument in Galatians 3. It didn't take long. However, I had to set the stage or else I'd lose our guests right off the bat.

---

95   Charles Colson, *The Body: Being Light in the Darkness* (Dallas: Word Publishing, 1992), 335–6.

It could be that Reformed preachers tend to get too deep too fast and for too long. This, again, is a wisdom issue. We are wise to assume pervasive biblical ignorance today. Since that is the context in which we preach, our preaching must take that ignorance into account. "To preach truths and notions above the hearer's capacity," warns Gurnall, "is like a nurse that should go to feed the child with a spoon too big to go into its mouth."[96] This leaves us with just two more brief recommendations.

7. Begin preaching those books of the Bible that are the most accessible

Calvin preached on the gospels and Acts exclusively on Sunday mornings, when he knew he had his broadest audience. Don't launch into a Sunday morning series on Leviticus or Deuteronomy. Calvin's pattern has informed my own practice over the past quarter of a century. I began in 1987 with Mark, then Acts, followed by John, Matthew, and Luke. With few exceptions the gospels and Acts have provided the content for my Sunday morning preaching for 25 years. Like Calvin, save the more difficult books (some New Testament epistles, most Old Testament books) for Sunday evening or weekdays. During these same years I have preached all the epistles except 1 & 2 Corinthians, Genesis through Job, plus several minor prophets. This pattern has worked well both for Calvin and for us.

8. Vary the sermon diet

A colleague preached a series on the Minor Prophets. Several books into it he began to see the preponderance of the theme of judgment and realized, with 9 more to go, what he'd gotten

---

96   Gurnall, *Christian in Complete Armour*, II:168.

himself into. Preach *a* minor prophet. Then preach *a* psalm or a section of the Psalter. Then might follow an epistle, an Old Testament narrative book, or a gospel. Longer books can be made to "feel" shorter by highlighting a series within the series. Matthew's gospel, for example, might include a series on the Beatitudes, the Lord's Prayer, the Parables, and the Olivet Discourse, all in the course of sequential preaching. In the middle of a long series one might break for a topical series on a biblical theme (e.g. the covenants), a theological theme (e.g. grace), or a "practical" theme (e.g. the Christian home). Don't fall into a rut.

How to preach

We move on to how to preach, examining not so much the content as the details of method. What are some of the keys to effective preaching?

1. Preach persuasively

The task of the preacher is not unlike that of the lawyer arguing a case before a judge and jury. He must aim at persuading the minds of his listeners. His goal is to convince them of gospel truths. According to Motyer there are 97 verbs used in the New Testament for communicating God's truth, 56 of which are declarative, such as *kērussō*, to herald, *didaskō*, to teach, *laleō*, to speak, *parakaleō*, to appeal, encourage, *deomai*, to plead, beseech, *peithō*, to persuade, *noutheteō*, to counsel. The Apostle Paul directs Timothy to "rebuke" (*epitimaō*, to warn), addressing the conscience regarding wayward behavior; "exhort" (*parakaleō*, to beseech, encourage), addressing the will regarding right conduct; and "reprove" (*elenchō*, to convince), addressing the mind (2 Timothy 4:2). Various ways of speaking are to be employed in order to make the truth plain and persuasive.

We find the Apostle Paul at Thessalonica in Acts 17:2–4, where we are told he "reasoned" (*dialegomai*), meaning "to argue a case," says Motyer, "in the sense of presenting and supporting a point of view with the aim of winning the other person over" (cf. Acts 18:4 and 19:8 where it is used with "persuading"). It means "marshalling and presenting evidence as compellingly as possible."[97] "Explaining" (*dianoigō*, lit. "opening" as in KJV, expound), is used of opening deaf ears (Mark 7:34), unseeing eyes (Luke 24:31), a closed heart (Acts 16:14), an uncomprehending mind (Luke 24:45), and even of opening the Scriptures to the understanding (Luke 24:32); and "Proving" (*paratithēmi*, lit. to put alongside), "giving evidence" (NASB), means to "set it out," says Motyer, "as a coherent, persuasive case, a well-prepared and well-served meal for the mind" (cf. Mark 6:41; Luke 10:8; Acts 16:34; Luke 23:46; 1 Timothy 1:18).[98] Our full powers of persuasion are to be employed. Attention should be paid to connective words such as "and," "therefore," and "so that," whereby what Motyer calls "the logic of the Holy Spirit," that is, "how, in His mind, one thing follows another, how one causes or gives rises to another."[99]

Of course the results are up to God. We water and plant, but God causes the growth (1 Corinthians 3:7). Regeneration, conversion, and sanctification are all supernatural works of God. Yet, God works through means, and there is a relationship between a compelling presentation and results. While we do not indulge "persuasive words of (worldly) wisdom," we are to preach clearly, plainly, logically, and convincingly (1 Corinthians 2:4; NASB). Make the case. Spurgeon insists, "It is not enough

---

97 Motyer, *Preaching?*, 32.
98 Ibid.
99 Ibid. 59.

to be so plain that you can be understood, you must speak so that you cannot be misunderstood."[100] The pattern of preaching found in the New Testament leads Motyer to ask of preachers the following helpful questions: "Have the hearers understood (cf. Matthew 13:51)? Has the Bible been properly and fully made plain (cf. 2 Timothy 4:17)? Has the material been set out in an orderly fashion (cf. Acts 11:4; 18:26)?"[101]

2. Preach with urgency

We've mentioned that worship services should be led with a sense of urgency. Sermons should be preached in the same way. The preacher should study the text so as to become convinced of the message that God has for the congregation in that passage. Once he knows what God is saying in the text, there ought to be a great urgency about communicating it. After all, God is speaking. Eternity is at stake. J. C. Ryle spoke of the "life and fire" that characterized Whitefield's preaching. "There was a holy violence about him," he explained.[102] By way of contrast, our preachers at times drone on as though they were lecturing on the Code of Hammurabi. A sense of urgency ought to animate all that we say. Abraham Kuyper cites the Latin proverb, *pectus est quod disertum facit*, "in the end, it is your heart that makes your eloquent." The proverb means, he says, "only those who are affected can affect others."[103] If the preacher is to move others, the truth upon which he preaches "must have seized and moved and stirred him."[104] Reformed Baptist minister Al Martin once remarked, "a man

---

100 Spurgeon, *Lectures to My Students*, 26.
101 Ibid. 33.
102 Cited in Stott, *Between Two Worlds*, 249.
103 Kuyper, *Worship*, 193–194.
104 Ibid. 194.

who yells 'fire' from a burning building has a natural eloquence." Do we believe that there is a fire? Do we believe that souls are in danger? Then the voice and manner of our preachers will take on a natural, passionate eloquence. We have no confidence in the contrived mannerisms that are the result of a classroom course on elocution. What we seek is the passion that is born of conviction regarding the great themes of time and eternity. Carrick speaks of the "almost *explosive* quality" of the preaching of Lloyd-Jones. Preaching, Carrick says, is "essentially a passionate, not a dispassionate activity."[105] He cites J. I. Packer's concern for the "calm and chatty intimacy" which the modern pulpit seems to have learned from the media. He cites John R. de Witt's lament that "the so-called 'conversational style' has brought death to the pulpit."[106] In his discussion of the interrogative, Carrick describes how Jonathan Edwards "interrogates his hearers," and "almost *hounds* them."[107] Lloyd-Jones himself speaks of "the element of attack" in preaching that distinguishes it from a lecture."[108] Too much preaching is innocuous and anaemic. "To me," the great John Murray of Westminster Seminary said, "preaching without passion is not preaching at all."[109]

Because the truths of the Reformed faith (really of the Christian faith) are interrelated and interdependent, it is possible for Reformed ministers to be convinced every time they enter the pulpit that they are preaching the most important of messages. How many times did Martyn Lloyd-Jones begin a sermon saying,

---

105 Carrick, *The Imperative of Preaching*, 50, 51.
106 Ibid. 52.
107 Ibid. 73.
108 Lloyd-Jones, *Preaching and Preachers*, 71.
109 Cited by Hulse, "The Preacher & Piety" in Logan (ed.), *Preacher and Preaching*, 88 (from Murray's *Works*, Vol. 3, 72).

"I am going to speak to you tonight about the most important subject in all the world." He believed he was, because he saw at a glance the interrelatedness of all of truth. Our preachers should not enter the pulpit until they are convinced that they have a message from God that is vital for the people of God. Every time they preach they should carry with them the burden of knowing that the people of God must know what their text teaches and understand its implications. Listen to Richard Baxter (1615–1691) as he rebukes our lack of urgency:

> If we were heartily devoted to our work, it would be done more vigorously, and more seriously, than it is by the most of us. How few ministers do preach with all their might, or speak about everlasting joys and everlasting torments in such a manner as may make men believe that they are in good earnest! It would make a man's heart ache, to see a company of dead, drowsy sinners sitting under a minister, and not hear a word that is likely to quicken or awaken them. Alas! we speak so drowsily and so softly, that sleepy sinners cannot hear. The blow falls so light that hard-hearted sinners cannot feel. The most of ministers will not so much as exert their voice, and stir up themselves to an earnest utterance. But if they do speak loud and earnestly, how few do answer it with weight and earnestness in matter! And yet without this, the voice doth little good; the people will esteem it but mere bawling, when the matter doth not correspond. It would grieve one to the heart to hear what excellent doctrine some ministers have in hand, while yet they let it die in their hands for want of close and lively application; what fit matter they have for convincing sinners, and how little they make of it; what good they might do if they would set it home, and yet they cannot or will not do it.

O sirs, how plainly, how closely, how earnestly, should we deliver a message of such moment as ours, when the everlasting life or everlasting death of our fellow-men is involved in it! Methinks we are in nothing so wanting as in this seriousness; yet is there nothing more unsuitable to such a business, than to be slight and dull. What! speak coldly for God, and for men's salvation? Can we believe that our people must be converted or condemned, and yet speak in a drowsy tone? In the name of God, brethren, labor to awaken your own hearts, before you go to the pulpit, that you may be fit to awaken the hearts of sinners. Remember they must be awakened or damned, and that a sleepy preacher will hardly awaken drowsy sinners. Though you give the holy things of God the highest praises in words, yet, if you do it coldly, you will seem by your manner to unsay what you said in the matter. It is a kind of contempt of great things, especially of so great things, to speak of them without much affection and fervency.[110]

John R. de Witt sees the same need of urgency today: "If eternal issues are dealt with in a tedious manner, delivered in a matter of fact tone of voice without vigour and conviction," he warns us, "hearers are not likely to be willing to take what is said seriously."[111] "'Passionless preaching,'" says Motyer, "is a contradiction in terms."[112]

3. Preach authentically
Phillips Brooks (1835–1893) defined preaching as "truth through personality."[113] I have noticed amongst some of my colleagues

---

110 Baxter, *The Reformed Pastor*, 147–48
111 de Witt, "A Few Thoughts on Preaching,", 138.
112 Motyer, *Preaching?*, 112.
113 Brooks, *Lectures on Preaching*, 5.

in the ministry a regrettable transformation as they make the transition from small group study to the pulpit. In the small group they are animated, interesting, engaging, in a word, they are themselves. Their personalities shine in that setting, enhancing and enlivening their teaching. But when they walk into the pulpit, they change. Their personality disappears. They seem bound-up, unnatural, stiff. They are not themselves, and as a result, they are not nearly as effective as they could be. Some younger men make the mistake of trying to be Rev. So and So, junior. They mimic the senior man's style, his phrases, his manner, his illustrations, and so on. Rarely will this work. The junior man is not the senior man. He cannot preach just like the Rev. Senior does. Young preachers can learn from other preachers. Indeed good preaching is as much caught as taught. Yet they mustn't try to be them. They can't be them. "A preacher must in the first place be *himself*, and not imitate someone else," says Abraham Kuyper, "for it is precisely the *self* that is choked by imitation."[114] A preacher can be himself on fire, but not another.

Reformed pastors must aim to so immerse themselves in the texts that they are moved to become enlivened, animated, eloquent versions of themselves. Let the text preach to the preacher first. As it does, it will inspire thoughts and phrases that are natural. It will inspire illustrations that arise organically from his own experience. This is why illustrations from books of illustrations rarely work well. They are not personal. We cannot preach someone else's experience. A preacher can only preach effectively his own experience. When the truth fires the heart suitable language and illustrations will come. Because the sermon's content has come naturally, it will be easier for the preacher to

---

114 Kuyper, *Our Worship*, 167.

deliver the sermon naturally. A preacher must use the gifts that God has given him, and be himself.

This brings up another matter of authenticity. Why are so many preachers smiling as they preach? Heaven, hell; righteousness, sin; God, Satan; it doesn't matter: there they stand, mindless smiles plastered on their faces. Perhaps they just have a smiley personality? No, their smile isn't perpetual in private. When did a smile become the obligatory facial expression when preaching? Smilers are not only not being their true selves, but their smiles don't fit their subjects either. The serious, urgent, demanding content of the Bible often requires the preacher project a mood different from the one communicated by a smile. Don't smile when warning of the danger of going to hell. Your listeners may not take you seriously. Don't smile when describing the trials and sorrows of life. Those listening may think you are flippant and resent your insensitivity.

Others of us may need to be asked, why are we mad all of the time? Why do we *never* smile? Why is there never a pleasant, never mind a joyful look on our face? In other words, we simply urge, be yourself, your better self, the self you should be in the context of the subject matter of your preaching. Authenticity in preaching must be characteristic of the Reformed pulpit.

4. Review and repeat constantly
"Truth needs to be driven home by the hammer-blows of repetition," Stott maintains.[115] Learn to say the same thing five different ways like the Apostle Paul does in Galatians 2:16:

---

115 Stott, *Between Two Worlds*, 246.

> *Nevertheless knowing that a man is not justified by the works of the Law but through faith in Christ Jesus, even we have believed in Christ Jesus, that we may be justified by faith in Christ, and not by the works of the Law; since by the works of the Law shall no flesh be justified.*

He says that we are justified by faith not five but six times in one verse! He says it negatively, positively, and every which way. Scripture constantly does this. It can talk about the circumcised heart, about regeneration, about being born again, about being baptized by the Spirit, about being a new creation. It says the same things over and over again, but in dozens of different ways, from Genesis right through to Revelation, the same things over and over. Again, John MacArthur is a genius at this. He'll say, "You must *repent*. You must *turn* from your sins. You must tell God that you *are sorry*. You must *give up* the old ways." Preachers mustn't say the same things the same ways. If they do people will lose interest. They should instead say the same things with variety, using both simple and sophisticated vocabulary so as to accommodate all. "What does the Bible say about *eschatology*? What does it say about the *end times*? Can we know what will happen at the *end of the world*? What does it teach us about the *last days*?"

Not only should our preachers use repetition but they should also review constantly. Main headings should be reviewed periodically. Even the best listeners can miss major points and lose touch with the direction of the sermon. It helps if the preacher says periodically, "Here is what we have seen so far. First ... Second ... Third ... Now fourth we see that he says ... ." This allows everyone to catch up, to see again how the whole sermon hangs together, and may even help the preacher to realize where he is going! More than once I have finally realized my main point in the process of such a review. A quick recap helps everyone.

5. Apply the text throughout

"It hardly need be said that a sermon without application, without relevance to those who hear it, is in truth not a sermon at all," J. R. de Witt maintains.[116] J. I. Packer agrees: "Preaching is essentially teaching *plus* application (invitation, direction, summons); where the plus is lacking something less than preaching occurs."[117] Because preaching is not just exposition, but communication to a given people in a given place and a given time, it must include application. Further, proper preaching not only includes application, but is itself application. It builds a bridge of comprehension from the world of the Bible to our world today. It explains the meaning, and with the meaning the relevance of biblical texts in the present. This is application.[118] All true preaching, then, is *prophetic*, addressing the times. It is not merely translation. It is the living God speaking to us today through the voice of the preacher. "Preaching that lacks application is the bane of the modern Reformed pulpit," laments Geoffrey Thomas.[119]

Again, we feel compelled to lay some of the blame for this at the feet of the extreme advocates of redemptive-historical preaching. They have at times urged the proclamation of the *historia salutis* (what Christ has accomplished for us in history, at the cross) at the expense of the *ordo salutis* (what Christ applies in us by His Spirit). As we have seen, they have taught something approaching the bare indicative, neglecting the response of the believer called

---

116 J. R. de Witt, "A Few Thoughts on Preaching," 19.
117 Packer, "Why Preach?" in Logan (ed.), *The Preacher & Preaching*, 3.
118 Stott, *Between Two Worlds*, 246.
119 Cited in Carrick, *The Imperative of Preaching*, 149.

188   *Serving with Calvin*

for by the *ordo* (e.g. faith, repentance, mortification, vivification, perseverance). Too often redemptive-historical preaching has taken the form of a *lecture* on redemptive history rather than a sermon for a congregation. It is a mistake, says D. E. Johnson in his comments on the teaching method found in the Book of Hebrews, to assume that the Holy Spirit will "mystically disclose to (our) hearers the response they should make to the majestic truths unfolded in (our) theological discourse(s)."[120] All preaching should aim at application and response. "Doctrine is but the drawing of the bow," says Thomas Manton (1620–1677), expressing the historic Reformed view, "application is hitting the mark."[121] Preachers should aim at their listeners' believing or doing what the passage requires of them, which the preacher for his part urges. As we have seen, all gospel indicatives imply gospel imperatives. Stott reminds us: "New Testament apostles make it plain that 'truth' brings with it moral demands: it is to be 'done' not merely heard, to be obeyed not merely believed."[122] Whether stated or unstated, it is the preacher's job to identity the applications of the indicatives and preach them. "It is of little service to supply men with information unless we urge upon them the practical inferences therefrom," says Spurgeon.[123] "Where the application begins," he maintains, "there the sermon begins."[124]

What is meant by application? Motyer provides a seven-fold definition: "The Word of God brought home to the hearers as truth to be *believed*, a way of life to be *followed*, a rule to be

---

120   Johnson, *Him We Proclaim*, 178.
121   Thomas Manton, *A Practical Commentary on the Epistle of James* (1871; Edinburgh: The Banner of Truth Trust, 1963), 357; cited by Guy Waters, "Preaching Like Peter?" Reformation_21 web site, posted November 18, 2013.
122   Stott, *Between Two Worlds*, 247.
123   Spurgeon, *Commenting and Commentaries*, 31.
124   Cited by John F. Bettler, "Application," in Logan (ed.), *Preacher & Preaching*, 333.

obeyed, a promise to be *embraced*, a sin to be *avoided*, an example to be *followed*, and a blessing to be *enjoyed*."[125] All of this is what congregations need to hear.

We recommend that preachers not wait until the end of the sermon to make application. Dr. James Baird used to urge preachers to answer the question, "So what?," every five minutes. An effective way to do this is to make careful application of each heading in one's outline. Each *point* has a *point*, we assume. Make its point overt with careful, practical application as one progresses through the sermon. Think of that businessman who is tempted to open his day-timer and review the next week's responsibilities, or the mother who has a roast in the oven. Keep their attention. Preachers need to show their congregations the relevance of the text. The relevance is there. A response is required. Tell them what it is frequently.

6. Include exhortation

By "exhortation" we mean more than application. Those who have heard the meaning of the text explained, and have heard of its application for today, must be exhorted to believe and implement all that God requires of them. The Apostles "exhort" (*parakaleō*),[126] and "admonish" (*noutheteō*), the latter defined by D. E. Johnson in his exposition of Colossians 1:28 ("admonishing ... teaching") as "an urgent, passionate appeal to hearers to respond appropriately to God's truth" (cf. Acts 20:11).[127]

Richard Baxter (1615–1691) and Jonathan Edwards (1703–1758) from long ago, and Martyn Lloyd-Jones (1899–1981) of recent memory, were particularly effective exhorters. Baxter preached

---

125 Motyer, *Preaching?*, 103 (my emphasis).
126 See *Worshipping with Calvin*, chapter 5, "Preach the Word."
127 Johnson, *Him We Proclaim*, 83.

with what Packer called "hands and feet," climbing all over his listeners, urging, pleading, exhorting.[128] Baxter's "Treatise on Conversion" is extraordinary in this respect.[129] For sustained, passionate pleading and persuading it is nearly beyond belief. Both Edwards and Lloyd-Jones had a way of getting inside one's head, anticipating one's questions and objections, stating them better than one could for oneself, and then answering them. Read Edwards' "Men Are Naturally God's Enemies."[130] Every possible objection to the thesis of his title is answered as he pleads for all to come to Christ.

Read any of Lloyd-Jones' sermons. In a particularly memorable sermon he criticized sharply the Arminian evangelicals for their tactics. Then he turned his rhetorical guns on the Calvinists who made up his audience. He said things like this: "You've become timid about the free offer of the gospel. You are afraid of sounding like an Arminian and that is a thing abhorrent to you. But listen to the Apostle Paul—'save yourselves from this wicked generation,' he says. 'Save yourselves!' But you've become learned. You've become theologians. You've read the Puritans, and are now an intellectual. But where is your fire? 'Your Calvinistic preachers are boring,' a lady told me with regret. I had to admit that she was right. We're quoting the Reformers. We're quoting the Puritans. We're quoting the Princeton theologians *and our people don't know what we're talking about.* Lord have mercy upon us!" He is all over his congregation. He is pleading. He is exhorting. He is

---

128 J. I. Packer, *A Quest for Godliness: The Puritan Vision of the Christian Life* (Wheaton, IL: Crossway Books, 1990), 13.

129 Richard Baxter, *The Practical Works of Richard Baxter*, Vol. II (Ligonier, Pennsylvania: Soli Deo Gloria, 1990), 397–500.

130 Jonathan Edwards, *The Works of Jonathan Edwards*, Vol. I (1834, Edinburgh: The Banner of Truth Trust, 1974), 131–142.

urging. This is what the Reformed pulpit must be doing. "Why won't you believe? Because the gospel lacks evidence? Go on now. It is not an intellectual problem, now is it? The problem is spiritual, not intellectual. You don't want to believe. You don't want to give up your lifestyle. You don't want God telling you what to do. You want to be your own man, the captain of your own ship. But where has that gotten you? Your life is a mess, isn't it? You're empty." Go after them. Make generous use of the second person, as the Apostle Peter does in Acts 2: "Jesus Christ whom *you* crucified." Plead, urge, exhort. Work on the congregation from every angle, repeating your text, urging their compliance, answering their objections. Don't let anyone escape.

Some voices today denigrate exhortation. They say that it is useless to tell people to *stop* doing *this* and *start* doing *that*. Yet, once again, this claim is not consistent with apostolic practice. The Apostle Paul is not shy about telling Timothy, without laying much theological groundwork, to "*flee* youthful lusts and *pursue* righteousness, faith, love and peace" (2 Timothy 2:22). "*Flee*" from these things, you man of God," he tells Timothy regarding the love of money, "and *pursue* righteousness, godliness, faith, love, perseverance and gentleness." (1 Timothy 6:11). The Apostle Paul exhorts! "*Fight* the good fight of faith," he continues, and "*take hold* of the eternal life to which you were called." "I charge you in the presence of God," he says, "that you keep the commandment without stain or reproach" (1 Timothy 6:11–14). There is a time to exhort.

Is it valid at times simply to tell people what to do without rehearsing their motives? Sometimes they've heard the gospel over and over and over again. Sometimes they've grown numb to the gospel, like the members of the old revivalistic Bible churches with their weekly altar calls. The time comes to exhort, not endlessly repeat what most everybody already knows. Timothy is to "Instruct those who are rich," in effect to *not do this* but *do that*. "Instruct" then, he says, "not to be conceited," and so on, and "to do good, to be rich in good works, and to be generous and ready to share." (1 Timothy 6:17–19). "Instruct (them) to *do good*!" This is not "law" except in its third use. This is not "moralizing" but simple Christian morality. This is not "works" except as "good works" that flow from faith (James 2:14ff). "We request and exhort," the Apostle Paul tells the Thessalonians regarding sanctification and especially sexual purity (1 Thessalonians 4:1–8).

As a teenager I got home rather later than usual one evening. After some interrogation and adequate answers (or so I thought) my father said simply, "Don't let it happen again." That was all I needed. Sometimes we just need to be told to stop. "Quit doing that" is not the most empathetic form of counseling but it can be effective. "Stop depriving one another," the Apostle Paul tells married Corinthian couples (1 Corinthians 7:5). "Abstain from every form of evil," he tells the Thessalonians (1 Thessalonians 5:22). "Turn away from evil and do good," the Apostle Peter tells his readers, citing Psalms 34:14 (1 Peter 3:11). Exhortation may play a positive role in the believer's life. The Apostle Paul reminds us of how he was "exhorting and encouraging and imploring each one of you as a father would his own children." Why? Why such strong admonitions? "so that you may walk in a manner worthy of God who calls you unto His own kingdom and glory" (1 Thessalonians 2:11–12). He exhorts and implores because such urgings contribute to the success of his listeners' worthy walking. We need preachers who similarly will exhort us and implore us. "We command you," he says (2 Thessalonians 3:6). "We command and exhort in the Lord Jesus Christ," he says of undisciplined busybodies, that they "work in a quiet fashion and eat their own bread" (2 Thessalonians 3:11–13). Don't neglect exhortation. "The old preachers," said Lloyd-Jones, "were great exhorters."[131]

7. Explain the context but don't dwell on it

We have urged that one should provide historical-biblical-theological context in one's preaching. However, we don't think that there is much value in dwelling on it. By "dwelling on it," we mean talking for fifteen minutes or more in a thirty minute sermon about what was "long ago and far away," as Jay Adams would put it. After all, the point of understanding what God did to them back then is so that we can understand what He is doing today for us. The preacher should tell the people what the text means for believers and unbelievers *today*. Bring the passage to bear upon the present in a hurry. This is why we urge preachers not to wait for the end of the sermon to make application. Instead they should draw points of application out of each point, the way that Matthew Henry does in his commentary on the whole Bible. As we have urged, preachers should apply and exhort as they progress through their passages. Reformed preaching, as mediated to us by Calvin and the Puritans, is careful not to allow context to crowd out application and exhortation.

8. Use quotations sparingly

The succinct, brief, poignant quotation can be a valuable asset to a preacher. The Apostle Paul uses one in Acts 17:28. Quotations from respected authorities can lend *credibility* to one's proclamation. It makes a difference if an Augustine, Calvin, Edwards, Hodge, or capable modern scholar holds the same

---

131 Cited in Iain H. Murray, "Raising the Standard of Preaching: Notes of a Memorable Address," in *The Banner of Truth Magazine,* March 2011, Issue 570 (Carlisle, PA: The Banner of Truth Trust), 18.

views as those which the preacher is urging. Quotations can also add *clarity* to one's presentation. Luther's identifying the Christian's righteousness as an "alien righteousness" clarifies the issue of justification. Even the Latin (which ought especially to be used sparingly) *simul jus et peccator* is particularly illuminating: the justified sinner is *at once just and sinner*. C. S. Lewis' "chronological snobbery," Neil Postman's "amusing ourselves to death," David Wells' "no place for truth" and "losing our virtue," Daniel Patrick Moynihan's "defining deviancy down," Calvin's "factory of idols" (of the human heart), Thomas Chalmers, "the expulsive power of a new affection," are examples of phrases which illuminate and can boost the impact of a sermon. Normally, quotations should be short and pithy, as in the preceding examples. Long quotations are difficult for congregations to follow. Paragraphs from the Puritans or church fathers may distract more than clarify, detracting from the message rather than enhancing it.

Care should be taken when using quotations from popular culture. It is one thing to find in popular culture expressions of despair or decadence. These can be illuminating, even a powerful addition. One thinks of the popular novelist Jack Higgins' response to his success at its height: "I wish someone had told me that when one gets to the top that there is nothing there."[132] However it's quite another thing to cite popular culture in a positive sense. For example, a recent sermon on election mined Dan Fogelberg's song, "Longer," for language with which to describe the unchanging and eternal love of God:

---

132   Cited in Alister E. McGrath, *Intellectuals Don't Need God and Other Modern Myths* (Grand Rapids, MI: Zondervan Publishing, 1993), 15.

Longer than there've been fishes in the ocean
Higher than any bird ever flew
Longer than there've been stars up in the heavens
I've been in love with you

There are multiple problems with this. Is God "in love" with us? The word "in" restricts the meaning of love to romantic love. Does God have romantic affections for His people? This is confusing at best. God's love in the Bible is not *eros*, sensual love, but *agapē* or *philia*. In Latin translation it is *caritas* not *amor*. Gordon MacDonald, former pastor of Grace Chapel in Lexington, Massachusetts, and current editor at large of *Leadership Journal*, recognizes the problem in describing why he is inclined to use the word "devotion" rather than "love" for Jesus. "It is difficult to escape the sentimental flavoring in the word *love*," he explains. "And I do not find sentimental love in that follow-me relationship initiated with his disciples."[133] Beyond this, why draw parallels between the human romantic love of an unbeliever with the pure and eternal and unchanging love of God? Why not cite Scripture if something is to be said about the love of God? Why not cite an insightful Christian? Citing the sentimental and dishonest lyrics of a pop artist fails to pass the blush test. At least quotations of this sort should be qualified by some explanation, such as "Fogelberg is groping toward the eternal. He seeks it in human love. But we know that such love is only found in God's love," etc. We don't advise citing the Beatles to prove that "all you need is love." Burt Bacharach and Hal David may think that "what the world needs now, is love, sweet love," but they have no particular

---

133 Gordon MacDonald, "How to Spot a Transformed Christian," in *Leadership Journal,* Summer 2012, 32.

expertise. Maybe their lyrics come close to "love never fails," but they are no authority. "As the Beach Boys say, ..." adds nothing substantive, and in fact detracts from the sermon. It distracts from the Bible and raises questions about a preacher who finds it necessary to use pop idols to buttress what should be a biblical argument.[134]

9. Preach sermons of moderate length

Some concessions should be made to the video generation if it is to thrive under expository preaching week after week. By "moderate length" I mean thirty minutes. Spurgeon warns us: "A man with a great deal of well-prepared matter will probably not exceed 40 minutes; when he has less to say he will go for 50 minutes, and when he has absolutely nothing he will need an hour to say it in."[135] Calvin's sermons seem to have been about 30 minutes long. Even a weak preacher can be effective if he restricts himself to half an hour. Less than thirty minutes, it seems to me, is too much like a "sermonette," which as John Stott famously says, breeds "Christianettes." However, if Reformed churches are going to feature sermons that are more than thirty minutes in length, they must, of necessity, be good, real good. Of course there are exceptions. There are cultural variables as well. We've heard Luis Palau, the Latin American evangelist, speak for 45 minutes *before he got to his sermon.* He then preached for an hour, and no one noticed! John MacArthur can preach for forty-five minutes to an hour. If after two or three years of regular preaching the people

---

134 J. R. de Witt makes the same point with respect to illustrations: "I have always believed that illustrations drawn from the cinema or the theatre have no place in the pulpit; likewise that one should be discriminating in making references to popular literature" ("A Few Thoughts on Preaching," 19).

135 Spurgeon, *Lectures to My Students*, 135.

are crying out for longer sermons, go ahead and extend the time. However, lacking that, most of our preachers better stick to about thirty minutes.

Motyer summarizes our concerns. "The *reason* for preaching is the will of God ... the *context* of preaching is the Bible ... the *objective* of preaching is the application ... but the *art* of preaching is the presentation."[136] Good preaching is an essential element of historic Reformed worship. It is the key to the church's health and fruitfulness. It is the key to the preacher's "success" in his calling and to the growth of the church. It is crucial that those leading historic Reformed worship services preach well.

---

136 Motyer, *Preaching?*, 89.

❧ Chapter 5 ❧

Administering the Elements—2

We have examined reading Scripture and preaching. We move along to our third element.

Prayer

Public prayer is an element of our worship that deserves careful preparation. It's a second form of pulpit speech, alongside of the sermon, which is meant to edify the congregation. It is, says Isaac Watts, "one considerable part, if not the chief duty, of public worship."[1] Leading in public prayer may be seen as a gift of God to be developed through practice, as well as a skill to be cultivated through both the study of the devotional language of the Bible as well as through one's private prayer disciplines. "Public prayer is no doubt the most demanding aspect of a minister's conduct

---

[1] Watts, *Guide*, 62.

of public worship," cautions J. Graham Miller (1913–2008), for many years minister of St. Giles Presbyterian Church in Sydney.[2] Geoffrey Thomas reminds us that "the private devotional life of the minister lays the foundation upon which is erected his public prayers upon the Lord's Day and in all his pastoral duties."[3] We have said a great deal about the prominence of prayer in a historic Reformed worship service.[4] Now we must elaborate respecting *what* to pray, and *how* to pray in public services.

What to pray

1. *Faithfully pray the "full-diet" of public prayer.* "Ever since the days of Origen," writes W. G. Blaikie, referring to the third century church father, "four divisions have usually been specified—adoration, confession, thanksgiving, and supplication. All public prayers," he continues, "must embrace more or less of these divisions."[5] To these four we have noted two more: the prayer of illumination and the benediction. Each of the prayer genres should come to expression in the public services of the church. None of them should be neglected. Congregations need to hear the praises of God, the confession of sin with assurances of pardon through the cross of Christ, thanksgiving, comprehensive (five-fold) intercessions, a prayer for illumination, and the parting blessing from God.

If churches will commit to the "full-diet," the time in the public assembly given to prayer will gradually expand. One reason why such little time is spent in prayer in gatherings purporting

---

2   Quoted in Iain H. Murray (ed.), *A Day's March Nearer Home, Autobiography of J. Graham Miller* (Edinburgh: The Banner of Truth Trust, 2010), 297.
3   Geoffrey Thomas, "Powerful Preaching," in Logan (ed.), *Preacher & Preaching*, 394.
4   See *Worshipping with Calvin*, Chapter 5, "Pray the Word."
5   Blaikie, *Work of the Ministry*, 175.

to be services of worship is that whole categories of prayer go unexpressed. Prayers are perfunctory and undefined. They came to be called "opening" and "closing" prayers, and the "prayer before the offering." Nothing distinguishes one from the other. Meandering "thanks" with a couple of "help us'es" and a few "just really"s are repeated in all three prayers, at the beginning, at the end, and in the middle of the service, with no particular aim, and with the yawning inattention of the congregation.

Keep the categories separate, in the minds of those leading if not in the service itself. Every service should devote time to praise, confession of sin, thanksgiving, intercessions, illumination, and benediction. As the categories are kept in mind, and in a number of cases the prayers distinguished and separated, the result will be prayers that are defined, sharpened in focus, and, as a consequence, meaningful to the congregation. Make the "opening" prayer a distinctive prayer of praise. Limit it to praise. Don't try to do everything in this prayer. Make the "pastoral prayer" a prayer of confession of sin and pardon, of intercession, and illumination. Limit it. Make the prayer before the collection a prayer of thanksgiving, and no more. Conclude with a clear benediction. Limit the scope of each prayer to its classification. Then develop each prayer within its category. Develop biblical language for praise, confession, thanksgiving, and so on. By praying the "full-diet," the prayer life of the congregation will be greatly enriched.

2. *Focus public prayer on spiritual concerns.* David Powlison, a leading counselor at the Christian Counseling Education Fellowship complains that too often "prayers from the pulpit sound like a nursing report at shift change in your local hospital."[6]

---

6   David Powlison, "Praying Beyond the Sick List," in *By Faith*, Issue 8, April 2006, 27.

By way of contrast New Testament prayers are almost entirely concerned with spiritual health (as in Ephesians 1, Philippians 1, Colossians 1). When an interest in physical health is expressed, it is often related to spiritual health (as in Matthew 9:1–8; 1 Corinthians 11:27ff; James 5:13–20). It is not that physical health ought not to be a concern in our prayers, but it's a matter of proportion. The primary concern of public prayer ought to be the glory of God, the sanctification of the saints, and the conversion of the world. As we travel about to various churches, we are astonished to observe how little time is spent in public worship services praying for those goals which are the primary ends of Christian ministry. How much time is spent in public services confessing sin? How much time is spent pleading for spiritual growth and maturation of the members of the church? How much time, if any, is spent praying for the regular services of the church, for the efficacy of the Word of God read and preached, for the edification of the saints and conversion of unbelievers? One could go on. The focus of public prayer should be on the eternal, the spiritual, the ecclesiastical, the ministerial and the missional.

3. *Aim at edifying the congregation through public prayer.* Because the Lord's Day worship service is a *public* service, the prayers in those services are of necessity public and partake of the qualities of public ordinances. This means that public prayer must edify the public. Prayers offered in public are audible, not silent, and must be intelligible because they aim not at personal but public edification. Their purpose is to bless both God and the congregation. There are two audiences, one on earth and one in heaven. This is precisely the Apostle Paul's point in 1 Corinthians 14:14–19. If one prays "in the Spirit" (whatever exactly that means) so that one cannot be understood, the prayer may be a sincere expression of thanksgiving, but (and here is the crucial

point) "the other man is not edified." Better are five intelligible words that may "instruct others" than "ten thousand words in a tongue" (1 Corinthians 14:17, 19). Public prayer, while addressed to God, is for public edification and instruction. It is (again) another kind of pulpit speech, closely related to preaching.

Moreover public prayer is a means of grace in the Reformed tradition.[7] The writer to the Hebrews urges us to "draw near" to God that "we may receive grace to help in time of need" (Hebrews 4:16). We "draw near" in prayer to receive grace and help. Prayer is a means of grace both in that God responds to prayer with His gracious gifts and that it edifies those who hear it. Consequently, when public prayers are offered, the outlook of the minister should not be that he is merely engaging in private devotions which the congregation overhears. Rather, his outlook should be more like that which characterizes his preaching. He aims to edify. He chooses themes and language carefully. He understands that prayer is pulpit speech that has all the potential to benefit the congregation as does the sermon. The reason why the long prayers of the Puritan tradition were so widely appreciated was because they were powerful and moving. Congregations were grieved, undone, filled with joy, and lifted to heaven all in the course of one prayer. This is the kind of careful, thoughtful, transforming public prayer that begs reviving today.

One additional consideration: pulpit prayers play a significant role in teaching members how to pray. Through the pastor's prayers they learn the *categories* of prayer (praise, confession, thanksgiving, etc.), the *language* of prayer (expressions of praise,

---

7   The Dutch and continental Reformed tradition has not classified it with the word and sacraments as one of three primary means of grace, as has the English-speaking Reformed tradition. Still, they have regarded it as an important means of grace, even if they have hesitated to elevate it to that higher status.

confession, thanksgiving, etc.), and the mood or *spirit* of prayer (humility, reverence, gratitude, etc.). He is their model for prayer. The edifying impact of public prayers are multiplied many times over as the minister's model of prayer is reproduced in the homes (family prayers) and closets (private prayers) of his congregation. Fill public prayers with edifying content, because of both their immediate impact on those listening, but also because of their rippling effect, as they are reproduced throughout the congregation.

4. *Fill public prayers with the language of Scripture.*[8] A key to edifying impact in public prayer is the use of scriptural language. Our prayers are to *praise* God for that which Scripture reveals to be true about Him, *confess* that which Scripture condemns, and give *thanks* for that which Scripture particularly highlights as God's gifts to us. We *seek* in prayer for that which Scripture commends or commands, and *plead* for that which Scripture promises. Scripture supplies the content and language of our prayers. Previous generations strongly believed this, including reaching back to the *Apostolic Tradition* (third–fourth century) and *Apostolic Constitutions* (fourth–fifth century), among others. Yet, with so much that is good in the Reformed tradition, this too has slipped away from us. Matthew Henry, Isaac Watts, and Samuel Miller wrote their classic works on prayer concerned that prayer be filled with "sacred dialect," as Watts puts it. Their concern is typical of the whole Reformed tradition. Scottish theologian, Patrick Fairbairn (1805–1874), for example, urges that the whole prayer "should be cast much in the mould of Scripture,

---

8 Some of this material previously appeared in Terry L. Johnson and J. Ligon Duncan, III, "Reading and Praying the Bible in Corporate Worship," in Philip G. Ryken, Derek W. H. Thomas (eds.), *Give Praise to God: A Vision For Reforming Worship* (Phillipsburg, NJ: P&R Publishers, 2003), 148–169.

and should be marked by a free use of its language."[9] Southern Presbyterian theologian, R. L. Dabney (1820–1898), says, "Above all should the minister enrich his prayers with the language of Scripture," explaining,

> Besides its inimitable beauty and simplicity, it is hallowed and sweet to every pious heart by a thousand associations. It satisfies the taste of all; its use effectually protects us against improprieties; it was doubtless given by the Holy Spirit to be a model for our devotions. Let it then abound in our prayers.[10]

Thomas Murphy (1823–1900) agrees,

> The prayer of the sanctuary should be thoroughly saturated with scriptural thought and expression. The language of the Bible is that which the Spirit prompted, and which must therefore be most in accordance with the mind of God. For the same reason it must be Bible language which is best calculated to express those devotional feelings which are the work of the Spirit in the heart.[11]

W. G. Blaikie (1820–1899), a disciple of Thomas Chalmers (1780–1847) and a founding minister of the Free Church of Scotland, urges "copious use of Scriptural expressions in prayer." This, he says, "is of essential importance," being "one of the most indispensable exercises" and "most earnest endeavors" of the minister. "Not to be able to throw his petitions into the language of the Holy Spirit," he continues, "*is to fail in one of the most important means of edification which a Christian congregation*

---

9   Fairbairn, *Pastoral Theology*, 317
10 Dabney, *Sacred Rhetoric*, 358
11 Murphy, Pastoral Theology, 213

can enjoy."[12] John Broadus (1827–1895), professor of homiletics at the Southern Baptist Seminary in Louisville, whose pastoral manual was once the most popular and widely used text book on homiletics in the United States, passing through 22 editions before being revised in 1897 and again in 1943, counsels,

> The minister should be consistently storing in his memory the more directly devotional expressions found everywhere in the Bible, and especially in the psalms and Prophets, the Gospels, Epistles, and Revelation ... most of us greatly need in our prayers a larger and more varied infusion of Scripture language.[13]

The voices from the ancient church, joins with those from the English, Scottish, and American Reformed traditions, Presbyterian, Congregational, and Baptist in agreeing that scriptural language is crucial in public prayer. Still, perhaps some remain unpersuaded, or are concerned that what worked in the past may not work today. Consequently we cite the authority that trumps all others.

This is the pattern found in Scripture itself. This is not merely the opinion of the Fathers, the Reformers or of eighteenth-and nineteenth-century evangelical theologians. It is also the pattern that we see in Scripture. The biblical saints learned God-pleasing and church-edifying devotional language from the Bible. They often used the language and themes of Scripture to interpret and express their experience. Consider for instance Moses seminal revelatory experience in Exodus 34:6–7.

---

12   Blaikie, *Work of the Ministry*, 176–177, my emphasis.
13   Broadus, *Preparation and Delivery*, 368–69

Then the Lord passed by in front of him and proclaimed, "The Lord, the Lord God, compassionate and gracious, slow to anger, and abounding in lovingkindness and truth; who keeps lovingkindness for thousands, who forgives iniquity, transgression and sin; yet He will by no means leave the guilty unpunished, visiting the iniquity of fathers on the children and on the grandchildren to the third and fourth generations."

The echo of this revelation is heard on at least eleven additional occasions in the Old Testament as later prophets learned from Moses how to praise God (Numbers 14:18; 2 Chronicles 30:9; Nehemiah 9:17, 31; Psalms 103:8; 111:4; 112:4; 116:5; 145:9; Joel 2:13; Jonah 4:2; etc.). Similarly, Mary at the annunciation drew upon the Song of Hannah (Luke 1:46–55, cf., 1 Samuel 2:1–10; Solomon at the dedication of the temple incorporated Psalm 132:8–9 (2 Chronicles 6:40–42); Nehemiah (chapter 9) drew upon the prayer of Daniel (Daniel 9:5ff) and the promises of God through Moses (Deuteronomy 30:1–5; Leviticus 26:33ff); Jesus on the cross used the words of Psalms 22:1 and 31:5 (Matthew 27:46; Luke 23:46); and the early church in the face of persecution prayed Psalms 146 and 2 (Acts 4:24–30). In each case the language of Scripture provided the language for prayer.

Where then are we to learn the language of Christian devotion if not from Scripture? That this is less than self-evident to a tradition whose defining principle has been that worship must be regulated by God's word is surprising indeed. Since our minds are "factories for idols," borrowing again Calvin's phrase, we must be taught the proper language of prayer.[14] Do the disciples not ask Jesus, "Lord, teach us to pray" (Luke 11:1)? Doesn't the presence

---

14   Calvin, *Institutes*, I.xi.8, 108.

of the Book of Psalms in the Bible indicate our need to be taught how to praise God? Were not the psalms not provided to teach the people of God the language of devotion which God is pleased to hear? If Jesus in the supreme crisis of his life drew upon the Psalter in order to understand and express His devotion and experience, then we can do no less.

Precedent in history and Scripture is not the only reason for filling our prayers with Scripture. There are practical reasons as well.

1. *There is a special efficacy in Scripture-filled prayer.* No prayers more accurately reflect the will of God than those which use the language which God Himself puts into our mouths (1 John 5:14–15). It is, as Murphy said, "most in accordance with the mind of God." No request is more sure to be granted than that which expresses what God Himself has promised to fulfill. No petition is more sure to be answered than that which pleads for that which God already commands. Pray the promises and commands of Scripture. This principle is evident in James 1. Does God command that we be wise? Of course He does. It follows then that we should ask for it. "But if any of you lacks wisdom, let him ask of God, who gives to all men generously and without reproach, and it will be given to him" (James 1:5). Similarly, pray the promise of 1 John 1:9, that if we confess our sins God is faithful and just to forgive our sins and cleanse us of all unrighteousness. Claim the promise of John 3:16 in prayer, that "whosoever believeth in Him shall not perish." Plead that the people of God will be holy even as God is holy (1 Peter 1:16). Plead that they will love one another and bear one another's burdens (Galatians 6:2). Faith comes by hearing the word of God doesn't it (Romans 10:17)? The word of Christ prayed in the

hearing of the congregation will be efficacious to the salvation of their souls.

2. *There is a special comfort in scriptural prayer.* It is one thing to pray, "Lord, please be with us through this day." It is quite another to pray, "Lord remember Your promise, 'I will never leave nor forsake you'" (Hebrews 13:5). The saints can sense the difference. It is one thing to pray, "As we begin our prayer, we thank You for the privilege of bringing our petitions to You." It is quite another to pray, "We come at Your invitation, O Christ, for You have promised, 'Ask, and it shall be given to you; seek, and you shall find; knock, and it shall be opened to you.' And so we come asking, seeking, and knocking" (Matthew 7:7–8). It is one thing to pray in the midst of tragedy, "Lord we know that You have a plan." That is a true, valid, and comforting thing to pray. Even so, it is quite another to pray, "O Lord, you have numbered the hairs upon our heads. You are working all things after the counsel of your will. Not even a sparrow may fall from a tree apart from you. You cause all things to work together for good for those who love you, and are called according to your purpose" (Matthew 10:29–30; Ephesians 1:11; Romans 8:28). As Dabney said, Scripture language "is hallowed and sweet to every pious heart by a thousand associations." Reformed worship will more effectively comfort the hearts of God's people as its ministers echo the promises of Scripture in their prayers.

3. *Scripture-filled prayer reinforces the ministry of the word.* As noted above, one reason why previous generations of evangelicals were more biblically literate than ours is that there was more Bible content in their services than in ours. What a difference it would make if Protestant ministers called the people to worship with Scripture, invoked the presence of God with scriptural praise, confessed sins using Scripture language, built their intercessions

around the five categories found in Scripture, used by the early church, and revived by the Reformers, and concluded with a scriptural benediction.[15] This done, Sunday morning and evening, fifty-two weeks a year, year after year will build a strong church, one characterized by scriptural literacy and spiritual maturity. If a church prays in this way its growth may be slower than is acceptable to many. It may require that one take a longer view than is customary today. One may not gather large crowds overnight. But in the long run a church that builds a foundation of prayer like this on the words of Christ, will endure like a rock, and not be shaken.

How to pray

How may Reformed ministers become proficient in praying in public, or in particular, praying in the language of Scripture? We may offer several recommendations.

1. *Cultivate the art of free prayer.* The older authors, especially Samuel Miller, nineteenth century Old Princeton's second professor and colleague of Archibald Alexander, urged ministers to develop the skill of free prayer through practice. One learns free prayer by doing it. At the same time, they warn against over-reliance upon written prayers as death to developing and maintaining this gift. They argue this in principle and with anecdotes about ministers who once prayed freely with great unction, but who joined liturgical churches, and because they needed only to read the *Prayer Book's* prayers, week in and week out, lost their abilities to pray extemporaneously. Learn to pray

---

15   See Terry Johnson, *Leading in Worship* (Oak Ridge, TN: Covenant Foundation, 1996), 10 n. 15, 34 n. 5, 22–38, and 38–57; or, Johnson, *Leading in Worship*, Revised and Expanded Edition (Powder Springs, Georgia: Tolle Lege Press, 2013), 308 n. 15, 315 n 5; 23–43; 45–80. .

aloud in public by praying aloud in public. It is an art. Cultivate it through use.

Free prayer is also cultivated through private prayer. Pulpit prayer grows out of and is a reflection of closet prayer. We've seen how Thomas Murphy calls public prayer an "echo" of what one "has learned in the closet," and his claim that only those who are "mighty in private" prayer will be "mighty in public."[16] For Samuel Miller it was an axiom that "None can hope to attain excellence in the grace and gifts of prayer in the public assembly, unless they abound in closet devotion, in holy communion with God in secret."[17] Pray in private, pray the full range of prayer types in private, and pray long in private. Public prayer grows out of closet prayer.

2. *Utilize the devotional language of the Bible.* The prayer language of Scripture should be learned and incorporated in public prayer. This can be done by concentrating on two disciplines.

i. Study and use the *prayers in Scripture.* Are there any better prayers of praise than those of David in 1 Chronicles 29 or the composite prayer of the Apostle Paul in 1 Timothy? Listen to them:

> Thine, O Lord, is the greatness and the power and the glory and the victory and the majesty, indeed everything that is in the heavens and the earth; Thine is the dominion, O Lord, and Thou dost exalt Thyself as head over all. Both riches and honor come from Thee, and Thou dost rule over all, and in Thy hand is power and might; and it lies in Thy hand to make great, and to strengthen everyone.

---

16 Murphy, *Pastoral Theology*, 214,215.
17 Miller, *Thoughts on Public Prayer*, 261.

Now, therefore, our God, we thank Thee, and praise Thy glorious name. (1 Chronicles 29:11–13)

Now to the King eternal, immortal, invisible, the only God, be honor and glory forever and ever. Amen ... He who is the blessed and only Sovereign, the King of kings and Lord of lords; who alone possesses immortality and dwells in unapproachable light; whom no man has seen or can see. To Him be honor and eternal dominion! Amen. (1 Timothy 1:17; 6:15–16)

Are there any better prayers of confession than David's Psalm 51, or Daniel's in Daniel 9? Are there any better prayers of illumination than those of Psalm 43:3 and Ephesians 3:18–19?

O send out Thy light and Thy truth, let them lead me; let them bring me to Thy holy hill, and to Thy dwelling places. (Psalm 43:3)

May (we) be able to comprehend with all the saints what is the breadth and height and depth, and to know the love of Christ which surpasses knowledge, that (we) may be filled up to all the fulness of God. (Ephesians 3:18–19)

Are there any better prayers of intercession for the saints than Paul's for the Ephesians, Philippians, and Colossians (Ephesians 1:15–23; Philippians 1:9–11; Colossians 1:9–11)? The following is a partial list of the major prayers found in Scripture whose study will pay spiritual dividends:

Abraham—Genesis 18:23–33 (intercession)

Moses—Exodus 15:1–18 (praise); 32:11–14 and 33:12–17 (intercession); Numbers 11:10–15 (complaint); 14:11–19 (pleading)

Hannah—1 Samuel 2:1–10 (praise)

David—2 Samuel 7:18–29 (thanksgiving); 2 Chronicles 29:11–20 (praise)

Solomon—1 Kings 3:6–9 (for wisdom); 8:22–53, 54–61 (praise); 2 Chronicles 6:14–42 (praise and petition)

Hezekiah—2 Kings 19:14–19 (intercession)

Jeremiah—Jeremiah 32:16–25 (praise and questioning)

Ezra—Ezra 9:5–15 (confession)

Nehemiah—Nehemiah 1:5–11 (confession and petition); 9:5–27 (praise and petition)

Daniel—Daniel 9:1–19 (confession and petition)

Habakkuk—Habakkuk 1:12–17 (questioning)

Mary—Luke 1:46–55 (praise)

Zacharias—Luke 1:68–79 (praise)

Simeon—Luke 2:29–32 (praise)

Early Church—Acts 4:24–30 (praise and petition)

Paul—Colossians 1:9–12; Ephesians 1:1–23; Philippians 1:9–11 (praise and petition)

Church Triumphant—Revelation 4:8–5:14 (praise)

ii. Incorporate the *broader language of Scripture* in the church's prayers. Not only should we pray the prayers of Scripture, but both our terminology and content should reflect Scripture's terminology and content. Our worship should not open with the pastor praying whatever pops into his head. Instead he might pray, "O Lord we have come to worship and bow down, to kneel before You the Lord our Maker; for You are our God, and we are the people of Your pasture, the sheep of Your hand" (Psalm 95). Instead of praying, "Lord save our covenant children," he might pray, "Lord remember your promise to be a God to us and to our children, and so save our covenant children" (Genesis 17:7). We repeat ourselves: Pray back to God His promises. Pray back to God His revelation of His own nature. Pray back to God those things that He requires of us in His word. For example, why not turn Ephesians 5:1–17 into a prayer?

We pray that we might be imitators of God, as beloved children, and walk in love, just as Christ also loved us. We pray that immorality, and impurity, and greed might not be named among us; nor filthiness and silly talk, nor coarse jesting, nor anything else that is improper or not fitting. Help us to walk as children of light, in goodness, righteousness, and truth. Teach us what is pleasing to you. Use us to expose the unfruitful deeds of darkness. Guide us, that we might walk, not as unwise men, but as wise, making the most of our time, because the days are evil. Keep us from foolishness, and give us an understanding of your will.

Find key phrases and precious promises and turn them into prayer. There is almost no limit to what can be done. Even historical allusions can be profitably employed in prayer. Samuel Miller provides several examples:

In a time of struggle for the church:

O Thou who didst of old, deliver thy covenant people from the bondage of Egypt, and didst open a way through the sea for them to pass in safety; so may it please thee now to deliver thy afflicted and struggling Church, to disappoint those who seek her hurt, to sanctify to her all her troubles, and bring her out of them all with increasing purity, and peace, and joy.[18]

---

18   Miller, *Public Prayer*, 277.

Administering the Elements—2

To cry for freedom from the corruption of sin:

We are by nature carnal, sold under sin; but we rejoice to know that, as thou didst once bring thy people out of bondage, and make them the Lord's freemen in their own land; so thou hast promised, by the Lord Jesus Christ, to proclaim liberty to the captives, and the opening of the prison to them that are the bond slaves of Satan. We rejoice to read in thy word, that, as Moses lifted up the serpent in the wilderness, even so the Son of man has been lifted up, that whosoever believeth on him should not perish, but obtain eternal life.[19]

Especially helpful in the study of prayer in addition to the older volumes already cited are Richard L. Pratt's *Pray With Your Eyes Open*,[20] W. Graham Scroggie's *Paul's Prison Prayers*,[21] Donald Cogan's *The Prayers of the New Testament*,[22] Herbert Lockyer's *All the Prayers of the Bible*,[23] and Kenneth Boa's handbooks.[24] Better yet, study Henry's *A Method for Prayer*, especially the new edition revised and edited by Palmer Robertson entitled *A Way to Pray*,[25]

---

19   Ibid. 277–8.

20   Richard Pratt, *Prayer With Your Eyes Open* (Phillipsburg, N.J.: Presbyterian and Reformed Pub. Co., 1987).

21   W. Graham Scroggie, *Paul's Prison Prayers* (1921, rprt.; Grand Rapids: Kregel Publications, 1981).

22   Donald Cogan, *The Prayers of the New Testament* (New York: Harper and Row, Publishers, 1967).

23   Herbert Lockyer, *All The Prayers of the Bible* (Grand Rapids: Zondervan Publishing House, 1959). Thankfully while books treating public prayers have neglected the use of Scripture-language, the books on private prayer have not. Pratt's is especially good in this respect.

24   Kenneth Boa, *Handbook to Prayer: Praying Scripture Back to God* (Atlanta: Trinity House Publishers, 1993); *Handbook to Renewal: Renewing Your Mind with Affirmation from Scripture* (Atlanta: Trinity House Publishers, 1996).

25   O. Palmer Robertson, *A Way to Pray* (Edinburgh: Banner of Truth Trust, 2010).

216   *Serving with Calvin*

or Watts' *A Guide to Prayer*, and read them over and over again. The whole Bible is our prayer book.

3. *Plan public prayers.* This too is obviously necessary if the preceding points are to be realized, that is, if our ministers are to pray edifying prayers that utilize the actual terminology of the Bible. In addition, planning is also necessary if prayers are to be well-ordered and fresh. "Do not go to the pulpit and say the first thing that comes to hand," Spurgeon warns, "for the uppermost thing with most men is mere froth."[26] It is disheartening to hear the careless language, the imprecision, and the incoherence of many pulpit prayers today. We suspect, though we cannot prove, that many ministers give no thought whatsoever beforehand to what they intend to pray. Isaac Watts over 300 years ago complained of those who were unskilled in public prayer, who "rush always into the presence of God in solemn prayer without due forethought even when there is time allowed for it."[27] He laments the disrepute into which free prayer had sunk because of its incompetent practice by "those few bold, ignorant and careless men who have been guilty of such rash and thoughtless addresses to God, under a pretence of praying by the Spirit."[28] He notes their "crude, rash, and unseemly expressions in the presence of God" that are "unworthy of his divine majesty and unbecoming of our baseness," citing Ecclesiastes 5:2 ("let not your words be few").[29] He cites Matthew 6:7, insisting that "vain repetitions" are evidence not of our fervency, but of "the barrenness of our minds and the slightness of our frame."[30] W. G. Blaikie warned

---

26   Spurgeon, *Lectures to My Students*, 132.
27   Watts, *Guide*, 46.
28   Ibid. 60.
29   Ibid.
30   Ibid.

a hundred years ago of the inevitable "repetitions, clumsinesses, circumlocutions, and other encumbrances" when prayers are unplanned, as well as "uncouthness, flabbiness ... expletives, repetitions, and redundancies."[31] William Willimon complains today that "Many of our pastoral prayers are a maze of poorly thought out, confusing clichés, hackneyed expressions, shallow constructions, and formalized, impersonal ramblings."[32] All of the old commentators are of one mind on the need of "studied" or "conceived" public prayers. One ought no more pray without preparation than preach, they would insist. "Some method must be used," says Watts, "in order to protect us from confusion, so that our thoughts are not ill sorted, or mingled and huddled together in a tumultuous and unseemly manner.[33] Fairbairn says, "I would earnestly advise a certain measure of special preparation for the devotional work of the sanctuary."[34] He encourages the use of an outline, and even the practice of writing out one's prayers, not in order to read them, but in order to organize one's thoughts. W. G. T. Shedd says the minister "ought to study *method* in prayer, and observe it. A prayer should have a plan as much as a sermon."[35] He continues,

---

31 W. G. Blaikie, *Work of the Ministry*, 167, 176, 179.
32 William H. Willimon, *Preaching and Leading Worship* (Philadelphia: The Westminster Press, 1984), 44.
33 Watts, *Guide*, 63. He continues, "It will be of use to prevent tautologies or repetitions, when each part of prayer is arranged in its proper place. It will guard us against roving digressions, when we have arranged our thoughts in order throughout every step of our prayer. We can judge what sort of subject properly and naturally follows what we are at present speaking, so that there is no need to fill up any empty space with content that is not proper or not suited to the purpose."
34 Fairbairn, *Pastoral Theology*, 318.
35 Shedd, *Homiletics*, 271.

In the recoil from the formalism of written and read prayers, Protestants have not paid sufficient attention to an orderly and symmetrical structure in public supplications. Extemporaneous prayer, like extemporaneous preaching, is too often the product of the single instant, instead of devout reflection and premeditation. It might, at first glance, seem that premeditation and supplication are incongruous conceptions; that prayer must be a gush of feeling, without distinct reflection. This is an error. No man, no creature, can pray well without knowing what he is praying for, and whom he is praying to. Everything in prayer, and especially in public prayer, ought to be well considered and well weighed.[36]

R. L. Dabney (1820–1898) agrees:

"I deem that the minister is as much bound to prepare himself for praying in public as for preaching. The negligence with which many preachers leave their prayers to accident, while they lay out all their strength on their sermons, is most painfully suggestive of unbelief toward God and indifference to the edification of their brethren." He labels the idea that one should trust in the leading of the Holy Spirit in prayer rather than prepare ahead of time "a remnant of fanatical enthusiasm."

"To speak for God to men is a sacred and responsible task. To speak for men to God is not less responsible, and is more solemn .... The young minister should no more venture into the pulpit with an *impromptu* prayer, than with an *impromptu* sermon."[37]

---

36 Ibid.
37 Dabney, *Sacred Rhetoric*, 346–7, 360.

Both Dabney and Miller (like Murphy) encourage the discipline of what they call "devotional composition," "not so much to recite these written prayers in the pulpit," explains Dabney, "as to train his own taste, and to gather a store of devotional language."[38] Among modern writers Robert Rayburn agrees: "If a minister wishes to be effective in leading the prayers of his congregation he must prepare for his public prayers."[39]

4. *Be authentic.* Authenticity in prayer is crucial. While one must pray with the congregation's edification in mind, this is not the same as calculating the phrases and expressions most likely to impress one's listeners. The primary audience for one's prayers is still God. Praying so as to impress the crowd, as opposed to edify, is not an uncommon mistake today. The "groan factor," the concurring sighs and moans that are often eagerly sought in small group prayer, has negatively impacted public prayer. Several generations have learned to affect an over-wrought earnestness that is designed to register audible approval. This factor can become so controlling that those leading in prayer began to compete with each other. Authenticity is crucial in preaching. It is also crucial in prayer. One's phrasing and tone should be biblical, yet natural. Given that the primary concerns of prayer are spiritual and eternal, issues of heaven of hell, there is a degree of urgency and earnestness that is not only appropriate but necessary. However, this earnestness must be authentic, natural to one's own God-given personality and disposition.

Inauthenticity is not a new problem. "Every devout heart will express itself in prayer in simple language," insists Blaikie.[40] He labels elaborate rhetoric in prayer an "abomination." "Eloquent

---

38 Ibid. 360; see also Miller, *Public Prayer*, 288ff.
39 Rayburn, O Come Let Us Worship, 199.
40 Blaikie, *Work of the Ministry*, 176.

prayers," he warns, "must ever be regarded with suspicion." He retells the story of an American newspaper that "revealed more than (it) probably intended when (it) described 'the most eloquent prayer that was ever addressed to a Boston audience.'" "Let prayer be uttered as in the very presence of God," counsels Blaikie. This means "an undertone of felt unworthiness." It means "the voice will have a touch of contrition, while a plaintive, fervent tone of entreaty will characterize the prayer throughout."[41]

5. *Pray briefly in public.* "Long prayers either consist of repetition, or else of unnecessary explanations which God does not require, or else they degenerate into downright preaching," Spurgeon warns.[42] We should not try the patience of our people by rambling on and on. Even the nineteenth century writers recommend brevity.[43] Murphy recommends that the main prayer should be five minutes, or no more than eight. Samuel Miller complains of the "excessive length" of some prayers.[44] Blaikie warns, "when attention fails devotion ends." He counsels that prayers last no longer than 5–10 minutes, and repeats George Whitefield's remarks to an excellent minister whose prayer was unreasonably long: "You prayed me into a good frame, and you prayed me out of it."[45] Similarly Spurgeon recounts, "I have known men tantalize us with the hope that they were drawing to a close, and then take a fresh lease 2 or 3 times; this is most unwise and unpleasant."[46] Careful planning will help avoid the "verbiage and repetition" about which Shedd complains.[47] It

---

41 Ibid. 177–178.
42 Spurgeon, *Lectures to My Students*, 61.
43 Warren agrees, *Purpose-Driven Church*, 256.
44 Miller, *Public Prayer*, 187.
45 Blaikie, *Work of the Ministry*, 178.
46 Spurgeon, *Lectures to My Students*, 61.
47 Shedd, *Homiletics*, 272–3.

will also guard against the frequent and mechanical repetition of favorite phrases, titles of God, and any other formula of words, of which Dabney complains.[48] He writes, "This mechanical phrase is obnoxious to every charge of formalism, monotony and lack of appropriate variety, which we lodge against an unchangeable liturgy, while it has none of its literary merit and dignified and tender associations."[49] Wandering prayers, meandering at length here, there, and everywhere, will also be corrected by planning.

6. *Pray, don't preach or announce.* Dabney warns of the "painful absurdity in our going about formally to instruct God of his doctrinal truth," or our seeming "to preach to God instead of praying to him."[50] Shedd warns of "didactically discoursing in prayer."[51] Murphy calls it "a great abuse of public prayer to use it for preaching to the audience or for rebuking them, or even, as is often done, for giving information to the Lord."[52] It would be an abuse of public prayer to rebuke the congregation by reminding God to "enlighten the minds of those who fail to come back for the Sunday night service. Show them how wrong they are and how discouraging their non-attendance is to those who come." We've heard ministers pray, "Lord, we thank you for the prayer meeting which is held in the chapel on Wednesday evening at seven o'clock, just after the fellowship supper and just before choir rehearsal. And we know that you want all your people to come unless providentially hindered. Help us to make it a priority." This is "a great abuse of public prayer" (not to mention silly), and must be avoided.

---

48 Dabney, *Sacred Rhetoric*, 347–8.
49 Ibid. 348.
50 Ibid. 355.
51 Shedd, *Homiletics*, 273.
52 Murphy, *Pastoral Theology*, 211–212.

7. *Use public terminology.* Choose suitable language in addressing the Almighty. The old authors denounce, with surprising vehemence, the use of over-familiar language in prayer. Watts urged that one's language be "decent and neat, but not pompous or gaudy; simple and plain, but not careless, unclean or rude."[53] He counsels that one "avoid low and coarse and too familiar expressions," particularly the impropriety of "a too familiar mention of the name of Christ." Avoid, he says, the "low and trivial" and "unseemly."[54]

Jonathan Edwards saw the emergence of this problem during the Great Awakening in the 1740s and wrote against it. "There is in some persons," he said, "a most unsuitable and insufferable boldness in their addresses to the Great Jehovah, in an ostentatious and eminent nearness and familiarity."[55] Evangelicalism continued to manifest an undue familiarity in the succeeding decades, attracting the rebukes of the nineteenth century writers. "Familiarity is the worst of faults in prayer," says Shedd.[56] Dabney heaps scorn on "Half-educated or spiritually proud men" who "frequently indulge in an indecent familiarity with the Most High, under the pretense of filial nearness and importunity."[57] Spurgeon counsels that one avoid "an unhallowed and sickening superabundance of endearing words." He says, "When 'Dear Lord,' and 'Blessed Lord,' and 'Sweet Lord,' come over and over again as vain repetitions, they are among the worst of blots." He wishes that "in some way or other," those who

---

53 Watts, *Guide*, 80.
54 Ibid. 81.
55 Quoted in Murray (ed.), *A Day's March Nearer Home*, 299; from Jonathan Edwards, *Treatise Concerning the Religious Affections*, Selected Works of Jonathan Edwards, Vol. III (1746, London: The Banner of Truth Trust, 1961), 289–290.
56 Shedd, *Homiletics*, 273.
57 Dabney, *Sacred Rhetoric*, 349.

indulge such "fond and familiar expressions," could come "to a better understanding of the true relation existing between man and God."[58] He urges that one be "scrupulously reverent" in one's language.[59]

The counsel of these pastoral guides has largely gone unheeded. If anything, the language of "God is my buddy," "the Almighty is in my hip-pocket," has gotten exponentially worse. "Warm, back-scratching use of words in prayer and preaching," have become characteristic of much of modern Christianity, complains J. I. Packer in his biting critique of our times.[60] However, if, even the "spotless and glorious angels in heaven ... cover their faces before his throne" (Isaiah 6); and if Elijah, "who had so much holy familiarity with God, at a time of special nearness to God ... wrapped his face in his mantle" (1 Kings 19:12–13); and if Moses, who spoke to God face-to-face, and "who was distinguished from all the prophets in the familiarity with God that he was admitted to," and who "at a time when he was brought nearest of all, when God showed him His glory ... 'made haste, and bowed his head toward the earth, and worshiped'" (Exodus 34:8); and if the publican, "stood afar off, durst not so much as lift up his eyes to heaven; but smote upon his breast saying, O God be merciful to me a sinner," then, says Edwards, "It becomes such sinful creatures as we, to approach a holy God (although with faith, and without terror) with contrition and penitent shame and confusion of face."[61] Modest, restrained, reverential language in public prayer is another of the great needs of our time.

What, then, does the prayer life of the public assembly of the

---

58 Spurgeon, *Lectures*, 57.
59 Ibid. 58.
60 J. I. Packer, *Hot Tub Religion* (Wheaton: Tyndale House Publishers, 1987), 69.
61 Edwards, *Religious Affections*, 289–290.

church look like when it all comes together? As the pastor *invokes* the presence of God, he should fill his praise with the language of Scripture. The congregation needs to hear him humbly exalting the greatness and majesty of God. The great biblical prayers of praise should be studied and the psalms should be mined for their rich devotional expressions. Week by week the minister's invocation should provide for the congregation a vision of the power and glory and goodness of the Triune God whom they worship, a God for whom nothing is impossible, a God who can do all things, and God to whom homage and adoration is due.

As the minister moves on to the *prayer of confession*, deep, expansive, detailed language of Scripture should be used. Churchgoers come to services each week bruised and battered by sin. They come burdened with guilt, knowing something of what they ought to be and their failure. Let them hear, in the minister's voice, humble grief for sin expressed on their behalf as he confesses idolatry, greed, covetousness, pride, lust, selfishness, jealousy, envy and gossip. The minister should give voice to their failure to love God with all their heart, mind, soul and strength and their failure to love their neighbor as themselves. The language of David, for example, might be used:

> *I know my transgressions, and my sin is ever before me. Against you, you only, have I sinned, and done what is evil in your sight. I was brought forth in iniquity, and in sin my mother conceived me.*

With David the congregation might be led to plead:

> *Be gracious to us, O God, according to your lovingkindness; according to the greatness of your compassion blot out our transgressions. Wash us thoroughly from our iniquity, and cleanse us*

from our sin. Purify us with hyssop, and we shall be clean; wash us and we shall be whiter than snow. Hide your face from our sins, and blot out all our iniquities. Deliver us from blood guiltiness, O God, the God of our salvation. Create in us clean hearts, O God, and renew a steadfast spirit within us. Restore to us the joy of your salvation, and sustain us with a willing spirit. O Lord, open our lips, that our mouth may declare your praise (Psalm 51).

The saints are struggling to believe the gospel and struggling to experience forgiveness. They may have confessed their sin privately, and yet they have not found relief. Often the problem is that they have not gone deeply enough. Their brokenness has been healed superficially with flippant promises that "'All is well, all is well'; but there is no peace" (Jeremiah 8:11). They need to hear their minister earnestly acknowledging and grieving sin and claiming the promises of God on their behalf. I mentioned in *Worshipping with Calvin* hating the *Book of Common Prayer* my first six months as a student in Britain. Eventually I learned to love it, and even to look forward to going to chapel each day in no small part so that I could pray Cranmer's beautiful general confession. I found it "therapeutic," though I hesitate to use the word, to deal with God with my sins in congregational worship each day. This is what churchgoers need to experience in their worship. They need to deal with God. The pastor needs to lead them there with praise and then confession. Let them hear a weighty confession of sin with a rehearsal of the promises of God. Let them hear expressions of thanksgiving for the promise of 1 John 1:9, that "if we confess our sins, God is faithful and just to forgive us our sins and to cleanse us from all unrighteousness." Let them hear thanks that Jesus "bore our sins in His body on the cross" (1 Peter 2:24), that "He gave His life a ransom for many" (Matthew 20:28), that though He knew no sin He became sin "that we might become the righteousness of God in Him" (2 Corinthians 5:21). Let them give thanks through their minister that they now have "no condemnation" and "peace with God" in Christ (Romans 8:1, 5:1). The extended promises of Psalm 103 might be prayed:

> *The Lord is compassionate and gracious, slow to anger and abounding in lovingkindness. He has not dealt with us according to our sins, nor rewarded us according to our iniquities. for as high as the heavens are above the earth, so great is His lovingkindness toward those who fear Him. As far as the east is from the west, so far has He removed our transgressions from us. (Psalm 103:8, 10–12)*

John D. Witvliet, director of the Calvin Institute of Christian Worship, suggests that "intercessory prayer may be the single act of worship most in need of reform (or resuscitation) in the church today."[62] If so, then we must reform it. As the service moves on to petitionary prayer, the congregation should hear compassion and urgency in the pastor's voice as he prays that the ideals of the Christian life might be realized in their lives. They need to hear him praying week after week that they might be holy even as God is holy (1 Peter 1:15–16), that they might be imitators of God as beloved children, and walk in love (Ephesians 5:1ff), and conformed to the image of Christ, bearing the fruit of Spirit (Galatians 5:22–23). Let them hear him pleading that they'll not love the world nor the things of the world, and that they'll not be seduced by the lust of the eyes, the lust of the flesh, and the boastful pride of life (1 John 2:15–16).

---

62 *Reformed Worship Magazine*, March 2008, No. 87, 40.

The pastor's prayers should comprehend the four other areas of intercession (in addition to the sanctification of the saints) found in Scripture, used by the early church, and revived by the Reformers. The church should pray for (1) the civil authorities; (2) the Christian ministry (Matthew 9:36–38; 1 Timothy 2:1–2; (3) the salvation of all men (1 Timothy 2:1, 3–4); and (4) the afflicted (2 Corinthians 1:3–4, 11; James 5:13–18).[63] They need to hear the breadth of the church's prayers. They need to hear our prayers circle the globe as we pray for the progress of Christian missions, for ministers and missionaries, for the nation, and for the needy.

What about the prayer of *illumination*? Doesn't the congregation need to be reminded that "the natural man does not accept the things of the Spirit of God" (1 Corinthians 2:14)? Won't the saints benefit from a weekly reminder that we are dependent upon the Holy Spirit if we are ever to understand the word of God? Illumination should be sought before Scripture is read and preached. We should pray that eyes will be opened, (Psalm 119:18) that ears will be unstopped, that stony hearts will be replaced with hearts of flesh, that stiff-necks will be loosened. We should pray that the eyes of the heart might be enlightened (Ephesians 3:18), that the Lord might teach us His truth (Psalm 86:11–12), and give us understanding (Psalm 119:33).

Finally, they need to hear the blessing of God pronounced upon them. They may be blessed with the Apostolic benediction (2 Corinthians 13:14) or the Aaronic (Numbers 6:24–26) or some other (e.g. Hebrews 13:20–21). But they should leave with one or other of these scriptural blessings ringing in their ears. Will that

---

63 See *Worshipping with Calvin*, Chapter 5; *Leading in Worship*, 10, n. 15; *Leading in Worship* Revised & Expanded Edition, 308, 315 n. 5; 34–39; 72–76.

not encourage them as they leave? Does this not conclude the service on the gospel's optimistic note?

Perhaps it is clearer now why we have said that the minister needs to lead in prayer? Who in the congregation is trained to pray in this manner? Who is most aware of the pastoral needs of the congregation? Who has been set apart for three years of biblical and theological education? Who spends extended time each day in the study of Scripture? Who labors daily on his knees in private prayer for the souls of the saints? Who consequently is capable of praying in the rich devotional language of Scripture as well as in a manner that is theologically sound? Public prayer is not merely a matter of anyone at all standing up and praying off the top of his head. The first thing in most of our minds, as Spurgeon once said, is "mere froth." It makes sense to have the minister pray even as it makes sense to have the minister preach and administer the sacraments. The prayers that we envision are those offered by a man called by God, who saturates his mind with the word of God, and spends hours each week on his knees before God. Even as the church has deemed it wise to apply the New Testament admonitions to "guard the gospel" by entrusting its proclamation through word and sacrament only to those ordained to do so, so also it is both pastorally and theologically wise to leave leadership in prayer in the hands of the minister (1 Timothy 6:20; 2 Timothy 1:12, 14).

Has public prayer been given the attention it deserves? Do not underestimate the powerful difference public prayer can make. Isaac Watts asks,

"Christians, have you never felt your spirits raised from a carnal and vain temper of mind to a devout frame by a lively prayer? Have you not found your whole souls overspread with holy devotion and carried up to heaven with most abundant pleasure by the pious and regular performance of him that speaks to God in worship? And when you have been cold and indifferent to divine things, have you not felt that heavy and lifeless humour expelled by joining with the warm and stirring expressions of a person skillful in this duty? How sweet a refreshment have you found under inward burdens of mind or outward afflictions, when in broken language you have told them to your minister and he has spread them before God in such words as have expressed your whole souls and your sorrows? And you have experienced a sweet serenity and calmness of spirits; you have risen up from your knees no more sad-faced."

Again Watts asks, "Who would willingly remain neglectful of attaining an instrument so sweet and successful in advancing religion in its powers and pleasures in their own hearts and the hearts of all men round about them?"[64] Is it clear that public prayer is a means of grace that builds the church? Commit to the practice of "studied prayer," as the Puritans called it, or to employ Mather's term, "conceived prayer." Plan the church's prayers, fill them with scriptural language and allusions, and watch the sanctifying impact that they make upon the congregation.

Singing

Chuck Fromm, widely recognized as among the most important leaders of the original contemporary Christian music movement originating in Costa Mesa's Calvary Chapel, has written an article entitled "Setlist or Hymnal" for *Worship Leader* magazine, of which he is CEO/Publisher. "What is the hymnal of your church?" he asks. He issues what we see as the critical challenge:

---

64 Watts, *Guide*, 174–175.

"Are your hymns representative of historical Christianity as well as modern?" Further, "Are the songs you singing representative of the multicultural, multiethnic, multigeneral nature of the kingdom of heaven?" Once again, "Do the hymns carry deep theological truth as well as beautiful metaphoric imagery?"[65]

His concerns are ours. Historic as well as modern selections? Diverse ethnic/cultural origins? Deep theological/biblical content? Beautiful poetic/metaphoric expression? His is an argument for a good traditional hymnal wherein time has filtered out the unworthy, the aesthetic and theological judgment of the church has been exercised, and contemporary contributions are tested and gradually gain acceptance.

Many of the world's greatest composers and songwriters were Christians. Bach, Handel, and Mendelssohn, as well as Lowell Mason and many others, have left a treasury of music for the church, music that is durable, that has stood the test of time. Respecting *lyrics*, priority should be given to those which God has given us in His word, that is, the psalms and biblical hymns. Traditional hymns, typically rich in biblical content, have come to us from a variety of *authors*: the church fathers, the monastic orders, the Reformers, the evangelical hymn writers of the eighteenth century (Watts, Charles Wesley, Toplady, Newton, Cowper, Doddridge, etc.), as well as some more modern writers. Our hymns have come to us from a variety of *origins*: Western, Central, Southern, and Eastern Europe, Great Britain, Turkey, Syria, Egypt, and North Africa; and from a variety of *churches*: all the Protestant denominations, Roman Catholicism, and Eastern Orthodoxy. Our first counsel is to give preference to traditional psalmody and hymnody. As we discuss criteria for song selection,

---

65   Chuck Fromm, *Worship Leader*, September 2012, Vol. 21, No. 6, 102.

we'll flesh out this preference. For now we urge, when choosing hymns, do not compromise quality for the shifting sands of popularity. Honor the *tradition* of the church. Honor the *collective wisdom* of the church. Honor the *aesthetic judgment* of the church. Honor the gift of God's providence that the church's treasury of song represents. Honor traditional hymnody and psalmody for its rich biblical content and its catholic breadth.

Can we establish criteria for selecting the best song choices? Hymnal-compilers have been identifying their principles for inclusion for generations. Read the introduction to most any hymnal. Song selection "is not a matter of taste," says T. David Gordon, "it is a matter of serious aesthetic, theological, and liturgical principle."[66] For the Christian beautiful music will reflect the nature of God, the Source of all truth, righteousness, and bounty.

Criteria for evaluation

While the treasury of hymns is an invaluable source of congregational signing, it is not an infallible source. Nor does respect for the treasury preclude additions to it over time. The "canon" evolves. Judgments must be made. We may establish at least the following criteria by which to evaluate a given song:[67]

1. *Is it singable?* Is the tune simple enough for a congregation to learn after working at it for a relatively short period of time? Notice we don't say that it must be so simple that it can be mastered the first time through. But neither should it be so complex or difficult (not always the same thing) that the

---

66 Gordon, *Why Johnny Can't Sing Hymns*, 176.

67 For similar criteria see D. T. Williams, "Durable Hymns," in *Touchstone* (July/Aug 2009). He lists categories of biblical truth, theological profundity, poetic richness, musical beauty, and fitness.

congregation is still stumbling after years of use.[68] This is essentially what Richard Baxter said over 300 years ago: "I think it unlawful to use such strains of music as are light (i.e. easy, frivolous, frothy, as opposed to weighty), or *as the congregation cannot easily be brought to understand*." He prefers "plain, intelligible church music."[69] In this respect a significant number of contemporary tunes on the one hand, as well as some classical music on the other, fail the test. Some of the popular Scripture songs are lovely when sung by solo performers, but because of irregular rhythms are poorly sung by congregations. Many contemporary tunes are *moaned* not *sung*. They fail to encourage vigorous, full-throated singing. There are classical tunes that must be classified as outstanding musically, but require trained choirs to be properly sung. "Complex syncopations, difficult melodic leaps, and excessively wide melodic range make a tune difficult for a congregation to sing," argues John Ferguson of St. Olaf College. "These attributes have nothing to do with the genre of the music, but have everything to do with whether the congregation will sing them well and with confidence."[70] "Too many of the more recent praise choruses seem to ignore all the rules of good composition, giving us not well shaped melodies but just one note after another," says D. T. Williams. They are often "not very singable," he maintains.[71] The hymnal itself contains a number of selections that are difficult. Often the words are excellent, but the

---

68 "The singing ought to be free from the faults which make it intolerable to persons of cultivated musical tastes, but it ought not to be of a kind in which only persons of cultivated musical taste can join," R. W. Dale, *Nine Lectures on Preaching*, 273.

69 Baxter, "Christian Directory," *Works*, Vol. 1, 705.

70 Cited in Plantinga & Rozeboom, *Discerning the Spirits*, 118. He continues, "Some tunes from chorale anthems and some tunes from the Contemporary Christian Music scene are equally inappropriate for just these reasons" (118).

71 D. T. Williams, "Durable Music," *Touchstone*, 21.

tunes are unfortunate. There are dozens of hymns and metrical psalms in search of excellent music. The Reformation rightly restored *congregational* singing to the life of the church, replacing specialized choirs and vocalists. The first test of any hymn must be, can a congregation sing it?

2. *Is it biblically and theologically sound?* Truth is paramount. The church learns much of its theology through its songs, as Luther noted long ago. Luther said, "next to the Word of God, music deserves the highest praise."[72] The church also learns the language of Christian experience through what it sings. Instinctively we turn to our songs both in time of crisis and great joy to find adequate language to express our response. It is vital that what we sing be theologically sound. A generation ago the hymn "At the Cross" was quite popular. It has this line:

It was there by faith,
I received my sight,
And now I am happy all the day.

Is it true that once we come to the cross we are "happy *all* the day?" How many people were damaged by the false expectation that this song creates, that they would always be happy? How many people were unprepared when the inevitable sorrow, sadness, trouble, and trials of life came their way? "At the cross" poorly describes the nature of Christian experience. It misleads. The beloved Christmas carol, "Away in a Manger," has this line:

The little Lord Jesus,
No crying He makes.

---

72   Cited in Begbie, *Resounding Truth*, 98; from *Luther's Works*, Vol. 49, 428.

Traditional Christology says that Jesus was "truly God and truly Man." He experienced the full range of human experiences, without sin. How many people, particularly those who theologize no more deeply than what they sing, have been led to think of Jesus as only remotely human because of this carol? If Jesus was truly human, then he cried as an infant, as all infants do. However, the carol would have us think that Jesus didn't feel the normal pains and emotions that people feel, and so couldn't possibly understand us. This Jesus is made of marble, He is without feeling. Yet the Jesus of the Bible is able to sympathize with us precisely because He suffered and was tempted in *all* ways as we have been. On this basis He is able to sympathize with us as our faithful High Priest (Hebrews 2:17–18; 4:15–16). What we sing must be biblically accurate and theologically orthodox. Our songs must faithfully express both Christian doctrine and experience. "The best texts," says D. T. Williams, "helped (believers of previous generations) interpret their own religious experiences in biblically sound ways."[73] It is imperative that our songs be theologically and biblically accurate.

3. *Is it biblically and theologically mature?* Paul rebukes the Corinthians (1 Corinthians 3:1ff) and the writer to the Hebrews scolds his readers for their failure to move on from "milk" to "solid food," for needing reinstruction regarding "elementary principles of the oracles of God," for failing to "press on to maturity" (Hebrews 5:11–6:2). Before his death James Montgomery Boice complained of the great hymns of the church being replaced by "trite jingles that have more in common with contemporary advertising ditties than with the

---

73   D. T. Williams, "Durable Music," *Touchstone*, 20.

psalms."[74] There is perhaps a place for children's choruses and campfire songs. However, that place is the Sunday School and summer camp, not the public worship services of the church. This is particularly true for churches in the Reformed tradition. Reformed Protestantism is blessed with a great and sophisticated theology. Yet it can only be sustained if it is constantly being reinforced in our public worship. Our doctrines and practices are communicated and learned in our primary congregational gatherings or they are not being communicated and learned in any significant sense at all. Yes, there may be some who are picking up the Reformed faith through their own private reading or through small, specialized study groups. However, for the bulk of the congregation Reformed thought and piety will remain foreign if it is not being learned in public worship. Consequently our sermons certainly, but also our Scripture reading, our administration of the sacraments, our prayers and our songs must reinforce our distinctive teachings, or those distinctive teachings will slowly evaporate from congregational consciousness. Not just our preaching but our prayers and songs and sacraments must express the conviction that God is sovereign, that salvation is by Christ alone, faith alone, and by grace alone, and that our final authority is Scripture alone. All of this is to say that it is crucial that the church's songs be substantial enough to express accurately mature Christian belief as well as the subtlety of Christian experience.

Reformed Protestantism historically has shown a decided preference for metrical psalms and time-proven biblical hymns. Of the latter, those of the eighteenth century, the "golden

---

74 James Montgomery Boice, *Whatever Happened to the Gospel of Grace?* (Wheaton, IL: Crossway Books, 2001), 180.

236   *Serving with Calvin*

age" of hymn writing, are a particularly good example.[75] The hymn-writers of the eighteenth and early nineteenth centuries "still felt strongly the obligation to make sure that their words were scriptural if not Scripture," as D. T. Williams points out. They matured in an environment of exclusive psalmody and consequently brought to their work habits of rigorous biblical fidelity. They often "included the biblical references that justified their content at the end of every verse or even every line."[76] Simplistic, sentimental, repetitious songs by their very nature cannot carry the weight of Reformed doctrine and will leave the people of God ill-equipped on occasions of great moment. The problem with them, and with many of the late-nineteenth century gospel songs as well, is not when they were written, as though there were something inherently wrong with anything modern, but their form and consequent content. Their form cannot easily accommodate serious thought.[77] The Reformed faith, by way of contrast, cannot survive the absence of serious thought.

The psalms teach us what God-approved songs look like. They are rich in theological content. They teach us to sing "of the lovingkindness (Hebrew *hesed*, grace) of the LORD" (Psalm 89:1), of His faithfulness and the works of His hands (Psalm 92:2, 4), of His greatness, splendor, majesty, strength, and beauty (Psalm 96:4–6), of His justice (Psalm 101:1). The Psalms are full of both

---

75   *Christian History Magazine* devoted an entire issue to the hymns of the eighteenth century.

76   D. T. Williams, "Durable Music," *Touchstone*, 20. Boice adds, "The compositions of Martin Luther, James Montgomery, John and Charles Wesley, or Isaac Watts are clearly better than the repetitious babble of so many writers of today's ubiquitous praises choruses. Why should we commit ourselves so tenaciously to what is manifestly poor?" (*Whatever Happened to the Gospel of Grace?*, 188).

77   "Recent choruses sometimes limit themselves by being so simplistic and repetitive that theological reflection never has a chance to get started." Ibid.

the attributes and works of God (e.g. Psalms 145–150), as well as Christian experience. We find the language of confession and pleas for mercy (Psalms 6, 25, 32, 51, 130, 143), and cries for help (Psalms 3, 4, 5) and thanksgiving (Psalms 65,100,136), as well as lament and complaint (Psalms 3, 4, 10, 13, 64, 77, 88, etc.). Our songs are a means by which "the word of Christ richly dwell(s) within (us)," and by which we teach and admonish one another (Colossians 3:16).

Dr. Douglas Kelly tells of an oft repeated scene in eighteenth- and nineteenth-century Scotland, of families split by the massive migrations to North America waving good-bye to each other, as both those on the docks and those on the ships launching out to sea sang the stirring Twenty-Third Psalm, concluding,

> "Goodness and mercy all my life shall surely follow me;
> And in God's house for evermore my dwelling-place shall be."

It is noteworthy that Martin Luther King, Jr., as he came to the stirring conclusion of his "I Have a Dream" speech, delivered from the steps of the Lincoln Memorial (August 23, 1963), drew upon two hymns to find the language with which to express the powerful themes of the occasion. He recited the first stanza of the national hymn, "My Country 'Tis of Thee" with great effect. His incomparable conclusion was a phrase taken from a spiritual: "Free at last! Free at last! Thank God Almighty, we are free at last!" Similarly, his last speech, the "Mountain Top" speech on the eve of his assassination (April 3, 1968), drew again upon the church's hymnody to express his sentiments at that weighty moment, reciting the last line of the "Battle Hymn of the Republic": "Mine eyes have seen the glory of the coming of the Lord." Among his most famous lines, which he used frequently in his speeches and which became the title of a biography about King was another line from a spiritual based on Jeremiah 8:22: "There is a balm in Gilead, to make the wounded whole."

During the time of his imprisonment by the Nazi government, 1943–45, prior to his martyrdom, Dietrich Bonhoeffer made repeated references to the comfort that he drew from the psalms and the great hymns of his faith. He made specific mention of "Praise to the Lord the Almighty:"

> Praise to the Lord, who o'er all things so wondrously reigneth,
> Shelters Thee under His wings,
> Yea, so gently sustaineth!
> Hast thou not seen
> How thy desires e'er have been
> Granted in what He ordaineth?

"Bonhoeffer knew many of Gerhardt's hymns by heart," says his biography Eric Metaxas, "and they would sustain him during his imprisonment."[78]

As T. David Gordon's daughter slowly died of leukemia over an eight-week period, he regularly held tiny Marian in the crook of his arm while with the other he held a hymnal as he sang to her. He makes mention of singing "Abide with Me" one morning from memory, until he broke down on the last stanza. He speaks of "the comforting, courage-begetting gift of a well-written hymn."[79] David Powlison gives thanks for the role that public worship has

---

78 See Eric Metaxas, *Bonhoeffer: Pastor, Martyr, Prophet, Spy: A Righteous Gentile vs. the Third Reich* (Nashville, TN; Thomas Nelson, 2010), 178; cf. 440, 463, 483. Gerhardt is Paul Gerhardt, among the greatest of the Lutheran hymn writers (1607–1676).

79 Gordon, *Why Johnny Can't Sing Hymns*, 24.

played in his Christian growth, particularly those "wise, well-crafted hymns that invite me to think as well as sing." He cites Katarina von Schlegel's "Be Still, My Soul" and its honesty. She "gives honest voice to her anguish and bafflement. She also gives honest voice to her hope and joy. And she gives honest voice to her reasons for hope amid grief. The Lord is on your side, even in this. He is your best, your heavenly friend, who will not bereave you. He rules this storm, too. He soothes these dark emotions. He will restore to you love's purest joys. Katarina von Schlegel gives all these gifts to us." Powlison concludes, "I look forward to meeting her, and I will thank her for helping me."[80]

It matters what we sing, just as it matters what we preach and what we pray. It is vital that our songs be biblically and theologically mature because they will often supply us with the language we will use to interpret and express our experience. What we earlier have referred to as biblical examples of praying Scripture were, more precisely, lyrics from scriptural songs. Mary at the annunciation drew upon the song of Hannah (Luke 1:46–55; cf. 1 Samuel 2:1–10); Solomon at the dedication of the temple incorporated Psalm 132:8–9 into his prayer (2 Chronicles 6:40–42); Jesus on the cross used the words of Psalms 22:1 and 31:5 to express both His grief and hope (Matthew 27:46; Luke 23:46); and the early church responded to persecution with the language of Psalms 146 and 2 (Acts 4:24–30). In each case the church's songs were interpreting experience and providing the language with which to express a faithful response.

"Times of tragedy and trial do not require novelty," says Timothy Quill with ironic understatement.[81] One might perhaps

---

80 David Powlison, "How *Does* Sanctification Work?" (Part 2), *Journal of Biblical Counseling*, 27:2 (2013).

81 Quill, "Liturgical Worship," in Pinson (ed.), *Perspectives on Worship*, 37.

240   *Serving with Calvin*

be able to justify singing the simple choruses as a temporary measure, designed to acclimate new believers to singing before moving on to more substantial songs. A limited use of such targeting the aptitude of the young and immature, aiming in doing so to eventually move them up to more serious songs, is understandable. However, the priority should always be the canonical psalms and theologically rich hymns.

4. *Is it musically appropriate?* Appropriateness or suitability are undefined but biblically sanctioned categories (see Chapter 3, "aesthetics"). There are those things that we are to know and do (or not do) based on the nature of things (e.g. 1 Timothy 2:9–10; Romans 13:13; Ephesians 5:4; etc.). It's actually a fairly obvious category. Think of trying to sing "O Sacred Head Now Wounded" to a tune like the Beach Boys "Surfin' USA." It doesn't work. It doesn't *fit*. It's not fitting, or suitable, or appropriate. Jeremy Begbie has helped us by identifying music's "fundamental embeddedness in the material world."[82] What it means to be in tune and on key arises out of the fabric of creation—ears that hear, voices that sing, and instruments that sound. The same is true for music that fits in some situations (parade ground) and not others (funeral service). We insist that some forms of music are appropriate for worship and others are not. We have noted that from Plato to Augustine to Calvin to the twentieth century the philosophers and theologians have agreed that musical forms are unequal in their suitability for public worship. The church has developed its music primarily over the last 500 years and the lyrics to go with it over the past 3000 years, going back to King David. We benefit from a treasury of "sacred music" from which to draw. Hard rock, romantic soft-rock, hip-hop, rap, and most other

---

82   Begbie, *Resounding Truth*, 186.

forms of pop music are simply inappropriate for divine worship. This is a subjective judgment for sure. However it goes beyond the subjective because music is ultimately rooted in the objective. Popular forms of music may be suitable for the bedroom or the dance floor, the pub or the workplace, but rarely will they be found suitable for the church's worship. This should not surprise us. Worship is so unlike any other human activity that we should not be startled to learn that musical genres created in other contexts and to serve other purposes should fail as vehicles with which to express divine praise. T. David Gordon's words should be carefully considered:

> If meeting our Maker and Redeemer is different from all our other meetings, why shouldn't the various aspects of that meeting be different from the aspects of other meetings? If God is "wholly other" than we, why would a meeting with him look as though we were "wholly like" us? If he is holy, why shouldn't the language we use when we approach him be holy? If he is sacred, why should we not attempt to construct music that sounds sacred, rather than profane? Why should the category of *sacred music* disappear?[83]

5. *Is it emotionally balanced?* This is perhaps the most subjective point in a very subjective section. However, there is a suitable balance between the emotive content and the cognitive content of our songs, and our prayers and sermons for that matter. Strong emotional appeal without strong biblical-theological expression is manipulation, not worship. Churches are employing the tricks of the propagandist, not the truths of the prophets, when they use syrupy songs devoid of theological content. Tunes ought not

---

83   Gordon, *Why Johnny Can't Sing Hymns*, 78.

overwhelm the words. John Stott was heard to say a few years ago that he would never allow the chorus "Alleluia," to be sung in his church for that reason.[84] The people were moved when they sang it, the congregation might be visibly *swaying*, but what were they *saying*? Almost nothing. They were singing a blank check, with each one filling in his own content. When repetition comes to this, lyrics bear more of a resemblance to eastern mantras than to Christian praise. Indeed while vacationing a few years ago I viewed on cable television simultaneously a "praise gathering" of a Guru in Oregon and on another station an extremely charismatic praise service. As I flipped from one to the other it was difficult to see any difference. Both started with high energy rhythms and gradually transitioned to a quieter, calmer motif. Both groups raised their hands. Both closed their eyes. Both repeated their peculiar sounds over and over again. Both swayed, or trembled as they did so. Are we not to love God with our minds? Some praise songs, says *World* magazine's Marvin Olasky, "should be shuffled off to a Buddhist temple."[85] Are not the songs with which we sing and make melody in our hearts also supposed to teach and admonish (Ephesians 5:19; Colossians 3:16)? Are we not to sing with the spirit and "with the mind also" (1 Corinthians 14:15)? What God has joined together ought not to be broken asunder.

On the other hand, the words ought not to overwhelm the tune either. Rich theological and biblical content joined to an unworthy tune is undesirable as well. Emotional balance is the goal. We find this balance of words and tunes in such hymns as "Joy to the World," "Hark the Herald Angel Sings," "Praise to the Lord the Almighty," "Crown Him with Many Crowns," "When I

---

84 Theological Students Fellowship Conference, London, January 1978.
85 Marvin Olaskey, "Joyful Noises," *World*, March 8/15, 2008, 92.

Survey the Wondrous Cross," "Here O My Lord I See Thee Face to Face," "How Sweet and Awful Is the Place." The music in each case underscores the content of the words.

6. *Is it aesthetically excellent?* It is exceedingly difficult to write an outstanding hymn tune. After 2000 years the church still only has a couple of hundred that are universally recognized (across cultures and generations) as outstanding. Many of the tunes in the hymnal, while serviceable, are less than outstanding. If history may be our guide, over 90% of today's compositions will not endure. They will go the way of "Father I adore you" and "Heavenly Father I Appreciate You," from the 1970s, and countless gospel songs from the late nineteenth and early twentieth centuries. Aesthetic judgments must be made. It doesn't matter when a hymn was written. Quality is what counts. Most of what is being written or composed today is frankly of poor quality. Much of it is used simply because it sounds contemporary, without regard for aesthetic standards. There are exceptions. For example, some of Getty and Townsend's work will likely find its way into the next generation of hymnals.[86] The exceptions, however, are few.

Aesthetic judgments indeed are made every Sunday in every church (again, see Chapter 3, "Aesthetics"). Ministers and musicians pick what they consider "good" tunes and reject those they judge "bad." The question is, will these judgments be made out of an informed, a developed aesthetic sense, or in the vacuum of the pop culture in which we are all immersed. We only know what a "big" tree is in relation to other trees. Those whose experience is limited to the Mojave Desert may think that an

---

86 "In Christ Alone" and "How Deep the Father's Love for Us" seem to be universally appreciated. The same can be said of Cook and Bancroft's "Before the Throne of God Above," and there will be others.

244   *Serving with Calvin*

apple tree is "big." As their experience broadens, as they see pines, oaks, and redwoods, their opinion of what is "big" will change.

Similarly, the aesthetic desert of pop culture encourages the development of a very limited aesthetic. "Good" within the limits of our all-pervasive and inescapable pop environment looks very different from "good" in the broader aesthetic environment of classical music, folk music, and the sacred music repertoire. Ministers and musicians will need broad and deep musical exposure if aesthetic standards are to be maintained, and the best songs are *to be sung.* The aesthetic sense of the evangelical church in the twenty-first century must grow, must mature. "If there are absolutes," said J. M. Boice, "all music cannot be equally good." He continues, "For in aesthetics, as in other areas, some music will be better than other music both in itself and for what we are trying to accomplish with it."[87]

It will be necessary for congregations as well as ministers and musicians to develop a sharper aesthetic sense. This can happen over time as they are exposed to the hymnal. Surrendering to existing "taste" or "style" preferences is an aesthetic dead end for the church, ensuring pop-shaped mediocrity and perpetual change. Tastes can be molded. Style preferences change through exposure. The experience of singing "The Spacious Firmament on High," with lyrics by the eighteenth century English poet Joseph Addison, to the tune "Creation," from Haydn's Oratorio by the same name, or "O God beyond All Praising," to the tune "Thaxted" from Gustav Holst's *The Planets*, or "We Are God's People," to the tune "Symphony" from Brahms' 1st Symphony, can be eye opening and aesthetically broadening. We are dismayed

---

87   J. M. Boice, *Whatever Happened to the Gospel of Grace?* (Wheaton: Crossway Books), 187.

to see the aesthetically deadening effects that popular culture is having on the church, and to realize that much of the church is oblivious that it is occurring. If aesthetic standards are to be maintained; if beauty matters; if it is important that our music and lyrics be outstanding, then ministers, musicians, and congregations will need to resist the intrusions of a popular, pagan, and mediocre culture and work to retain and develop the church's historic aesthetics.

7. *Is it demographically comprehensive?*[88] Or better, is it *catholic*? Reggie M. Kidd's, *With One Voice*, is a celebration of musical diversity in worship.[89] Kidd, a professor of theology at Reformed Theological Seminary, Orlando, portrays Christ as the "singing Savior," whose voice is heard in a range of styles from Bach to Bubba to the Blues Brothers.[90] We can agree with him up to a point. Every group may make its contribution to the church's songbook. The hymnbook, as we've seen, reflects this diversity. But having affirmed diversity, one is not relieved from the task of providing criteria for inclusion and exclusion. Not all songs are of equal quality. Neither are all styles equally appropriate for worship. Nowhere does Kidd discuss how one is to identify excellence or suitability. How, then, is the church to handle the flood of choices that it faces? He suggests two solutions, the first of which surrenders unity, the second of which surrenders excellence. A church may either sing in its preferred style (surrendering unity by catering to only one kind of person) or it may blend a diversity of styles (surrendering excellence in the absence of additional criteria for selection beyond diversity),

---

88 See *Worshipping with Calvin*, Chapter 8 on catholicity; Chapter 2, "Catholicity" of this work.

89 Kidd, *With One Voice*.

90 Ibid. 125ff; 144ff.

246 *Serving with Calvin*

resulting in a quota system, an ever changing and ever expanding repertoire with equal contributions by each preference group.

"Blended" worship has its capable advocates.[91] It seems to solve the problem of competing style preferences by providing something for everyone. Now everyone is happy! The reality, however, is that blending cannot meet all possible style preferences: classic, revival Baptist, Anglo-contemporary, Latino-contemporary, African-American contemporary, African-American traditional, Hip-Hop, hard rock, country, high-liturgical, and so on, and on, and on. The practical reality, for those who "blend," is that the preferences of one or two groups will be honored, and the rest will go without. Lawrence and Dever can claim that, "the style of music you use on Sunday mornings is incredible unimportant" because they have, consciously or unconsciously, followed the advice of Warren cited below (identify your target audience) and limited themselves to traditional and anglo-contemporary. [92] Those who do not fall into their preferred style (e.g. Cowboys and Hip-Hoppers) will conclude, this place is not for me.[93] Indeed Capitol Hill Baptist is a young, professional, largely Anglo congregation. As Timothy C. J. Quill argues in his response to Lawrence and Dever, the style

---

91 See Lawrence and Dever, "Blended Worship" in Pinson, *Perspectives on Christian Worship*, 218–268; Robert Webber, *Blended Worship: Achieving Substance & Relevance in Worship* (Peabody, MA: Hendrickson, 1994).

92 Ibid. 232.

93 This is exactly Dan Kimball's criticism of Lawrence and Dever, as he complains that their descriptions of blended services didn't seem very blended to him. Most of the songs, he observes, "sounded like 1980s praise music." He says, "If we are truly 'blended' then where are the hip-hop songs? Where is any global music influence? ... Why are there no African-American worship styles repeated?" Their blending, he says, seems "only a fairly limited and specific style of a primarily middle to upper class, somewhat suburban, clearly Reformed approach to worship" (in Pinson [ed.], *Perspectives on Worship*, 286).

of music a church uses *is* incredibly important, "as are all elements of style such as art, architecture, vestments, and ceremony." "Music is not neutral," he insists. "One cannot put a religious text to a different music style without affecting the text itself."[94]

We have argued that there are criteria for song selection that should be followed. Now we ask, shouldn't catholicity be a factor? Shouldn't tradition, that is, a history of valuable use, also be a criterion? Shouldn't aesthetic excellence count? And shouldn't demographic breadth matter? In other words, should not the church's treasury of "sacred music," with its biblical content and theological maturity, edited over centuries, compiled in standard hymnals, provide the church with the preponderance of its sung praise? The songs we sing should be those of the whole church, not the songs of a single demographic (racial, ethnic, generational). The songs we sing should be catholic. The songs selected should transcend the tastes of the generation or ethnic group that produced it and appeal universally.

Rick Warren urges ministers to choose a "style of music" according to "the kind of people God wants your church to reach."[95] He chose "contemporary pop/rock" because he wanted to reach the 40 and under crowd.[96] This is not a philosophy that we can imagine the Apostles expressing. The church's task is to set up shop in a neighborhood and to reach everyone it can, targeting the taste preferences of no group in particular in order to include all groups in general. The church's music, found in its hymnal and Psalter, belongs to no single group: it is not

---

94 Ibid. 219. Quill is associate professor of Pastoral Ministry & Missions at Concordia Theological Seminary in Fort Wayne, Indiana.

95 Warren, *Purpose Driven Church*, 280.

96 Ibid. 285. I take this to be what he means when he says, "Most people under forty don't relate to music before 1965."

248 *Serving with Calvin*

the music of the Swing-generation, of the Crooners, of Elvis, of classic rock, or what has developed since. To identify it with the older generation is simply false. Every generation has had to learn to love the church's music.[97] Consequently the church's music belongs to all groups universally. Indeed the best hymns have always had appeal across the various demographics (e.g. "Be Thou My Vision," "Amazing Grace"). The church's songs should partake of catholicity.[98]

Care should be taken even in youth gatherings not to create a musical environment that is at odds with that of the whole church. Youth should be taught to love the church's psalmody, hymnology and conventional instrumentation. While some use of contemporary forms may be justified in generationally-specific gatherings, care should be taken that these contemporary forms (style of music, type of instrumentation) not lead to division, as youth grow-up and inevitably anticipate that the forms with which they are familiar be used in the worship of the whole church. The strategy of combining old words with new tunes runs exactly this risk, as any pastor who has attempted to replace the

---

97 "Traditional worship forms are not, in fact, our preferred musical style when we listen to music. Such traditional forms are not 'our' music; they are the church's music, and they antedate us by many generations" (T. D. Gordon, *Why Johnny Can't Sing Hymns*, 76).

98 The problem with the vagueness of "Christ-centered worship" reemerges in connection with what Chapell calls "musical styles." Musical preferences, he says, are based on what we find appealing or appropriate. What we find appropriate, he says, is based on factors such as tradition, familiarity, our mission. The collective judgment of the catholic church, what promotes the communion of *all* the saints, or the "sacred music" tradition are not categories with which he deals. "New worship styles" are assumed to be necessary for "effective outreach." Rather than potential and new converts being expected to conform to the culture of the church, the church, it is assumed, must adapt to the culture of the world. Again, this resolves no issue in connection with those things which divide the church, and leaves it to congregations to fight out what "style" they will use.

old music of "Beneath the Cross of Jesus" or "And Can It Be" with newly-composed tunes can confirm.[99] The church's music should be demographically comprehensive.

Practical helps

One needs to proceed wisely in all matters musical. We are urging commitment to traditional psalmody and hymnody. Be careful, though, music is a minefield today. If a congregation is unaccustomed to psalms and traditional hymns, consider the following:

1. Initially *use only the most familiar, easy, and accessible of the traditional hymns and psalms. Trinity Hymnal, Trinity Psalter*, and *Trinity Psalter, Music Edition*, are excellent sources.[100] There are many, many to choose from that are theologically and biblically rich and accessible. Even the worst hymnals are gold-mines of religious verse and song.

2. Begin a *Psalter & Hymn of the Month* program, targeting the children. Urge their use in family worship so the whole family learns them.[101] Gradually a significant body of church song will be learned and loved.

99　I share Paul Jones' frustration when he asks, "Why would anyone think that Martin Luther's 'A Mighty Fortress' or Charles Wesley's 'And Can It Be' need new music?" (*Singing & Making Music*, 95). We would ask the same question of those who have changed the tunes of "Alas and Did My Savior Bleed," "Let Us Love & Sing & Wonder," "Man of Sorrows, What a Name," "There is a Fountain Filled with Blood," "Guide Me O Thou Great Jehovah," "For All the Saints," and "Crown Him with Many Crowns."

100　Potential editorial bias should perhaps prevent me, but because of its metrical and musical variety, size, and price, I recommend the *Trinity Psalter* (1994; Pittsburgh, PA: Crown & Covenant Publications, 1997), of all available Psalters.

101　See chart at the end of Terry L. Johnson, *The Family Worship Book* (1998; Fearn, Ross-shire: Great Britain, Geanies House, 2003), for a 10-year calendar for learning monthly hymns and psalms.

3. *Make use of recordings* to shape taste and familiarize the congregation with quality hymnody/psalmody. My recommendations are,

Hymns Triumphant Vol 1 and 2, Sparrow Records, 1981, 1984, which feature 67 of the best of classic hymnody

Psalms of the Trinity Psalter Vol 1 and 2, IPC Press, 1999, 2002, which feature 59 of the most beloved and accessible of the metrical psalms

The Psalms of Scotland, SCS Music Limited, 1988, which supplements one's repertoire of metrical psalms adding several versions and tunes not featured on the *Trinity Psalter* CDs

4. *Find ways of letting the proverbial "steam out of the kettle."* This can be done by establishing a "hymn sing" the 15 minutes before the evening service. This allows those who prefer the more sentimental selections from the hymnal to sing what they like. One can even pass out song sheets and use guitars—and then collect the song sheets and put away the guitars when the service proper begins. All of this can take place before the call to worship.

5. Add new songs to your church's repertoire as such meet the qualifications of "canonization," that is, that combine outstanding lyrics and music, are accessible, singable, suitable, beloved, orthodox, and demographically comprehensive.

Sacraments

The sacraments are one of three primary means of grace, along with prayer and the ministry of the word. They should not be relegated to the wee hours of the morning or to a week night.

They should play a central role in the life of the Reformed church.[102]

1. *Administer the sacraments regularly.* Since they are one of only three primary means of grace, the saints need all three if they are to thrive spiritually. The Lord's Supper should be administered "frequently," says the Westminster Assembly's *Directory.* The counsel of frequent administration is a direct result of a Reformed theology of the eucharist. Frequent administration provides regular occasions to present the gospel with God-ordained visual enhancements—the bread and the cup—proclaiming by so doing the sacrificial meaning of Christ's death and the promise of "the forgiveness of sins" through His blood "poured out for many."

There are a number of voices calling for weekly communion. Some are insisting that this is biblically required. A surprising contempt for historic Reformed practice has been displayed at times, by its advocates, with weekly administration assumed to be the only correct practice and anything less regarded as obviously defective.[103] Weekly communion, while advocated by Calvin, has, in fact, not been the practice of the Reformed church, not in Europe, not in Great Britain, not in North America, not anywhere else that the Reformed faith has gone.[104] One can hardly claim with any credibility that a church devoted to *sola*

---

102 See Hughes Oliphant Old, *Holy Communion in the Piety of the Reformed Church* (Powder Springs, Georgia: Tolle Lege Press, 2013). This massive study will be the definitive word on communion for generations to come.

103 e.g. Jeffrey J. Meyers, *The Lord's Service: the Grace of Covenant Worship* (Moscow, ID: Canon Press, 2003), 213ff; Clark, *Reformed Confession*, 283–284, n. 206; "The Evangelical Fall from the Means of Grace," in *The Compromised Church*, John Armstrong (ed.) (Wheaton, IL: Crossway, 1998), 133–47; Belcher, *Deep Church*, 139–40.

104 Other important advocates of weekly communion include John Owen, Richard Baxter, Jonathan Edwards, and Charles Spurgeon. Baxter argued that "Eucharistical worship is the great work of the day." He maintained that the Lord's

252   *Serving with Calvin*

Scriptura and the regulative principle abandoned itself to extra-biblical traditionalism at this critical point. There are sound reasons for monthly or quarterly communion, and those reasons should be considered respectfully.

Reformed Protestantism has demonstrated a decided preference for *intensity* of observance over *frequency*.[105] Personal preparation, self-examination, and contemplation have been encouraged with the utmost seriousness going back to the Reformers and continuing through the centuries. *Shorter Catechism* Q97 and *Larger Catechism* Q's 171, 174, and 175 are exemplary of Reformed sacramental piety:

> LC# 171: How are they that receive the sacrament of the Lord's Supper to prepare themselves before they come unto it?

> Answer: They that receive the sacrament of the Lord's Supper are, before they come, to prepare themselves thereunto, by examining themselves of their being in Christ, of their sins and wants; of the truth and measure of their knowledge, faith, repentance; love to God and the brethren, charity to all men, forgiving those that have done them wrong; of their desires after Christ, and of their new obedience; and by renewing the exercise of these graces, by serious meditation, and fervent prayer.

The older authors gave considerable emphasis on the need for personal preparation. Robert Bruce (1554–1631), a successor of John Knox at St. Giles in Edinburgh, and according to T. F. Torrance, "one of the most deeply spiritual and powerful ministers

---

Day should primarily be a day of thanksgiving with the Lord's Supper as the "chief part" (Baxter, "Christian Directory," *Works*, Vol. 1, 684).

105   See *Worshipping with Calvin*, Chapter 6.

of the Gospel Scotland has ever known," devotes one-third of *The Mystery of the Lord's Supper*, a collection of sermons preached in 1589, to preparation.[106] Thomas Doolittle (1630–1707) in his *Treatise Concerning the Lord's Supper*, spends nearly one quarter of his 179 pages (in our edition) urging communicants to prepare thoroughly for the table. Eight arguments are offered in one chapter for what he calls "painful and serious" preparations for the Lord's Supper, with multiple sub-points; nine questions "to excite us to greater diligence in preparation" in another chapter; and four directions with five questions (and multiple sub-points!) for "get(ting) our hearts rightly disposed to receive the Lord's Supper" in a third chapter.[107] Doolittle, who was converted under the ministry of Richard Baxter (1615–1691) in Kidderminster, urges self-examination *after* the sacrament as well as before. He devotes three chapters to post-communion reflection. "Reflection after the Lord's Supper is as necessary as examination before," he insists.[108] Thorough personal preparation was typical of the Reformed tradition.

Congregational preparation was also emphasized. Examination by sessions, use of communion tokens, the "fencing of the table" all underscore the Reformed emphasis on intensity, that is, on careful, in-depth observance of the Lord's Supper. Reformed churches in both Britain and North America developed the preparatory services, and even communion seasons to encourage

---

106 T. F. Torrance (ed.) in his Introduction to Robert Bruce, *The Mystery of the Lord's Supper: Sermons on the Sacrament Preached in the Kirk of Edinburgh by Robert Bruce in A.D. 1589* (Ross-shire, Scotland: Christian Focus Publications, 2005), 1.

107 Thomas Doolittle, *A Treatise Concerning the Lord's Supper*, (1709, Morgan, PA: Soli Deo Gloria, 1998), 34, 49, 61.

108 Ibid. 101.

254 *Serving with Calvin*

proper congregational preparation for the Table.[109] These services would typically begin on Thursday and continue each evening, culminating in the Sunday morning service. Both Sunday evening and Monday evening were then devoted to thanksgiving. Extended preparation and careful participation was thought to be required both by the importance of the eucharist and the severity of the biblical warnings respecting "unworthy" participation (1 Corinthians 11:27–32).

A preference for monthly or quarterly communion should not be interpreted as indicating diminished importance any more than should weekly observance of necessity indicates heightened importance.[110] There is no shortage of churches and even whole denominations in which weekly communion has become routine and mindless. There is an inherent tension between frequent observance and careful observance, which should not be dismissed lightly. We would urge that the Reformed church's reluctance to practice weekly communion be taken seriously, even if it is not to be followed slavishly.

Because of this tension, frequency should continue to be seen as a wisdom issue. Church life on the Lord's Day typically includes

---

109 See Schmidt, *Holy Fairs*; Kuyper, *Worship*, mentions pre and post communion services in the Dutch tradition (277); these are described in detail in *Worshipping with Calvin*, Chapter 6.

110 We should not say, with Robert Letham, that frequency is "a reliable gauge of how eagerly (the church) wants Christ" (*The Lord's Supper: Eternal Word in Broken Bread* [Phillipsburg, New Jersey: P&R Publishing, 2001], 60). The parallel with prayer and Scripture reading, which Letham and others argue (e.g. Rayburn, *O Come Let Us Worship*, 259), breaks down. Does he mean to say that we should receive the Lord's Supper daily, even multiple times daily, as may be the case with the word and prayer? This line of reasoning fails to recognize the differences between the various means of grace; Better is Chapell: "weekly Communion should not be considered a mark of orthodoxy or superior piety" (*Christ-Centered Worship*, 294).

an instructional hour before or after morning worship. Normally one will not want to compromise the sermon by reducing it to less than 30 minutes. Also, one will not wish to rush through the administration of the sacraments or partake without careful preparation. Word and sacrament together, uncompromised and unrushed, will probably require an hour and a half or more. Most churches will probably find such a commitment difficult to sustain. An hour of Sunday School plus an hour and a half of public worship on Sunday morning is too much for most congregations on a regular basis. Reports gathered from various sources, as well as our own experience in Reformed churches practicing weekly communion and yet maintaining a commitment to serious preaching, confirm our fears: communion is rushed and often irreverent.

The Westminster *Directory* was not being unfaithful to the Reformed tradition (as some might accuse) but rather fully consistent with it when it determined not to settle the issue of frequency. Yes, the Lord's Supper is to be observed "frequently." "But how often," it insisted, "may be considered and determined by the ministers and other church-governors of each congregation, as they shall find most convenient for the comfort and edification of the people committed to their charge."[111] Our recommendation is *monthly* communion, once a quarter in the morning, the other eight months in the evening. This honors the Lord's Supper as a vital means of grace without short-changing the sermon, while also recognizing the realities of church and family life which make careful observance difficult on a more accelerated schedule.

---

111   "The Directory for Publick Worship of God" in *The Westminster Confession of Faith and the Larger & Shorter Catechisms* (Glasgow: Free Presbyterian Publications, 1985), 384.

Baptisms also should be administered as frequently as is practical. Occasionally time constraints make a proper baptism inadvisable on a given Sunday. Otherwise, a baptism every week would be desirable. Why? Because it provides a regular opportunity to explain a covenantal understanding of redemption and of the whole Bible. Matthew Henry insists that baptism is an "edifying ordinance." "It is of great use to all," he says, "to be frequently reminded of their original corruption and of their baptismal covenant ... therefore ministers ought not to refuse their hearers the benefit they might derive from being spectators of this solemnity."[112] Infants in particular, passive and unaware, provide an unsurpassed picture of God's sovereign grace. The baptismal water reminds us of regeneration, the atoning blood of Christ, of the forgiveness of sins, of reconciliation with God, of gospel cleansing, of the outpouring of the Holy Spirit, and of the vast love of God which extends to the children of believers. It reminds us of justification, of sanctification, and of mortification and vivification. Baptized children have opportunity to "improve their baptism" by professing their faith, and communing members may do the same through contemplation of the promises and self-examination (See above *Larger Catechism* #167).[113]

2. *Administer the sacraments covenantally and ecclesiastically*— Administer the Lord's Supper as a meal which seals the covenant.[114] Not only is it a time when the gifts of God in Christ are enjoyed, when redeemed hearts are gladdened and tender

---

112 Henry, "Treatise on Baptism," *The Complete Works of Matthew Henry*. 2 vols. Edinburgh: J. Fullarton & Co., 1855. Reprint Grand Rapids: Baker Book House, 1979. Second reprinting, Grand Rapids: Baker Book House, 1997, I:531.

113 See Abraham Kuyper, *Our Worship*, ed. Harry Boonstra (1911, Grand Rapids: William B. Eerdmans Publishing Co., 2009), 247, for similar counsel.

114 We have developed this theme at length in *Worshipping with Calvin*, Chapter 6.

consciences reassured. It should also be a time of covenant renewal. "The sacraments are like contracts," says Calvin, "by which the Lord gives us his mercy and from it eternal life; and we in turn promise him obedience."[115] Two hundred years later, Stephen Charnock (1628–1680), says much the same, demonstrating continuity in the classic Reformed view of the Lord's Supper as a covenantal meal. "Evangelical sacraments seal the evangelical promises, as a ring confirms a contract of marriage," says Charnock. Citing Romans 4:11, he argues that the sacraments have a double reference. "God doth attest, that he will remain firm in his promise, and the receiver attests he will remain firm in his faith." God confirms his promises. We confirm ours. There are "mutual engagements in the Lord's Supper" in which "God obligeth himself to the performance of the promise, and man engageth himself to the performance of his duty."[116]

The invitation to the table should function as the Reformed "altar call," calling sinners to repentance, calling covenant children to commitment, calling the backslidden to renewal, and welcoming the faithful to table fellowship and spiritual nourishment with the risen Christ. Matthew Henry's *Communicant's Companion* is particularly insightful in this regard.[117] Covenantal communion is a powerful monthly

---

115 Calvin, *Institutes*, IV.xiii.6, 1259.

116 Stephen Charnock, *The Existence & Attributes of God*, II:288. He continues: "In every repetition of it, God, by presenting, continues his resolution to us, of sticking to this covenant for the merit of Christ's blood; and the receiver, by eating the body and drinking the blood, engageth himself to keep close to the condition of faith, expecting a full salvation and a blessed immortality upon the merit of the same blood alone" (II:288).

117 Matthew Henry, "A Communicant's Companion" in *The Complete Works of Matthew Henry*. 2 vols. Edinburgh: J. Fullarton & Co., 1855. Reprint Grand Rapids: Baker Book House, 1979. Second reprinting, Grand Rapids: Baker Book House, 1997, 1:284–412.

reminder of the need of those in earshot of the covenant to "do business with God," as we have put it.

We have also explained the covenantal aspect of baptism in *Worshipping with Calvin*. Baptism is the rite of admission to the visible church.[118] It is administered exclusively by the church, by its ministers, to the children of believers on the basis of the faith (and membership) of their parents.[119] Like the Lord's Supper, baptism also signifies privilege and responsibility. The traditional Reformed baptismal vows rightly indicate both the responsibility of the *parents* to rear their children "in the nurture and admonition of the Lord" and of the *church* to assist them (Ephesians 6:1ff). Children likewise are to "improve their baptism" by professing their faith and even older members are to do the same through sanctification and service (See *Larger Catechism* #167). Again, Matthew Henry represents the apex of Reformed pastoral theology in his *Treatise on Baptism,* and provides examples still today of how to administer baptism covenantally.[120]

3. *Administer the sacraments with scriptural simplicity.*[121] Avoid both the complicated, the exotic (like intinction) and the melodramatic (by overplaying the cuteness or emotion of a baptism). Jesus modeled two distinct sacramental actions

---

118 Westminster Confession of Faith, XXVIII.1.

119 Ibid. XXVIII.4.

120 Henry, "Treatise on Baptism," *Works*, 1:489–568; this is also in Matthew Henry, *Family Religion: Principles for Receiving a Godly Family* (Ross-shire, Scotland, UK: Christian Focus Publications, 2008), 129–287; see Kuyper, *Worship*, 247, for similar counsel.

121 For the recommended details of administration, see *Leading in Worship*, 59–77; *Leading in Worship Revised & Expanded*, 82–105.

involving first the bread and then the cup.[122] Each is accompanied by the command, "Do this" (1 Corinthians 11:24–25). In Matthew's account, each element is blessed separately as well (Matthew 26:26–27).[123] These elements and actions should not be confused. Intinction (the practice of dipping the bread into the cup) reduces the two sacramental movements ("take, eat," "drink from it") to one and cannot be justified. A generation ago Joachim Jeremias, in his brilliant study, *The Eucharistic Words of Jesus,* demonstrated that the separation of the symbols of Jesus' body and blood was a significant part of the sacrificial imagery that Jesus was invoking.[124] The blood and flesh were separated in Old Testament sacrifices. The former was sprinkled or poured on the altar, the latter consumed as a burnt offering. Their separation is an important element in conveying the sacrificial and atoning meaning of Jesus' death. This sacrificial symbolism should not be obscured by an unwarranted conflation. Our observance of the Lord's Supper should be "according to Scripture," consequently as

---

122 As long as a single loaf and a single cup are featured in the sacramental actions, it is a matter of indifference, *adiaphora*, if pieces of bread are pre-cut and the fruit of the vine is pre-poured in individual cups. It is overkill on Letham's part to identify these practices as "redolent of post-Enlightenment individualism," and as unwarranted changes which "violate and pollute" the sacrament! (*Lord's Supper*, 51). Similarly, leavened versus unleavened bread, wine vs. the unfermented "fruit of the vine," are all matters of *adiaphora* (cf. Chapell, 290–291). Wine, by the way, is not specifically named in the New Testament in connection with the Lord's Supper, though it may be safely assumed to be the beverage in question. However, the phrase "fruit of the vine" is, rather than *oinos*, which, it seems to us, provides leeway enough for a range of choices so long as the juice of the grape is used.

123 See Jeremiah Burroughs, *Gospel Worship: or the Right Manner of Sanctifying the Name of God in General* (1648, Pittsburgh: Soli Deo Gloria Publications, 1990), 344.

124 Joachim Jeremias, *The Eucharistic Words of Jesus* (London: SCM Press, 1966), 222–227. See also Leon Morris, *The Gospel According to Matthew* (Grand Rapids: Eerdmans Publishing Co., 1992), 649.

260 *Serving with Calvin*

close to the scriptural account as is practical. Intinction, a practice of the Eastern Orthodox Church that was not introduced into the Western church until the eleventh century, and then condemned by the Council of Clement in 1095, and again by the Council of London in 1175, ordinarily should not be practiced.[125]

Because the sacraments themselves are signs, their integrity as signs should not be obscured or cluttered with other activities whether they be relatives around the baptismal font, a walk with the infant up and down the aisles of the church, or pastoral counsel at the table. The Reformers' heightened appreciation for the biblical theology of the covenant led to a simplifying of the administration of church ordinances lest attention be taken away from the grace-giving signs themselves. "It was because the Reformers prized so highly the divinely given signs," says Hughes Old, "that they had such disdain for those signs of merely human invention which obscured them."[126] We repeat Calvin's conviction: "How much better would it be to omit from baptism all theatrical pomp, which dazzles the eyes of the simple and deadens their minds ..." Let it be simple, he says. Let nothing essential be omitted. Let the sacraments which God ordained "not (be) buried in outlandish pollutions" but rather let them "shine in (their) full brightness."[127]

We hear similar counsel from Matthew Henry, pointing out that the apostles administered baptism with "great plainness

---

125 Davies, *Dictionary of Liturgy & Worship*, 286.

126 Hughes O. Old, *The Shaping of the Reformed Baptismal Rite in the Sixteenth Century* (Grand Rapids: Eerdmans, 1992), 286.

127 Calvin, *Institutes*, IV.xv.19, 1319. See also Jeremiah Burroughs: "There should be no action intermingled in the time of the receiving of the Sacrament, nothing but minding the work that you are about, which is to remember the death of Jesus Christ and to discern the body of the Lord" (*Gospel Worship*, 347).

and simplicity," and recommending that we do the same.[128] He complains the "inventions of men" by which "the ordinance itself hath been thereby miserably obscured and corrupted."[129] "The spouse of Christ looks most glorious in her native beauty, and needs not the paint and tawdry attire of a harlot." These "appendages," he says, "instead of adorning the institution of Christ, have really deformed and injured them."[130]

Do not obstruct, obscure, or confuse the signs. Do not elevate the elements.[131] Do not use wafers. It is of doubtful wisdom to have communicants come forward as if to an altar rail. Because "the essential action of the Lord's Supper is the sharing of a meal," Old explains, "we serve one another rather than file up to some sort of altar to receive the bread and wine at the hands of the clergy."[132] Do not kneel. Communicants should be seated, ideally, though not necessarily, at a table. But they should be seated because this is our ordinary posture when eating a meal. Warfield, in his essay on the subject of posture at the Lord's Supper, cites the seventeenth century Scottish theologian and commissioner at the Westminster Assembly, George Gillespie (1613–48), who said, "we ought to come to the table or the Lord to receive the mystical food in the sacrament, as well as we come to our ordinary table

---

128 Henry, "Treatise on Baptism," *Works*, 1:531.

129 Ibid. 532.

130 Ibid. 533.

131 Letham, *The Lord's Supper*, claims that the Confession (XXIX.4) opposes elevating the elements only in connection with worshiping them but not elevating them "so that the people may see them" (43). This seems to us to miss the point. Because the Medieval church elevated the elements so that they might be worshiped, Reformed churches ought not to elevate them at all lest this sacramental gesture be understood as an invitation to adore the elements.

132 Hughes O. Old, *Leading in Prayer: A Workbook for Ministers* (Grand Rapids, Michigan: William B. Eerdmans Publishing Company, 1995), 232.

for our ordinary food."[133] "Had I my choice," says Baxter, "I would receive the Lord's supper sitting."[134] Writing over 250 years later out of the Dutch Reformed tradition, the great Abraham Kuyper (1837–1920) draws the same conclusion. "It is not absolutely necessary to sit at a table for the celebration of the Lord's Supper," he concedes, "though doing so is the most hallowed way to administer communion."[135] This is the historic Reformed view. We sit when we eat an ordinary meal, we do not kneel and rarely do we stand. By saying this we are not imposing a law. Rather we are reminding ourselves that the Lord's Supper should look like a meal. Mark Noll, church historian formerly of Wheaton College and currently of Notre Dame, tells of his Presbyterian church in the western suburbs of Chicago, which for years celebrated communion in the "Scots Form," that is, at tables, served by the elders. "This experience," in what he calls "retro-Calvinism," "was powerful beyond words" as well as "an intensively communal experience."[136] It is worth the care and effort required to maintain the proper symbols.[137]

---

133 B. B. Warfield, "Posture of the Recipients at the Lord's Super," in John E. Meeter, *Selected Shorter Writings of Benjamin B. Warfield—II* (Phillipsburg, New Jersey: Presbyterian & Reformed Publishing Co., 1973), 365; also Burroughs: "Those who communicate must come to the table as near as they can, as many as can sit about it, and all to come as near as they can" (*Gospel Worship*, 341). Also, "It is as if Christ should say ... 'this sitting with Me at My table is a prelude, a fore-signification of the communion that you shall have with me in My kingdom'" (*Gospel Worship*, 342, based on Luke 22:29–30).

134 Baxter, "Christian Directory," *Works*, 1:687.

135 Abraham Kuyper, *Our Worship,* 268.

136 Mark Noll, "Deep & Wide: How My Mind Has Changed," *Christian Century*, June 1, 2010, Vol. 127, No. 11, 32.

137 Chapell, *Christ-Centered Worship*, seems unwilling to decide if communion should be taken seated or standing, at the rail or at the table; if the host should or shouldn't be elevated; if the minister should stand in front of or behind the table; if the elements should be received by intinction or kept separate. His priority is "a

Baptism should look like a simple outpouring of water. "Washing with water is a plain thing," says Henry, "and the perfection of a gospel ordinance lies much in its simplicity."[138] The directories for worship in the Presbyterian tradition are clear and consistent. "The minister shall baptize the child ... by pouring or sprinkling of the water on the face of the child, *without adding any other ceremony.*"[139]

4. *Administer the sacraments in the context of counsel & instruction.* All first communions should be preceded with counsel or instruction. Non-communing children making their public profession of faith as well as adult converts should be thoroughly examined to determine the credibility of their profession of faith prior to admission to the Lord's Supper. Instruction is necessary, though one need not repeat the errors of the fourth century, where catechumens were required to demonstrate their "worthiness" to receive baptism and be admitted to the eucharist. Instruction is not a matter of worthiness but readiness. The aim should be to ensure that converts grasp the nature of the covenant into which they are

---

gracious spirit" and "healthy balance," lest we be "too hasty about innovation or too deferential to tradition." However, this indecisiveness leaves poor guidelines for churches, and ensures conflict among those who have differing convictions. Rather it belongs to church leaders to identify *adiaphora* and distinguish it from matters of principle. Historic Reformed practice has settled most of these issues. This openness to everything flaws what otherwise might have been a considerably more helpful book. It shows, in my estimation, both a deficient deference to Scripture and confidence in tradition.

138 Ibid. 491.

139 This language dates to the original *Directory for the Public Worship of God* (1645), my emphasis; the *Book of Church Order of the Presbyterian Church in America* uses the same language, almost word for word (see Sec. 56–6) (Sixth Edition [2012 Reprint], Published by The Office of the Stated Clerk of the General Assembly of the Presbyterian Church in America, Distributed by The Committee for Christian Education and Publication, Lawrenceville, GA).

entering, the covenantal meaning of the meal, and the level of commitment required.

A given family's first infant baptism should also be preceded by instruction. Zwingli established this principle nearly 500 years ago in the first major defense of infant baptism by a Reformed Protestant: "we do not allow children to be brought to baptism unless the parents have first been taught."[140] Often there will be confusion about why infants are baptized, and so the family's privileged status in the covenant will need to be explained (Genesis 17:17; Acts 2:38; Romans 4:11; Colossians 2:11; 1 Corinthians 7:14). Also, the responsibilities of the family need to be explained. Rearing one's children in the "nurture and admonition of the Lord" is no small task (Ephesians 6:1ff). The obligation to "pray with and for" one's children and to "teach them the doctrines of our holy religion," and make use of "all the means of God's appointment," are considerable and should be fleshed out.[141] Regular family devotions should be vigorously promoted.[142]

Above all parents must be urged to trust God for their children. They are to "claim God's covenant promises in (his/her) behalf and look in faith to the Lord Jesus Christ for (his/her) salvation, as (they) do for (their) own."[143] This is the undertaking of a lifetime. Covenant children belong to the covenant Lord. This outlook effects how we deal with our children throughout their

---

140 Ulrich Zwingli, "Of Baptism," in G. W. Bromiley, *Zwingli & Bullinger* in John Baillie, et. a. (ed.) *The Library of Christian Classics*, Vol. XXIV (Philadelphia: The Westminster Press, 1953), 146.

141 The language here is that of the baptismal vows of the Presbyterian Church in America. See *Leading in Worship*, 73–77.

142 See Johnson, *The Family Worship Book*.

143 This is the second parental baptismal vow of the Book of Church Order of the Presbyterian Church in America.

lifetimes. "Tell the children, and keep telling them, that they are the Lord's," urges William Still. Further,

> When they begin to question, do not resort to frantic affirmations, as if you were, or had become, unsure—you are standing by faith upon God's promise, not on your own wavering hope. Quietly, sweetly and with supreme assurance in the promises of God affirm that they are the Lord's, by birth into a Christian home, and by the prophetic gift of faith exercised; and that you as Christian parents are standing upon God's promise in order that they may grow up in the Lord and come to voluntary commitment to Him, acknowledging their sin and need of a Savior, gladly falling in with God's offer of mercy in Jesus Christ, and receiving Him as their personal Saviour. It would be right and proper, therefore, in circumstances of crisis and tension, simply to assert that these children are overtaken and overcome by the grace of God through the exercise of His gift of faith, and that, wriggle as they may, there is nothing they can do about it![144]

5. *Administer the sacraments with the word and prayer.* Word and sacrament in Reformed practice always belong together. The Lord's Supper should be accompanied by preaching as well as explanation of the nature of the Lord's Supper, distinguishing correct from defective views, as well as the qualifications of those who partake. The table should always be "fenced," that the unconverted, uninstructed, unprepared, unexamined, or unrepentant not partake in an "unworthy manner," lest they eat and drink judgment to themselves (1 Corinthians 11:27–29).

---

144 William Still, *Child Rearing within the Covenant of Grace* (Aberdeen, Didasko Press, n/d), 9–10.

Likewise prayer is essential. Remember Jesus said of the Holy Spirit, "He will take what is mine and declare it to you" (John 16:14). The efficacy of the Lord's Supper depends upon the work of the Holy Spirit. Consequently considerable prayer should be offered in connection with communion (e.g. the Communion Invocation, the Eucharistic Prayer, Prayer of Humble Access, the Prayer of Consecration, the Prayer of Dedication). The Communion Invocation of Richard Baxter's Savoy Liturgy is a strong example how the Puritans sought the illuminating and sanctifying work of the Holy Spirit in their communion services.

The meaning and mode of baptism should also be explained at the time of its administration, so that faith might be engendered, and so that biblical baptisms might not be confused with baptismal regeneration or with mere symbolism. Henry comments that every baptism be accompanied by the word of God (citing 1 Timothy 4:5). He says,

> The word is our warrant for what we do; and therefore should be read, as our commission, "Go ye and disciple all nations, baptizing them." The nature of the ordinance should be opened, and of the covenant of which it is the seal, and care taken to fix a right notion of the institution, and to raise the affections of the congregation.[145]

We repeat Calvin's admonition: "the sacrament requires preaching."[146]

Likewise, Clavin insists, prayer that is "suited to the ordinance" should be offered,

---

145 Henry, "Treatise on Baptism," *Works*, I:531.
146 Calvin, *Institutes*, IV.xix.6, 1454.

Acknowledging the goodness of God to us in making a new covenant ... and in appointing sacraments to be the seals of that covenant, ... giving him thanks, that the covenant of grace is herein so well ordered, that not only we, but our seed, are taken into it; dedicating the child to God accordingly; begging that he would honour his own ordinance with his presence, and sanctify and bless it to the child; that the washing of the child with water, in the names of the Father, Son, and Holy Ghost, may effectually signify, and seal, his ingrafting into Christ; and that he may thereby partake of the privileges of the new covenant, and be engaged to be the Lord's.[147]

All the Reformed baptismal rites include an extensive prayer for the sanctifying work of the Holy Spirit.

6. *Administer the sacraments in the context of catechetical instruction.* The Reformed tradition does not contemplate infant baptisms being administered without offering catechetical instruction at the age of discretion. Nor does it contemplate admission to the Lord's Table with catechetical instruction. The vows in Geneva required of parents that they promise, "when (the child) has come to the age of discretion, to instruct him in the doctrine that is received by the people of God."[148] As we've seen, more recent versions of the vows require that parents promise to "teach (the child) the doctrines of our holy religion."[149] We recommend that the church not only urge parents to catechize,

---

147 Ibid. 537.
148 Elsie Ann McKee (ed.), *John Calvin's Writings on Pastoral Piety*, The Classics of Western Spirituality (New York: Paulist Press, 2001), 156.
149 See note 377.

268   *Serving with Calvin*

but that catechetical classes be offered by the church. What Henry says to parents can be said by extension to the whole church:

> You are unjust to your God, unkind to your children, and unfaithful to your trust, if having by baptism entered your children in Christ's school, and listed them under his banner, you do not make conscience of training them up in the learning of Christ's scholars, and under the discipline of his soldiers."[150]

7. Finally, maintain a serious tone for the administration of the sacraments. There is some discussion abroad about whether the administration of the Lord's Supper is a "celebration," a remembrance of the source of our forgiveness, peace, joy, and hope of eternal life, and therefore to be observed with a light and joyful tone, or whether the more traditional somber tone is the more appropriate. Historically there can be no doubt that the latter has been the tone adopted across all the denominational traditions including the Reformed. The Scots Confession of 1560, for example, urges "great reverence" along with diligent self-examination.[151] Our Reformed forefathers often referred to the Lord's Supper as the "sacred solemnity" or "sacramental solemnity."[152] "Whoever goes to the Table," said the Scottish

---

150   Matthew Henry, "A Church in the House," in *The Complete Works of Matthew Henry*, 2 vols. (Edinburgh: J. Fullarton & Co., 1855; 1979; Reprint Grand Rapids: Baker Book House, 1997), 253; see also Johnson, *Catechizing Our Children* (Edinburgh: The Banner of Truth Trust, 2013) for a recommended calendar of catechism classes.

151   Macleod, *Presbyterian Worship*, 87.

152   E.g. Edmund Calamy & Richard Vines, *et. al. The Puritans on the Lord's Supper*, ed. Don Kistler (Morgan, PA: Soli Deo Gloria, 1997), 38, 120, 121; Jonathan Edwards, *The Life of David Brainerd* in *The Works of Jonathan Edwards, Vol. 7* (New Haven: Yale University Press, 1985), 388.

Reformer Robert Bruce (1554–1631), "ought to go with a sorrowful heart, for the sins wherein he has offended God."[153] Further, "They should come with great reverence to the Table."[154] Spurgeon refers to it as "this sacred meeting place," "this sacred eucharist," and "this hallowed ordinance."[155] Among more recent writers, Robert G. Rayburn (1915–1990) calls the Supper, "the central and most solemn act of the church's worship."[156] We would suggest that a tone of solemn joy should be maintained for the following reasons.

(i) The Lord's Supper is a "remembrance" as well as a proclamation of Christ's death. Set before communicants are the "awful emblems" of His suffering: shed blood and broken body.[157] While we rejoice in the benefits of Christ's death we cannot do so without solemnity as we recall His brutal execution and our sin which made His humiliation necessary. J. W. Alexander (1804–1859), in his "Sacramental Discourse" (1860), rejects the "superstitious mystery" and "unscriptural terrors" that have been "conjured around this ordinance by priestcraft and deception," yet he still claims for the Lord's Supper "a sacredness unlike any on earth." He asks,

"If the worshiper who prepared to enter the typical sanctuary must wash his body in pure water—how cautiously, how reverently

---

153 Bruce, *The Mystery of the Lord's Supper*, 42.
154 Ibid. 46.
155 C. H. Spurgeon, *Till He Come: A Collection of Communion Addresses* (Fearn, Ross-shire: Christian Focus Publications, n.d.), 106, 107.
156 Rayburn, *O Come, Let Us Worship*, 255.
157 Calamy, *The Puritans on the Lord's Supper*, 40.

should we draw near the place where the appointed emblems set forth Christ, evidently crucified in the midst of us."[158]

One can only imagine his response to partakers discussing their lunch plans before, during, and after receiving the elements.

Spurgeon seeks an appropriate balance urging us not to come to the table as if it were a funeral. "Let us select solemn hymns, but not dirges. Let us sing softly, but none the less joyfully." The mood is one of solemn joy. "We will mourn that we pierced the Lord, and we will rejoice in pardon bought with blood. Our strain must vary as we talk of sin, feeling its bitterness, and lamenting it, and then of pardon, rejoicing in its glorious fullness." He recommends communion songs which are soft, sweet, and strong. "There are no boisterous themes with which we have to deal when we tarry here. A bleeding Saviour, robed in a vesture died with blood—this is a theme which you must treat with loving gentleness, for everything that is coarse is out of place. While the tune is soft, it must also be *sweet*. Yet, it "must also be *strong*," he says. "There must be a full swell in my praise." [159]

(ii) The act of affirming or renewing covenant vows is an inherently serious exercise. "That you may be the more serious in this ordinance of the Lord's Supper," urges Nathanael Vincent (1638–1697), "remember that therein you solemnly renew covenant with the God of heaven, you give yourselves over to Him, disclaim all other lords and owners, and profess to take Him

---

158 J. W. Alexander, *God is Love* (1860; Edinburgh: The Banner of Truth Trust, 1985), 256–257.

159 Spurgeon, *Till He Come*, 155, 157, 160). See also Bridges: "Deeply let us cherish the godly reverence in his service, remembering that 'even our God is a consuming fire.' But let us never forget, that the holy ordinance is a means of acceptance to a rejoicing heart" (*Christian Ministry*, 460).

to be your Lord, your God, your Guide, your All."[160] Edmund Calamy (1673–1732) is particularly clear on this point. He warns us in connection with the Lord's Supper with words that apply to baptism as well: "Take heed of levity, as if it were a common, ordinary, and customary thing you were setting yourselves about, when you go to give up yourselves to God anew."[161] We are to engage in affirming our vows "with all the seriousness and solemnity we are able, to be His servants and subjects to our life's end."[162] Because we transact with God, "the utmost awe, reverence, seriousness and devotion" are necessary "whenever we set ourselves to this matter."[163] Similarly, Henry urges that baptism be administered "in a solemn manner."[164] He insists, "That inward awe, which should possess us in divine worship, must put a gravity upon the outward deportment."[165] Further,

Whispering, and laughing, and other irreverences of behavior, at this ordinance, are a provocation to God, an affront to the institution, a disturbance to others, and a bad sign of a vain and carnal mind.[166]

Nathanael Vincent broadly applies the warnings of 1 Corinthians 11:27ff (in connection with the Lord's Supper) to all our worship: "With what intention, vigilance, and godly fear should the Lord's people engage in His work and worship!"[167]

---

160 Nathanael Vincent, *Attending Upon God without Distraction*, introduced by Joel R. Beeke, edited by Don Kistler (1695; Grand Rapids, Michigan: Soli Deo Gloria Publications, 2010), 197.

161 Calamy, *The Puritans on the Lord's Supper*, 46.

162 Ibid. 42. See also Richard Vines, *Puritans on the Lord's Supper*, 120–121.

163 Ibid. 48.

164 Henry, "Treatise on Baptism," *Works*, I:562.

165 Ibid. 562.

166 Ibid. 563.

167 Vincent, *Attending Upon God*, 148.

If we understand the nature of baptism as a rite of covenantal admission and the nature of the Lord's Supper as a covenantal meal, requiring confirmation of the covenant and reaffirmation of covenant vows, we will maintain a solemn tone throughout their administration. "Everyone involved in (these) solemn service(s)," continues Donald Macleod, "should aim at order, efficiency, and reverence."[168]

This, then, is how we think the public ministry ought to be conducted. Each service should be carefully planned. Those leading services should know what they are doing and why they are doing it. They should know how transitions are going to be made. The service should not drag, but move along, without rushing. A mood of "reverence and awe" should be established, with each succeeding element of worship being approached with sobriety and urgency. The service should be saturated with Scripture and prayer. Pray, read, sing, and preach the language of the Bible. Public worship on the Lord's Day will make or break a church's ministry. These services, in a true sense, are the ministry of the church. In these services both the primary audience and the primary means of grace are present. Diligently use those means, and trust that God will bless His prayer-empowered word.

---

168 Macleod, *Presbyterian Worship*, 73; see also Rayburn, *O Come, Let Us Worship*, 265ff. Rayburn seems to have leaned quite heavily on Macleod in this section.

Where, then, should Reformed worship services be held? Granted they can be held anywhere, from an igloo at the North Pole to a grass hut in central Africa. Yet is there an ideal setting? When given an opportunity to design our churches, particularly their interiors, what should they look like? What setting is most conducive to the hosting of Reformed worship?

274

❧ Chapter 6 ❧

Preparing the Setting

The same theology that determines the shape of worship also determines the design of buildings in which those service stake place, and the types of furnishings and decorations that will adorn the interior. "Architecture for churches is a matter of gospel," says Donald J. Bruggink and Carl H. Droppers, authors of *Christ and Architecture*.[1] Moreover,

> A church that is interested in proclaiming the gospel must also be interested in architecture, for year after year the architecture of the church proclaims a message that either augments the preached Word of conflicts with it.[2]

---

1   Donald J. Bruggink and Carl H. Droppers, *Christ and Architecture* (Grand Rapids: Eerdmans, 1965).
2   Ibid. 1.

At the time of the Reformation the Protestant leaders altered the architecture and furnishings of the Roman Catholic churches which they inherited. As A. L. Drummond points out, "The majority of medieval churches were singularly ill-adapted to the preaching and congregational worship with their echoing vaults and long-drawn aisles."[3] Never were the changes merely matters of style. Statues were removed, altars were replaced with tables, and pulpits were erected because of the theological convictions of the Reformers, and because they "were acutely conscious of the power of architecture and the constant message that it held for the people." "It might fairly be said," continue Bruggink and Droppers, "that the Word of God challenged the architecture of medieval Romanism, and the Reformed responded with an attempt to transform these inherited buildings into structures more suitable for biblical worship."[4] When later they begin to build their own houses of worship. Reformed architecture came into its own.

External Style

There is a sense in which Reformed worship is compatible with most any style of architecture be it Romanesque, Gothic, Greek-Revival, Colonial, or Modern. Still, two principles remain important.

First, the architectural style should partake of the language of church architecture. Ideally it should say to the observer, this is a church, not a bank, not a big-box retailer, and not an office building. The church's architectural form is an aspect of the church's external witness to the community. This form should

---

3   A. L. Drummond, *The Church Architecture of Protestantism: An Historical and Constructive Study* (Edinburgh: T & T Clark, 1934), 19.

4   Bruggink and Droppers, *Christ and Architecture*, 2,3.

say clearly that this is a house of worship, that serious things take place here, and all are welcome to come.

Second, the church's building should contribute to rather than detract from the "overall quality of the built environment of a community," says David Gobel, Professor of Architectural History at the Savannah College of Art & Design.[5] "Churches," he continues, "must consider not only the architectural design of their building, but also its urban design—that is, its relationship to streets, blocks, and neighboring buildings of the community."[6] Only when it has done so can the church consider itself a good neighbor, and its buildings "an asset and an adornment to the city," contributing not only to the church's worship, but "to the beauty and welfare of the city of man."[7]

Interior Arrangement[8]

If congregations are to avoid designing buildings whose message conflicts with that which is preached, those buildings must be assembled from the inside out. What goes on inside determines the architecture. What happens when the people of God gather to worship "determines the arrangement of the interior furnishings and the outward shape of the building," argues Macleod.[9] As Rick

---

5   David Gobel, "Reforming Church Architecture," *New Horizons Magazine*, February 2011, 6–7.

6   Ibid.

7   Ibid.

8   In addition to Bruggink and Droppers, see Philip Bess, *Till We Have Built Jerusalem: Architecture, Urbanism, and the Sacred* (Wilmington Delaware: ISI Books, 2006); André Biéler, *Architecture in Worship* (Edinburgh & London: Oliver & Boyd, 1965); Drummond, *The Church Architecture of Protestantism*; James H. Nichols & Leonard J. Trinterud, *The Architectural Setting for Reformed Worship*, Revised Edition (Chicago, Illinois: Presbytery of Chicago, 1960).

9   Macleod, *Presbyterian Worship*, 128.

Serving with Calvin

Warren acknowledges, "The shape of your building will shape your service."[10]

Central Pulpit

The preeminence of the word of God in Reformed worship requires that the architectural focal point of the church building not be an altar, as it was in the medieval church and remains in Roman Catholic churches today, or not even the table in a Protestant church, but the pulpit. The Reformers were convinced that auditory priorities required that a Reformed church structure be designed for preaching and listening. This was accomplished in inherited structures in several different ways. Sometimes the pulpit was moved to the center, sometimes it remained on the side but was elevated and enlarged, sometimes a large sounding board was added, and sometimes it was the seating of the people that was moved to positions around the pulpit. The point in each case was to facilitate the spoken word. At the same time the result was also to make the pulpit the central architectural feature of the house of worship, or at least of the seated congregation. When they built new churches, the Reformers and their successors built so-called "auditory churches," churches made for preaching and listening.

Reformed Protestants did not think that in making these changes that they were introducing something novel. Central pulpits are found in the first formal church buildings, the basilicas of the third century. According to A. L. Drummond, in *The Church Architecture of Protestantism*, the Reformation's central pulpits "restored the real arrangement of the primitive churches." In the early basilicas as well as gothic churches before

---

10   Warren, *Purpose Driven Church*, 264.

the ninth century, "there can be no doubt that the bishop always preached or exhorted, in the primitive times, from his throne in the centre of the apse ... "[11] The pulpit, then, should be central and prominent. Pews should wrap around the pulpit. Protestant congregations cannot be content to gaze forward uncomprehendingly at the mystery of the mass. They must understand and believe. "Faith comes by hearing" (Romans 10:17). The design of the church must aid the hearing of the word, and in so doing, visibly underscore the principles of *sola Scriptura*, and *sola fide*.

Table and Font
The table and font should be placed at the base of the pulpit, the three together, representing the primary means of grace, with priority given to the word.[12] The table should be clearly a table, "a simple wooden table," as Barth insisted, and not an altar.[13]

Chancel's were split in the Middle Ages and continue to be split in Roman Catholic churches in order to allow an unobstructed view of the altar, the proper architectural focal point given a sacramental theology. However, a split chancel makes little sense in a Protestant setting. Altars, and anything looking like an altar, should be removed, thereby reinforcing the message of *solo Christo*, of the finality and sufficiency of Christ's death upon the cross as an atonement for sin (Hebrews 7:27; 10:10, 12). The pulpit should be placed in the center and not split, lectern on one

---

11 Drummond, *The Church Architecture of Protestantism,* 206, citing John Ruskin, *The Stones of Venice* (Geo.Allen, ed. 1898), ii. Appendix 6.

12 Kuyper concurs: *Worship,* 234.

13 Karl Barth, "The architectural problem of Protestant places of worship" in Biéler's *Architecture in Worship,* 92. Also, Nichols and Trinterud: "the table ought to be most clearly a table, and not a misplaced altar" (*Architectural Setting for Reformed Worship,* 20).

side, pulpit on the other. Neither should the pulpit be placed on a platform that might be mistaken for a stage. When congregations look forward they should see a place designed for preaching and prayer, and not mistake it for a place for performers providing sacred entertainment.

Choir & Organ

The Reformation moved the choir, when retained, to the back balcony or lacking such, to the rear or side of the sanctuary, to a position they called a "singing pew." The purpose of this move was to shift emphasis from a "beautifully sung service" provided by a religious elite to congregational singing. Where Protestant choirs persisted, they were, "primarily to assist the congregation in its singing," according to Bruggink and Droppers.[14] The best position for doing so was in the back. In addition, the choir was thereby identified with the congregation, not with the clergy, and was not given a clerical status. It is to be regretted that Protestants have gotten into the habit of dressing their choirs in robes like medieval monks. "The choir is only a part of the congregation. It is not an adjunct of the priesthood. It ought to be among the congregation, at least in symbol," insist Nichols and Trinterud.[15] The practice of placing the choir in the back was characteristic of Reformation era churches and was provided for architecturally in the centuries that followed. This design can be seen in the older churches of Scotland and Holland, those built by Sir Christopher Wren following the great London fire (1666), and the Colonial churches in America. The rear choir-gallery was typical of all Protestant churches until the mid-nineteenth century.

14　Bruggink and Droppers, *Christ and Architecture*, 393.
15　Nichols and Trinterud, *Architectural Setting of Reformed Worship*, 20.

Organs likewise, when retained by the Reformers, were left in the back of the church building, where they had been for several centuries. There, they would not compete architecturally with the means of grace. Like the choir, the organ was to assist the congregation in its praise of God, a task best done from behind.

Given that so much of the foregoing seems obvious, why is it that so few churches today are designed in a manner consistent with Reformed principles? First, it should be noted that many, if not most Reformed churches in Europe are. It seems only American Reformed Protestants have so completely lost sight of their architectural heritage. Second, Americans tend perhaps to be more pragmatic and less theologically-oriented, and have given less thought to the meaning of their architecture. Consequently, third, there were historical movements or fashions that were uncritically copied by the churches for pragmatic reasons.

The split-chancel choir was revived in Protestant churches through the influence of the Church of England's "high-church" Oxford movement of the mid-1800s. Its leaders provided for the return of the choir to the medieval position between the people and the restored "altar." What is regarded by many as "traditional" Episcopal architecture was actually a nineteenth century innovation, inconsistent with Protestant, and even Anglican practice for 200 years. But it was consistent with the Roman Catholic leanings of the Anglo-Catholic Tractarians. This architectural fashion has been unthinkingly mimicked by others since, without regard for the displacing of the pulpit, the restoration of the altar, and the undesirable distance it puts between the people and the Lord's table.

The "theater plan" of choir placement became popular in "low-church" circles, that is, the placement of the choir behind the pulpit, in tiers, through the influence of the late nineteenth century and early twentieth century revivalists. D. L. Moody, Billy Sunday, and Billy Graham preached in large auditoriums with stages on which were featured both the preaching and "special music." The popularity of those "crusades" prompted churchmen to mimic both the format of these services and the design of the buildings. However, when choirs are placed behind the pulpit, they, with, perhaps, the organ pipes, become "the most significant visual element in the front of the church."[16] Bruggink and Droppers comment that this practice is little more than a century old and that "throughout the prior nineteen centuries of Christ's Church the choir was placed in almost every position throughout the church room *except above and behind the pulpit!*"[17] They go so far as to call it "choirolatry." It is, for the heirs of the Reformation, an unthinking challenge to the prominence that ought only be given to the pulpit, table, and font, as the symbols of the means of grace. Yet today this arrangement is found in the vast majority of American Protestant churches. Remarkably, even the most conservative Southern Presbyterian congregations of 1950s and early 1960s built split-chancel buildings with the choirs behind the pulpit.[18]

Behind the mindless mimicking of the successful religious gatherings of the evangelists, Bruggink and Droppers find an even less admirable motivation for the new arrangements. They cite the testimony of Joseph Edwin Blanton, of "wide architectural and musical erudition," saying,

It is the ... desire of congregations to be entertained, I believe,

---

16   Bruggink & Droppers, *Christ & Architecture*, 395.
17   Ibid. (my emphasis).
18   e.g. Granada Presbyterian Church, Coral Gables, Florida; First Presbyterian Church, Jackson, Mississippi, and Trinity Presbyterian Church, Montgomery, Alabama.

which has fixed, more or less, the location of the choir in the chancel.[19]

They see a connection between the innovations of the high-church party and the low-church in this respect.

In low-church Protestantism, the pulpit may be central, but the parishioner, like his high-church counterpart, goes to church with the expectancy of the drama of the service, except that his drama is not one of ecclesiastical awe and mystery but of a performance by choir and minister in which the personalities involved are given the opportunity to play a larger part in relation to their function in the service.[20]

In the last 150 years these aberrant fashions have swept the field and become the norm among Protestants, and in so doing obscured the clear message communicated by the older Protestant architecture. More recently, the choir has been replaced by the praise band, as the architectural focal point.[21]

The choir and organ and organ pipes once again should be placed in the rear of the building and not compete with, or rather supplant, the pulpit as the architectural focal point. We note with some irony once more that the neo-orthodox have understood what evangelicals have missed. Karl Barth, for example, insists, "Since the organ and choir are accessories appreciated to a greater or lesser degree and may in principle be dispensed with, they should not appear in the field of vision of the assembled community."[22] Remove the trapping of entertainment from places

---

19 Ibid. 398.

20 Ibid.

21 See Timothy Quill, in Pinson (ed.), *Perspectives on Christian Worship*, 272. He laments this development and adds, "Music has been 'sacramentalized' and becomes the chief means of experiencing God's presence" (272).

22 Barth, "Architectural Problems of Protestant Places of Worship," in Biéler's, *Architecture in Worship*, 93.

of worship. Do not allow the setting of worship to be mistaken for a house of mirth. Do not build stages and platforms and place bands and singers upon them. Do not mimic the format and tone of late-night comedy show presented to an audience relaxing in theater seating. The historic architectural language of central pulpit and pews in reverential arrangement should not be compromised.

Our counsel cannot be mandated by a single biblical text. These are wisdom issues. Often in matters small distinctions make a significant difference. The psychological difference between a choir, chamber group, or even soloist, performing up front, on a stage, microphones in hand, and that made by the same groups and individuals in the back balcony out of sight, is large indeed, and important. Every practical step should be taken to ensure that through architecture and furnishings churches do not give what Bruggink and Droppers call "a garbled account of the gospel."[23] Reformed churches have made effective use of a variety of materials: wood, stone, brick, stucco; and, as we've noted, a variety of styles. There is room for considerable diversity. Yet architectural style and interior arrangement must have theological integrity. "The architecture of any church building ought to speak plainly and well the message of the Christian Gospel as it is understood by those Christians whose common meeting place it is."[24]

The furnishings, decorations, and the arts

The place of worship should also be characterized by decorative simplicity. It is our view that the cultural momentum toward the

---

23   Bruggink and Droppers, *Christ and Architecture*, 4.
24   Nichols and Trinterud, *Architectural Setting for Reformed Worship*, 19.

pictographic in the twenty-first century is not to be conceded and accommodated, as it was in the fourth to ninth centuries, but resisted and defied. The preference for the visual is in church history a slippery slope which eventually overwhelms the verbal. The Reformers' arguments are still valid.[25] The use of the unauthorized visual media, whether in the form of liturgical drama or liturgical art, implies the inadequacy of God's word, leads to idolatry, is in violation of Scripture, and is distracting. Scripture and history led Reformed Protestants to these conclusions. Their convictions are worth pondering as we witness today a re-imaging, or re-visualizing of Christian ministry. The transformation of the plain-style meeting house of the broadly Reformed tradition (Presbyterian, Congregationalist, Baptist, and even Methodist), with its plain-style interior and simple services, into a mega-church filled with video screens, banners, pictures, stage props, and liberal use of drama, dance, media, and Power-Point is a striking development. The Reformed tradition from Zwingli to the twentieth century was disciplined, that is, restrictive in its use of visual art. The Reformers carefully read Scripture and church history and rejected not just all *cultic* (i.e. devotional) use but also all *illustrative* (i.e. didactic) use of visual art in worship and only permitted careful use of *decorative* art. Calvin "eliminated the visual arts from the worship and meditative life of the church," observes John Leith.[26]

We have noted that today churches at a rapidly increasing rate are incorporating the use of video in their services and are creating staff positions with titles such as "Director of Worship Arts" encompassing dance, drama, video, and music. Seminaries

---

25   See *Worshipping with Calvin*, Chapter 6.
26   Leith, *Introduction to the Reformed Tradition*, 175.

286   *Serving with Calvin*

and study centers are establishing their "Centers for the Study of Worship & Art" and "Institutes of Worship Arts," and holding conferences with similar titles.[27] Reformed theologians, even conservative Reformed theologians, are defending this re-imaging of Christian worship without giving serious consideration of Reformed Protestantism's cautions.[28] American Protestant churches are being swept along in the cultural tide that is transforming western civilization from an essentially typographic, or word-based culture to a pictographic, or image based culture.[29] "Generation Xers are hungering for a new style of worship," says Arthur Hunt, "that bears a closer resemblance to MTV than to their parents' old-time religion."[30] The *Atlanta Constitution* reports that the 12Stone Church in Lawrenceville, Georgia, somewhat typically of today's larger churches, has built a 2,500 "worship experience center" where the message is reinforced by five huge high-definition screens and a $250,000 acoustical system. Dave Ronne, 12Stones "Director of Redemptive Arts," explains their philosophy: Studies indicate that retention of a message increases when information is seen as well as heard.[31]

This revived use of visual media is unprecedented in both the broadly Protestant and Reformed tradition, which of all Christian traditions has been preeminently typographic.[32] "The printing

---

27   e.g. Fuller Seminary's Brehm Center for Worship, Theology, and the Arts (see *Fuller Focus*, Fall 2004, Vol. 12, No. 3, 4–9).

28   e.g. Frame, *Worship*, 72–74.

29   See Postman, *Amusing Ourselves to Death*.

30   Arthur W. Hunt, III, *The Vanishing Word: The Veneration of Visual Imagery in the Postmodern World* (Wheaton: Crossway Books, 2003), 23.

31   Rebecca McCarthy, "Gwinnett's 12Stone church features glitzy amenities, Starbucks," *Atlanta Journal Constitution*, January 22, 2008.

32   Carlos M. N. Eire says of the Reformed church, "The stripped, whitewashed church in which the pulpit replaced the altar became the focal point of a cultural

press was the mechanical engine that drove the Protestant Reformation," Hunt reminds us.[33] The pressure to join the current trend is considerable. Yet the arguments for an increasingly sensual and visible worship sound familiar to those aware of the history of worship. Consequently we continue to approach the use of visual art with great caution.

Devotional art

The devotional use of art must continue to be prohibited for Reformed Protestants. Despite the claims to the contrary made by the Eastern Orthodox and medieval church, visual art may not be seen as a means of divine revelation or as a means of grace. Mark Driscoll of Mars Hill Fellowship in Seattle comes perilously close to the Eastern, if not pagan, view when he claims that "art is that region between heaven and earth that connects the two."[34] This is a regrettable claim. The church does not possess *acheiropoietic* art, that is, art made without human hands, as claimed by Eastern Orthodoxy, nor did God inspire sacred art as a means of communicating divine truth. He might have, but didn't. He inspired writers, not painters or sculptors. The devotional use of art fails all four of our tests: It implies the inadequacy of God's word as revealed truth, it leads to idolatry, it violates Scripture, and it is distracting. Karl Barth, widely recognized as the twentieth century's greatest and most influential theologian,

---

      shift from visual images to language," in *War Against the Idols* (Cambridge: Cambridge University Press, 1986), 315.

33   Hunt, *The Vanishing Word*, 85.

34   Quoted in Plantinga and Rozeboom, *Discerning the Spirits*, 34.

insists, "Images and symbols have *no place at all* in a building designed for Protestant worship."[35]

Decorative art
Churches are going to be decorated, either suitably or unsuitably. We discussed aesthetics earlier, noting the interrelatedness of the true, the good, and the beautiful.[36] Abraham Kuyper righty applies the last of these to our buildings.

> When we therefore arrange and furnish our worship spaces and conduct our activities in them, there is not one good reason why we should consider ourselves exempt from the obligation that rests on all of us to ask in every case not only what is *true*, not only what is *good*, but also what is *beautiful*.[37]

The beautiful is always subordinate to the true and the good. External, visible beauty is always subordinate to internal, invisible beauty. "Art," he says, "must serve the church, not be its master." Yet, given these qualifications and conditions, our concern for beauty is valid and necessary. "The church," says Kuyper, "must use art."[38] How should churches be decorated? Our answer would be that churches should be decorated simply and beautifully. This means that the finest materials ought to be used and the finest

---

35 Barth, in Biéler's *Architecture in Worship*, 93. Barth continues, "They too can serve only to dissipate attention and create confusion. It is only the community met together for "worship" in the strict meaning of the word—that is for prayer, preaching, baptism and the Lord's Supper—and above all the community in action in every day life, which corresponds to the reality of the person and work of Jesus Christ. No image and no symbol can play that role."

36 See Chapter III, Aesthetics.

37 Kuyper, *Our Worship*, 49,50.

38 Ibid.

craftsmanship employed within the framework of simplicity and, says Karl Barth (1886–1968), "without the necessity of recourse to extraneous ornamentation."[39]

The church has understood the need for simplicity in its buildings and restraint in the decorating of its worship spaces, not only in its early centuries but also during periods of spiritual health in the Middle Ages. The Cistercian monastic movement of the twelfth century emphasized "the eloquence and beauty of simplicity."[40] The Cistercians gave renewed attention to the study of Scripture and the church fathers, which they deemed had been neglected. They focused on biblical theology rather than a theology driven by philosophical concerns. Their preaching, as exampled in Bernard of Clairvaux (1090–1151), was biblical exposition. He was concerned to preach the text. Old finds his preaching to be even "a premonition of Puritan plain-style at its purest."[41]

The Cistercians' concern for simple biblical preaching spilled over into concern for simplicity in all areas of life, including architecture, art, and liturgy. "This simplicity of artistic expression goes hand in hand with a recovery of preaching," observes

---

39 Karl Barth, "Architectural Problems of Protestant Places of Worship," in Biéler, *Architecture in Worship*, 93. Barth's whole statement is, "The shape, dimension and colour of the doors, walls and windows, and of the seating can and must contribute to the concentration of those taking part in the service. These factors should help to orientate the worshippers towards the message and worship which draws them together, without the necessity of recourse to extraneous ornamentation. It is only thus that the whole building will be 'worthy' and 'beautiful.'"

40 Hughes O. Old, *The Reading & Preaching of the Scriptures in the Worship of the Christian Church*, Volume 3: The Medieval Church (Grand Rapids: Eerdmans Publishing Company, 1999).

41 Ibid. 275.

Old.[42] "Cistercian preaching, as Cistercian art, has a classic straightforwardness."[43]

The Cistercians simplified the liturgy, the church calendar, clerical vestments, and church furnishings. "St. Bernard in particular fulminated against curious carving, stained glass, painting on wall or pillar, elaborate altar-cloths," Drummond points out.[44] Their buildings featured no statues, no gargoyles, centaurs, or griffins, and no elaborate decorations. Their altars were bare. "Functionalism was their architectural gospel," says Old.[45]

Similarly the simplicity of life emphasized by the Cistercians was also emphasized by the thirteenth century preaching orders, the Franciscans (founded 1209 by Francis of Assisi) and Dominicans (founded 1216 by Dominic). Both groups emphasized what might be called "apostolic simplicity." If the Franciscans gave emphasis to scriptural preaching and the Dominicans to doctrinal preaching, both were concerned to be biblical. The churches built by these preaching orders (the Franciscans and Dominicans) were designed to facilitate preaching. Their auditory concerns anticipated those of the Reformers even as their rejection of ostentation anticipated the Reformers concern for simplicity. The monasticism of the thirteenth century was "saturated with the Puritan attitude toward life," Drummond maintains.[46]

Three hundred years later the Reformation revived the same concern for simplicity: a simple gospel, unostentatious living,

---

42   Ibid. 256.

43   Ibid.

44   Drummond, *The Church Architecture of Protestantism*, 9.

45   Old, Class lectures, Erskine Theological Seminary, April 11, 2007.

46   Drummond, *The Church Architecture of Protestantism*, 9.

simple and functional buildings, simple and undistracting furnishings and decorations. Each of these groups, the early church, the Cistercians, Franciscans, Dominicans, and Reformers, were concerned with biblical preaching. Consequently each was concerned not to allow architectural ostentation distract attention from the proclamation of God's word.

The plain-style New England meeting house provides a classic example of what we mean. Beautiful woods, colors, and textures may be used. Skilled architects and interior designers are needed to maximize efficiency and beauty. Some ornamentation may even be in order. But simplicity should not be compromised. Nothing in the place of worship should call attention to itself and thereby distract attention from the God-ordained means of grace: the word, sacraments, and prayer. Form should follow function. Pulpit, table, and font should be given architectural prominence. Stained glass, banners, statuary, pictures of biblical scenes or characters from church history should be avoided, not so much because they are prohibited as because they are distracting and consequently unwise. Functional efficiency and undistracting beauty are the hallmarks of a proper Christian use of decorative art in worship services. Macleod speaks for the Reformed tradition when he says, "Simplicity is more likely than anything else to evoke a sense of the majesty of the unseen."[47]

Illustrative & didactic art

Art designed to illustrate a biblical passage or enhance a biblical lesson or otherwise serve the ministry of the word may be useful today in an educational setting. However, it should not be employed in the space devoted to worship, where, we have noted

---

47   Macleod, *Presbyterian Worship*, 132.

above, it is likely to distract attention from the means of grace and could be misused as a devotional aid leading to idolatry.

Graphic art

Bulletins, hymnals, Psalters, and prayer books, used during the worship service, ought to be more rather than less beautifully designed. The personal computer has sparked a revolution in graphic design. What was considered acceptable just a few years ago is now considered substandard by most everyone. Cheap or "cheesy" graphic design can be its own kind of distraction, even saying to visitors that "no one here cares about excellence!" Outside of the worship service the work of graphic designers is also needed in the layout of web sites that are "user friendly" and appealing. Artists and designers are also needed in the design of letterhead, brochures, advertisements, and other church literature or publications.

Graphic arts could also be effectively utilized outside of worship in the layout and design of study Bibles, biblical study aids, and other Christian books, be they doctrinal, historical, or pastoral. Similarly, painting and photography could be carefully employed to illustrate or emphasize the message of these various books. Care should be taken never to portray God. Neither should the human face of Jesus be prominently displayed, since his facial appearance is unknown and its portrayal always involves the projection of the artist's ideals, thereby compromising the biblical portrayal of Christ (Galatians 3:1). Design work should be understood not as an alternate means of communicating, but, as is the case with music, that of enriching and supporting the ministry of the word. The development of skilled artists, photographers, and graphic designers will always be a need of the Reformed church.

Performing arts

Liturgical dance and drama may be understood as having an illustrative or didactic intent. They are meant to teach or illustrate scriptural or moral lessons by making those truths visible, much as the elaborate ceremonies introduced in the fourth century by Cyril of Jerusalem were designed to provide for the churches of late antiquity and the Middle Ages. Yet as is the case with extra-biblical ritual, devotional art and ostentatious decorative art, the performing arts fail important tests, namely the objections of the Reformers to images: (i) their use implies the inadequacy of God's word; (ii) their use leads to idolatry, in this case a different kind of idolatry, that is, the idolatry of confusing entertainment with worship; (iii) their use lacks scriptural and historical warrant (despite the claims of their advocates); (iv) their use is distracting in that they deprive the worship service of the time that might have been devoted to the ministry of the word read, preached, sung, prayed, and administered (in the sacraments). Just as God commissioned writers and not sculptors or painters, so also He ordained preachers, not choreographers, dancers, or playwrights. There is considerable irony in the growing momentum behind the use of the performing arts in worship, what might be considered the contemporary low-church alternative to the drama of the liturgy in the high-church. The liberal wing of the church contributed most of the earliest advocates for drama in worship. Fred Eastman, Professor of Biography, Literature and Drama (!) at Chicago Theological Seminary, and Lewis Wilson, who specialized in religious drama and religious journalism with Eastman at Chicago, published *Drama in the Church* way back in 1932, with a revised edition in 1942.[48] They called upon Protestants to abandon the patristic and Reformation era bias against drama and restore the positive Medieval outlook. Their arguments sound familiar. The (liberal) church was losing its influence and its preaching was increasingly ineffective. The use of drama would revitalize the ministry and mission of the church. This reasoning should be resisted. There may be a place for drama, skits, and plays in non-liturgical settings and on weeknights and Saturdays. Youth groups, Christian schools, and other organizations may find legitimate use for non-liturgical didactic drama. It's less clear that dance can fulfill any didactic function.[49] Regardless, the performing arts should not be given access to the services of worship of Reformed Protestantism.

Modern Innovations

How are these principles to be applied to the use of images electronically projected upon large screens? Overhead projectors, slides, DVDs, "PowerPoint" are readily available. Should they be used? Some issues can be answered straightforward in light of principles already considered.

Images of God, facial images of Jesus, would still be strictly forbidden. Images are images whether they be third century mosaics or twenty-first century film-clips. Admittedly images of biblical characters or personalities from church history would be less risky, less susceptible to idolatry, when flashed upon a screen in worship services than when in a permanent form as in a fresco,

---

48 Fred Eastman & Louis Wilson, *Drama in the Church: A Manual of Religious Drama Production* (1932; New York: Samuel French, 1942).

49 For more on this, see Terry L. Johnson, *Reformed Worship: Worship that Is According to Scripture: Revised & Expanded* (Greenville, SC: Reformed Academic Press, 2003), 64–66.

mosaic, or statuary. Similarly film clips used for illustrative or didactic purposes would also be less vulnerable to the concerns of the second commandment. However to say that a practice is "less risky" is hardly an endorsement, and the same objections to their use in worship remain: their use implies the inadequacy of God's Word, they lack scriptural warrant and they are distracting. They should be excluded from the place of worship.

The question of temporary, electronically projected images is: are they consistent with a religion revealed through the word? Are they compatible with a religion spread through the "foolishness of preaching" (1 Corinthians 1:21 KJV)? Can the time used to project these images be justified, given the priority of the word (John 17:17; Romans 10:17)? In other words, why would a church that takes seriously the theology of the word want to use part of the finite time devoted to the public assembly to project images rather than pray, read Scripture, sing praise, preach, or administer the sacraments? The evidence is already piling up that the "law of diminishing returns" has set in, that young people have been saturated with images and are increasingly immune to their intended message, and real communication with youth takes place the old fashioned way: person to person.[50]

Finally, the projection upon large screens of the image of the one preaching within worship spaces, in overflow rooms, and in off-campus or remote sites (sometimes across the state, and even across the country, via satellite), raises questions about another kind of idolatry of which Bonhoeffer warned, the idolatry of hero-worship. Neil Postman, as astute observer of electronic media, warned, "The power of a close-up televised face, in color,

---

50 Michael Horton, *A Better Way Rediscovering the Drama of God-Centered Worship* (Grand Rapids, Michigan: Baker Books, 2002), 228ff.

makes idolatry a continual hazard. Television is, after all, a form of graven imagery far more alluring than a golden calf."[51] We would do well to take his warning seriously.

The technological sophistication of churches today is impressive. However, it is not at all obvious that complex electronics trumps biblical simplicity. There is a sobering sense in which we can say that the church has been down this road before, in the era of the Fathers, in the Middle Ages (spurring the Cistercian call to simplicity) and the Renaissance/Reformation era.

The issues which we face today are similar. In the name of outreach the ministry of the church is being pushed in the direction of the visual, whether the high-church ceremonial or the low-church technological. Now, as then, the argument of the advocates of visual media is that this is the way to reach our civilization. Now, as then, the church has to decide if faith comes by *hearing* or *seeing* the word of Christ (Romans 10:17).

Facilities & Appearances

We've looked at the interior arrangement of Reformed houses of worship. We will now give a more general consideration to facilities and their appearances. When I first began my ministry with the Independent Presbyterian Church of Savannah in January of 1987, there was one baby in the nursery and one couple under 40 years old active in the church. The nursery had been last painted and decorated in the 1970s, and looked it. It was worn, tattered, stained, and dated. I told the leadership of the church, "The first thing we need to do is renovate the nursery." The rebuttal was, "Why? We don't have any infants."

---

51 Postman, *Amusing Ourselves to Death*, 123.

My response was, "No, and we won't have any infants, or the young couples that bring them, if we don't make the nursery an appealing place for them to leave their children." Bill Hybels, Rick Warren, and Randy Pope are geniuses at eyeballing church facilities from the perspective of visitors. They encourage us to ask a number of questions about our building, grounds, and reception of guests. Those who have urged the church to "contextualize" its ministry are correct up to a point. We minister in a given cultural context. We are foolish not to accommodate that culture where we can without compromising principle. Attention should be given to the following items.

Regarding buildings & grounds

Adequate parking—if parking is difficult, people may find a more convenient place to attend or stop attending altogether. This is particularly a problem for urban churches but one which must be solved.

Posted signs—have signs everywhere telling people where to find what they need.

Grounds—lawn should be mowed, gardens well groomed and weeded. Landscaping should be attractive.

Neatness—trash should be picked up, clutter removed. A neat, tidy appearance should be a priority.

Restrooms—clean, well-stocked modern facilities should be maintained.

Nurseries—as noted, clean, safe, attractive nurseries are a must.

Wear & tear—where paint is chipping or carpets fraying, touch-up or replacement (as the case may apply) is necessary.

The common theme moving through this list is the evidence that someone is paying attention. Sloppy, dirty, cluttered, unkempt facilities beg the question, does anyone care about this church and its ministry? And if, as evidenced by the deteriorating church facility, they don't, why, a visitor might ask, should I? Our heavily didactic ministry is difficult enough for outsiders. Don't throw additional obstacles in the way.

Regarding members

Friendliness—an ethos of friendliness should be encouraged from the pulpit. Visitors should be eagerly sought out and greeted by church members. Rick Warren encourages a "three-minute rule," where members agree to talk to only people they've never met the first three minutes after the service ends. Periodically I encourage members to note the visitors around them and greet them following the service. We are surprised and dismayed in our vacation-time visits to other churches by how often visitors (like us) are ignored. How can a church ever hope to grow if its members don't create a warm, welcoming environment for outsiders?

Official greeters—we appoint elder and deacon couples to serve as greeters on a given Sunday on a rotating basis. This serves to "grease the rails" of friendliness and helps set the tone for the entire congregation.

Growth-oriented—behind the pro-visitor ethos of a church is a pro-growth ethos. As a young minister I would never have believed that there were churches that didn't want to grow. Then I encountered a church, or at least a segment of a church, that didn't. The leadership was comfortable with a little growth. They were eager enough to add a few young couples. Yet they wanted nothing on a scale that might threaten the existing power structure. For a ministry to multiply and a church to grow, it must want to grow. If it does, the outlook on and treatment of visitors will follow suit.

Regarding the environment of the service

Sound—a tradition that depends as heavily on the ministry of the word as does the Reformed must have an adequate sound system. Modern ears are accustomed to amplified, even highly amplified sound. An excellent acoustical environment is crucial, and should be enhanced by listening aids for the hearing impaired.

A frequently overlooked dimension of the acoustical quality has to do with the singing environment. Modern churches have tended to carpet their buildings like domestic living rooms. Architects have tended to kill the acoustics with sound absorbing materials and then overcome the deadness with electronic amplification. The problem is that carpets and acoustical tiles suffocate congregational singing. Congregations are discouraged in singing when their experience is like that of shouting into a pillow. Hard surfaces should be maintained throughout worship spaces so as to encourage the experience of strong congregational singing. If the congregational singing of psalms and biblical hymns is an element of worship, an environment that encourages, rather than discourages, congregational singing should be maintained.

Lighting—one of my predecessors at the Independent Presbyterian Church used to keep the shutters on the large 30-foot high Palladian windows shut and then, to top it off, dim the lights for the sermon! Older members could testify to the excellent sleeping environment it provided. I protested to the church staff to no effect. After too many Sundays in dreary darkness I personally spent a morning opening dozens and dozens of shutters, downstairs and in the balcony. "Let the sunshine in!" I shouted tongue-in-cheek, as I secured the cooperation of the chairman of the diaconate to turn up the lights "full-blast." Do not underestimate the importance of a well-lit room. On the other hand, make sure that the lighting is soft, not harsh, human, not industrial.

Temperature—Warren warns with the "utmost conviction" that "temperature can destroy the best planned service in a matter of minutes! When people are too hot or too cold they stop participating. They mentally check out and start hoping for everything to end quickly."[52] He claims that the most common mistake churches make is to set the temperature too warm. Combine the above problem, dim lighting, with a warm room and the preacher faces a stiff challenge in just keeping the congregation awake. The room should not only be well-lit but slightly cool.

Seating—during the summer on Sunday nights our congregation meets at a nearby camp facility in the main lodge. I am a fanatic about the comfort and arrangement of the chairs. I don't want to get a "great deal" on cheap seats from the local warehouse. The adage is true: the mind can only absorb what the seat can endure.[53] This is not the place to cut costs. Also the arrangement can make all the difference in the world. The congregation should be packed in comfortably tight around the pulpit, close to the preacher and in sight of one another without personal space being violated. Ideally the arrangement should be nearly as wide as it is deep. Too deep and one has a tunnel effect, which discourages both communication and fellowship. Too wide and one fails to see a majority of the congregation at any given moment, and is forced frequently to look from side to side. Slightly long and nearly as wide serves both the auditory

---

52   Warren, *Purpose-Driven Church*, 268.
53   Cited by Warren, Ibid. 266.

(preaching, reading, praying, singing) and fellowship purposes of the service.

Announcements—a British friend of mine told a story about visiting a large Presbyterian church in the United States in which an elder gave about five minutes of announcements, and then was followed by another five minutes by the pastor as he repeated the same announcements again, but with greater emphasis. We limit our announcements to three, or at the most four, and restrict them to those which pertain to the whole congregation. We also urge that the congregation read the weekly newsletter and bulletin. Announcements will gobble-up worship time if allowed to do so. We start announcements several minutes before the worship hour so as to start the service itself right on time.

This concludes our discussion of preparing the setting of worship. Those of us on the "purist" end of the church spectrum should not underestimate the importance of these physical factors. Matthew Henry's counsel to "those who are serious in religion" is that when they are seeking to persuade others "to that which is good," they "should make it as cheap and easy to them as may be."[54] We repeat ourselves: our theology and worship is difficult enough. It's hard to be Reformed. We require twice on Sunday worship, a strict Sabbath, daily family worship, and the catechizing of children. Our services are heavily didactic. We should not drive people off by careless negligence. Some of us, perhaps, in the name of honoring the sovereignty of God, have gone Gnostic, treating people like disembodied spirits for whom the physical and aesthetic environment were of no consequence. If the proponents of historic Reformed ministry and worship wish to see their tribe increase, they must give focused attention

---

54 Henry, *Commentary*, 2 Ch 35:7.

to parking, grounds, restrooms, nurseries, upkeep and overall appearance of the physical plant. They cannot avoid issues of acoustics, lighting, temperature, and seating, as well as the overall friendliness of the congregation. There is nothing about these concerns that is incompatible with Reformed theology, a high regard for the sovereignty of God, or a priority placed on the work of the Holy Spirit. It is merely to practice biblical wisdom, to understand the nature of people and things, to take into account the physical and material dimension of the human experience, and accommodate that dimension as we rely on the supernatural work of the Holy Spirit working through the word.

When we have prepared the minister and the setting, our work is not yet through. The congregation also must be carefully considered. Every congregation has its own personality. Each church has its own culture. The whole project of reforming the church's ministry and worship could implode at this point. How then are we to proceed? Carefully. Very carefully.

❧ Chapter 7 ❧

Preparing the Congregation

Because this is a gimmick-driven and entertainment-crazed church environment, congregations are unlikely easily to embrace the serious, substantial, simple/spiritual worship of Reformed Protestantism. A multi-faceted approach to informing and persuading regular folks of the value of historic Reformed Protestantism is likely to be necessary. This has certainly been the case in Savannah, and our example may prove instructive for others.

Savannah background

At first blush the Independent Presbyterian Church of Savannah, with its classically Reformed architecture and large, solid-mahogany central pulpit, balcony with choir and organ in the back, looks like a place where historic Reformed worship would be easy to implement, if indeed it was ever unimplemented.

304 *Serving with Calvin*

But the fact is that when the present writer began his ministry there in January 1987, there was not a single member who would have identified himself or herself as Reformed in theology or ecclesiology. There were large numbers of mainline Protestants and a significant number of Columbia Bible College evangelicals. But no one was self-consciously Reformed.

Moreover, none of the classic elements of Reformed worship were present. The congregation knew nothing of *lectio continua* Scripture reading, of sequential expository preaching, of metrical psalm singing, of a full-diet of Scripture-based and enriched prayer, or frequent communion. Facing all the difficulties of a downtown church in a decaying urban setting, the congregation was slowly dying. Sunday morning attendance averaged 238 in 1986 in a facility that seats over a thousand, even plunging into the 130–140 range during the summer months. Sunday School attendance was under a hundred. Only a couple dozen of the faithful returned for Sunday night. Hostile factions were bitterly competing for larger pieces of a shrinking church-pie. As one of Savannah's most popular doctors said of his visit to the church in the mid-1980s, "It was the sorriest excuse for a church I'd ever seen." The facility, though magnificent, was deteriorating. Desperate to grow, the congregation called an inexperienced 31-year-old to lead it out of its troubles, thinking that youth would attract youth, and the church's decline would reverse.[1]

Savannah ministry

Shortly after arriving in Savannah a member of the secretarial staff urged me, "What are you going to do to make this church

---

[1] For those interested in more about this history, see David Calhoun's magnificent study, *Splendor of Grace* (Greenville, SC: A Press Printing, 2005), the history of the Independent Presbyterian Church from 1755–2005.

grow?" Her church background led her to anticipate an answer filled with novel programs and creative ministry. I gave her an old school answer: "We'll preach and pray." I took seriously the counsel of my mentor Dr. James Baird, then pastor of First Presbyterian Church of Jackson, Mississippi, who cautioned me: "Don't change anything for five years." For the most part, I didn't. I tweaked the order of service slightly, moving the announcements to before the call to worship. The other changes were equally subtle. I immediately began an expository series on the Gospel of Mark, following Calvin's pattern of preaching mainly the Gospels and Acts on Sunday morning. Several weeks later I began a second series of expositions on Sunday evening on Daniel, and a third for the Wednesday noon service on James. I also immediately started the practice of selecting as one of our three "hymns" in each Sunday service a setting of a metrical psalm from the hymnal, and identifying it as such in the bulletin in order to help the congregation grow accustomed to singing psalms. Finally I added an Old Testament reading to complement the New Testament or *vice versa*, depending on which Testament was being preached. It would be a few years before this reading would be *lectio continua* or before we would change from quarterly to monthly communion. But most of the elements of historic Reformed worship were in place within the first few weeks or months of my ministry. It was a stealth revolution.

Growth

What happened? We grew. Rapidly. Not spectacularly by mega-church standards. Yet all the numbers, people and income, doubled and tripled within a couple of years. We added 75 members a year, attendance increased to an average of 400 on Sunday morning (today it is 550+). We increased eight-fold on Sunday night, and Sunday School more than doubled. Our growth was noteworthy enough that a denominational church-planting official came to Savannah and took me to lunch to find out the keys to our growth. "What are you doing to grow the church?" he asked. I answered, "I inherited a beautiful facility and a fine order of service. Otherwise, I'm not doing anything unusual. We have no programs *per se*." He looked back at me surprised and somewhat perplexed. I continued, "We have a simple ministry of preaching and prayer that God is blessing. That is all." So it was and so it continues to be.

It helps to stay in one place for an extended period. I have referred to my first years in Savannah as a "seven years' war." Since then we have been an exceptionally happy, unified, and steadily growing congregation. We have gone from being a primarily elderly church in 1987 to where today 53% of our members (communing and non-communing) are under 40 years of age (32% are under 20), and 37% have been members for less than 5 years. Our largest single demographic is young families with children. Because we have a traditional building and service, we attract substantial numbers of retirees who have settled in the Savannah area. Typically they are mainline Protestants and frequently six months after joining with a barely credible profession of faith, they will say to me, "You know, I don't think I was a real believer before I joined this church." Fifteen percent of our in-town membership is 65 years of age or older, and 5% have been members for over 40 years.

The above statistics demonstrate that generational balance is a benefit of a ministry that features both a reverent, well-ordered traditional service and vigorous expository preaching. Because our service is designed for *no one group in particular* it is designed for *everyone in general*. Because we are targeting no single group we draw from across the demographic spectrum. We have managed to hang onto our original membership while adding just over 1500 new adult members in our 28 years. The vast majority of these new members have not come from a conservative Presbyterian background. Very few of them have had any prior contact with Reformed Protestantism, and fewer still had any prior knowledge of historic Reformed ministry and worship. Some were not Christians at all. Most of our new members have been mainline Protestants or low-church evangelicals from Baptist, Methodist, and Bible-church backgrounds. Far from being an impediment to growth, according to a recent sample survey of our congregation, 75% of our new members have joined *because* of our worship and preaching.[2]

Ministry today

Today we sing metrical psalms and classic hymns, preach sequential expository sermons, read Scripture *lectio continua*, pray extensively, administer monthly communion, and have an evening service. We also observe the Sabbath, catechize our children, and practice family worship like our Presbyterian forefathers. Our congregational life is simple, revolving around the activities of the Lord's Day. This is intentional. We aim to leave the midweek schedules of our members uncluttered by church activities. On Sunday we gather for Sunday School at 9:30 a.m., morning worship at 11:00 a.m., and evening worship at 5:30 p.m. Following the evening service each week we have a congregational meal, which greatly enhances the opportunities for fellowship in a largely commuter downtown church such as ours.

---

2   For full details see my dissertation, "A Study of Making the Case for Historic Reformed Worship," submitted to the faculty of Erskine Theological Seminary in candidacy for the degree of Doctor of Ministry in May 2008.

The Sunday evening service and fellowship supper move to our camp facility on Talahi Island from Labor Day to Memorial Day (the end of May to the first of September), further enhancing the fellowship and family life of the church. Mid-week Bible studies are also available for those whose needs go beyond those met through the Sunday services and daily family prayers in homes. The congregation is overwhelmingly happy and increasingly pleased over time with the shape of our ministry, with 94% of the current congregation using words like "comfortable," "appealing," "stimulating," and "moving" to describe their experience! This contrasts sharply with the seeker churches where hanging onto "churched Harry" is as big a challenge as attracting "unchurched Charlie."

Getting there

The problem we faced in 1987 was not unlike that of any church attempting to implement Reformed ministry and worship. I needed to convince a partially indifferent, partially broad evangelical and thoroughly unreformed congregation of the truth of the Reformed faith and the importance of Reformed ministry and worship. We needed as well to attract and retain new members, as would a church-planter. Neither the existing congregation nor those who joined had any appreciation for either the Reformed faith or Reformed worship. Neither was there a model of a church of our size and stature practicing Reformed ministry and worship anywhere in our region. We were without examples to follow. The need, then, was to build a consensus in both the existing congregation and the new members, a consensus that embraced both the Reformed faith and the ministry and worship that flows from it, without dividing the church or driving off significant numbers of members in the process. How was this done?

Worship services

Without a doubt the key to the successful implementation of Reformed ministry and worship has been the services themselves. When led with urgency, fervor, and an economy of language, the services are their own best argument. When given a range of choices (e.g. newsletters, books, pamphlets, special classes), 89% of our sample survey said that attending services was the most important factor in convincing them of the value of historic Reformed worship.

In *Worshipping with Calvin* we described what was for us "self-authenticating" encounters with the elements of historic Reformed worship. There is a "well, of course" quality to each of them: of course psalms should be sung; of course we should read Scripture in our worship; of course a proper sermon should explain a text of Scripture; of course our prayers should echo the praises, confessions, thanksgiving, and petitions of Scripture; of course the Lord's Supper should be frequently administered. All this makes perfect sense. Who would have thought otherwise? When ordinary folks hear strong congregational singing of biblical texts, hear a nuanced reading of Scripture, hear a carefully applied biblical exposition, or hear impassioned scriptural prayer, many will find the experience convincing, as I did as a young man, and as many in our congregation have. "This is what we are supposed to do in worship," they will say, as they witness the word sung, read, preached, prayed, and administered. There is no substitute for well-led services morning and evening each Lord's Day, to convince those unfamiliar or ignorant of the worship of Reformed Protestantism.

Inquirers' Class

All of our new members are expected to take our Inquirers' Class. It consists of seven sessions in which we move progressively, pyramid-like from the church catholic (a mini-history of the Christian church), to the church Protestant (the five so-called "Solas"), to the church Reformed.

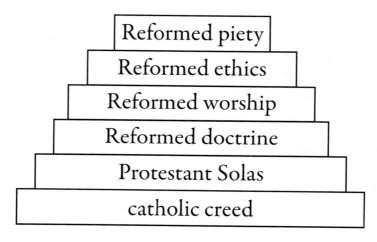

From the broad base of catholicity we progressively get more narrow, viewing our distinctives in the context of our shared heritage and theology with all of Christendom. One of our seven sessions is devoted to Reformed ministry and worship. I discuss from John 4 the importance of worship, the meaning of "spirit" and 'truth,' and then explain the "elements" of our service (i.e. preaching, singing, etc.), while distinguishing them from "forms" and "circumstances." Fifty-one percent of our surveyed respondents said that Inquirers' Classes played an important role in convincing them of the value of historic Reformed worship.

Officers' Training Class

This class is for officer candidates (though open to all men in the church) and is offered bi-annually. It consists of an inductive study of the *Westminster Confession of Faith*. Like the Inquirers' Class, it places worship and ministry (as described in I.6, XXI–XXII and XXVII–XXIX of the Confession) in the broader context of a comprehensive survey of Reformed theology. One hundred fifty men have completed this class in twenty-eight years. Today these men form the backbone of the church. As far as humanly can be discerned, these men ensure that the Independent Presbyterian Church will continue faithfully to preach the Reformed faith and practice historic Reformed ministry and worship into the distant future. Because of the more detailed discussion of worship issues in this class beyond what is possible in the Inquirers' Class, 89% of our surveyed officers said that this class played an important role in convincing them of the value of historic Reformed worship.

Pastor's writings

Periodically I have written newsletter articles and preached sermons, and then collected those articles and sermons and made them into pamphlets and books for the use of our congregation and beyond.[3] Forty-two percent have found our publications to be valuable in solidifying their convictions regarding Reformed worship. We recommend that pastors write for their congregation what they preach to their congregation. Pamphlets provide a

---

3　e.g. IPC pamphlets: "Worship & Music Today;" "The Lord's Supper;" "An Evangelical & Reformed Faith;" and books: Trinity Psalter; Reformed Worship; The Pastor's Public Ministry; Leading in Worship; The Family Worship Book; The Case for Traditional Protestantism, When Grace Comes Alive: Living Through the Lord's Prayer (Ross-shire, Scotland: Christian Focus Publications, 2003).

312   *Serving with Calvin*

handy resource to which church members can turn to solidify their convictions.

Reformation & Heritage Sundays

Each year we observe three historic services, one recalling our Reformation heritage, the other two our Georgia and Scottish heritages. The first of these we instituted. The latter two we inherited. Frankly, three such services is overkill. However, we have attempted to redeem them by adapting historic Reformed orders of service for use on those Sundays. We rotate the use of two of the following on an annual basis: The Genevan *Form of Church Prayers* (1542), Knox's *Form of Prayers* (1556), the *Book of Common Prayer* (1552), the Westminster *Directory for the Public Worship of God* (1644), and Richard Baxter's *The Savoy Liturgy* (1661).[4]

The value in using these historic orders has been to provide perspective. Today's Christians are able to see first-hand what previous generations of Christians have understood about ministry and worship. The depth and substance of these services can be eye-opening. At the conclusion of one such service in a church with a rather informal Sunday night service, an older member came to me and said, "I wish we could do this every week." Since every generation tends to absorb uncritically the bias of its own era, a breath of liturgical sanity from the past can play a valuable role in stimulating a reassessment of the liturgical present. Openness to reassessment is exactly what we need as we attempt to restore historic Reformed worship today.

In addition to the above, periodically we have offered Sunday

---

4   For adapted forms of these orders see Johnson, *Leading in Worship*, 121–150; *Leading in Worship: Revised & Expanded*, 185–237. For the originals, see Thompson, *Liturgies of the Western Church*, 185–405.

School classes dealing with worship issues, and have from time to time promoted publications in our bookshop as well as recordings of classic hymns and metrical psalms.

Our approach, then, has been multi-pronged. Our survey of our congregation confirmed what we have observed. Our members by large majorities and across the various demographic categories have joined *because* of our historic Reformed ministry and worship; regard the worship services as the favorite part of the church program; grow increasingly positive in their outlook over time; find the preaching and singing (traditional hymnody and metrical psalmody) to be especially appealing; find very little that they would like to change; find little attraction in contemporary forms of worship; and have found actually participating in the Reformed worship the most convincing apologetic, though other means have contributed. We have been largely successful in achieving a high level of knowledge and conviction regarding the value of Reformed worship and in achieving a high level of awareness of and rejection of alternatives to Reformed worship. With respect to various means of reaching these goals, attending services has been far and away the most effective. However, the others means employed have also proven effective: pamphlets, books, Inquirers' Classes, Officers' Training, Sunday School, and other literature all received high marks from our surveyed members. The conclusion to draw, it would seem, is that a multi-faceted approach is wise, each means reinforcing the other in the overall effort to persuade contemporary people of the value of Reformed ministry and worship and its relative superiority to the alternatives.

314

❧ Chapter 8 ❧

Mistakes to Avoid

It remains for us to underscore several cautions about implementing historic Reformed worship. There are common pitfalls to avoid if we are to be "wise master builder(s)" like the Apostle Paul. Like the Apostle Paul, Reformed ministries recognize the sovereignty of God in church growth. The human agent is secondary.

I planted, Apollos watered, but God gave the growth. (1 Corinthians 3:6)

The kingdom of God grows because God "causes" (NASB) or "gives the growth."

So neither he who plants nor he who waters is anything, but only God who gives the growth. (1 Corinthians 3:7)

Still, the human agent and human means are not irrelevant. There is a relationship between the means and fruitful ministry.

> *According to the grace of God given to me, like a skilled master builder I laid a foundation, and someone else is building upon it. Let each one take care how he builds upon it.* (1 Corinthians 3:10)

The Apostle Paul builds only "according to the grace of God given to me," yet he builds as a "wise" (NASB) or "skilled master builder," and each servant of Christ must "be careful" (NASB), not careless, not indifferent, but "take care how he builds" upon the foundation which is Christ.

> *For no one can lay a foundation other than that which is laid, which is Jesus Christ.* (1 Corinthians 3:11)

Christ alone is the foundation, and yet one can wisely build the church out of that which is enduring or unwisely build the church out of that which will not endure.

> *Now if anyone builds on the foundation with gold, silver, precious stones, wood, hay, straw—each one's work will become manifest, for the Day will disclose it, because it will be revealed by fire, and the fire will test what sort of work each one has done.* (1 Corinthians 3:12–13)

The difference between the two sets of materials (gold, silver, precious stones vs. wood, hay, straw) is that one endures while the other is temporal. One is expensive and the other is cheap. One is difficult to work with but lasts while the other is quick and easy. One remains while the other burns up.

> *If the work that anyone has built on the foundation survives, he will receive a reward. If anyone's work is burned up, he will suffer loss, though he himself will be saved, but only as through fire.* (1 Corinthians 3:14–15)

Looking at the preceding discussion in 1 Corinthians 1 and 2, the cheap and easy approach to church building involves compromise that moves in one of two directions, or both. The first direction is to tone down the gospel and the second is to dress it up. The first involves *content*.

> *For the word of the cross is folly to those who are perishing, but to us who are being saved it is the power of God.* (1 Corinthians 1:18)

There are those for whom the gospel message is "foolishness." Corinthian Greeks, proud of their Greek intellectual heritage, found the gospel unsophisticated, unrespectable, simplistic by the standard of Greek philosophy. The returning editor of *Christian Century* magazine, in his recent "parting shot," denied the transcendent significance of the cross. This is the "Greek" outlook. There will always be those who will not find Christianity intellectually plausible.

> *For Jews demand signs and Greeks seek wisdom, but we preach Christ crucified, a stumbling block to Jews and folly to Gentiles* (1 Corinthians 1:22–23)

The simple message of "Christ-crucified" is "folly" to some, offensive to others, lacking, in the former view, subtlety, nuance, sensitivity, sophistication. Yet it is the wisdom of God and the power of God for salvation (1:24–25).

The second temptation to compromise is in the area of *delivery*. Verse 21 speaks literally of the foolishness of "preaching" (*kerygma*). Given the theme of 1 Corinthians 2:1–5, it is arguable that the Apostle Paul has in mind both the *method* of presentation and the *message*. He includes both at the beginning of his second chapter:

> And I, when I came to you, brothers, did not come proclaiming to you the testimony of God with lofty speech or wisdom. (1 Corinthians 2:1)

Notice both "speech" and "wisdom," delivery and content are in view. Next he focuses on content:

> For I decided to know nothing among you except Jesus Christ and him crucified. (1 Corinthians 2:2)

Then he returns to method:

> And I was with you in weakness and in fear and much trembling, (1 Corinthians 2:3)

When we remember the Greek love of rhetoric and their development of the rhetorical arts, the Apostle's point becomes clear. The Greeks appreciated, even demanded, the employment of sophisticated rhetorical methods. The Apostle Paul would have been familiar with them. Yet he refuses to use them. Why? He explains:

> *and my speech and my message were not in plausible words of wisdom, but in demonstration of the Spirit and of power* (1 Corinthians 2:4)

See the distinction again. His "speech" (*logos*) or "message" (NASB) and his "preaching" (*kerygma* content and delivery are both in view. He did not utilize "persuasive" (NASB) or "plausible words of wisdom," lest,

> ... your faith might not rest in the wisdom of men but in the power of God. (1 Corinthians 2:5)

A simple gospel (*content*) demands a simple delivery (*method*) lest the latter obscure or overpower the former, lest one's faith rest not on God but man's persuasive powers.

This is why we and the Reformers before us have urged simple services of the word. This is why we have favored a "plain style" of ministry in which the word is read, preached, sung, prayed, and seen, without embellishments, and in a plain setting.

Yet have we implemented historic Reformed worship wisely or unwisely? Have we been "skilled master builders"? At times we have been our own worst enemies. At times we have been bad advertisements for that which we champion, with poorly conducted and unappealing services.

General concerns

What are our concerns? We may begin with three general areas of application.

Faith or presumption?

First, we are concerned with the confusion of faith with

320 *Serving with Calvin*

presumption. Jesus teaches in the "Parable of the Seed" that the sower scatters seed and goes to bed. The seed grows *automatos*, "by itself," "he knows not how" (Mark 4:26–29). A stronger affirmation of the sovereignty of God in the growth of the kingdom of God can scarcely be imagined. We sleep, the kingdom grows. We rightly are thrilled by Luther's words:

> We should preach the Word, but the results must be left solely to God's good pleasure ... I opposed indulgences and all the papists, but never with force. I simply taught, preached, and wrote God's word; otherwise I did nothing. And while I slept, or drank Wittenberg beer with my friends Philip and Arnsdorf, the Word so greatly weakened the papacy that no prince or emperor ever inflicted such losses upon it. I did nothing; the Word did everything.[1]

My early years in Savannah the denominational officials were impressed with the growth of our congregation. They paid me a visit. "What are you doing?" they asked. "Nothing special," was my response. They were expecting some wonderful new ministry innovation to be unveiled. "We just preach and pray," I said.

Yet, there can be a problem with this. Trust in the power of God through ordinary means can become an excuse for negligence and sloth. Does belief in the sovereign grace of God mean that no attention need to be paid to *excellence*? Can we present to the world a Mayberry choir, unskilled musicians, Aunt Mabel solos, uninspired announcements and prayers by elders, microphones that don't work, and the whole stamped with mediocrity?

---

1   Martin Luther, *Luther's Works*, 51:77, found at a number of locations on the internet.

Does belief in the sovereign grace of God mean that no attention need be paid to *neatness* and *tidiness*? May our facilities be sloppy, messy, disordered with 1970s décor, smells, and stains? May our facilities be in such disarray (as I fear often they are) that they scream to visitors that no one cares about beauty, order, cleanliness, or what visitors might think?

Does belief in the sovereign grace of God mean no attention need be paid to *room dynamics*? We are not gnostics. We take seriously human nature as embodied souls living in a physical world. We should understand that it matters if the church gathers in a huge room with small numbers. Or in a basement without natural light. Or in a carpeted room with lousy acoustics that smothers the singing. Or in a room that is too hot or too cold. Or in a facility that is inconveniently located.

God can build a great church at any place and at any time. A congregation can meet in a tent, as did Calvary Chapel in Costa Mesa, California, in the early years of Chuck Smith's ministry, and Jesus can build a vast congregation. Yet this is no reason to discounting the importance of an excellent and public presentation, neatness, beauty, and proper room dynamics.

What we actually mean when we say that we simply preach and pray is that these fundamental means stir up the people of God to action. The preaching and praying inspires generous and sacrificial *giving*. We're not saying that all the church needs is preaching and praying and that it doesn't need money. No, the primary means inspire the secondary means.

The preaching and praying *motivates* outreach. The members of the congregation are inspired by the preaching to urge others to "come and see" their church and its ministry (John 1:46). The "gatherers" begin to gather their friends and acquaintances and bring them to church. This is essential if a church is to grow.

The preaching and praying inspires the congregation to care for its *facilities*. Members begin to care about what visitors see when they walk through the doors. Let's be careful about what we mean when we say that all we do is preach, pray and trust God. What we really mean is that we preach, pray, and trust God to motivate the congregation to care for all the secondary means by which a ministry grows.

Faithfulness or failure?

Rousas J. Rushdoony once wrote of some of the "split 'p'" Presbyterian congregations that for them the sign of faithfulness was failure. Motyer points out that in the 28 chapters of Acts there are 37 references to growth. This is why he suggests a more apt title for Acts would be "The Growing Church."[2] There is a *presumption of* growth in the New Testament. Is there a problem with complacency among the Reformed? We are concerned that too many pastors are content to lead remnant churches consisting of no more than a few dozen members. Are we satisfied with no growth, year after year after year?

Admittedly it is hard to be a traditional Presbyterian. Members are expected to attend services Sunday morning *and* Sunday evening. They're expected to observe a Sunday Sabbath *all day* long! They're expected to conduct daily family worship. They're expected to catechize their children. The leadership practices church discipline, corralling wayward members. Presbyterians are so uptight! Plus, they have no fun stuff, like praise bands, skits, light shows, or pyrotechnics. It has to be admitted, we'll never grow like the novelty-driven mega-churches.

Still, is the gospel the power of God (Romans 1:16)? Did Jesus

---

2   Motyer, *Preaching?*, 19.

not promise to build His church (Matthew 16:18)? Did He not commission us in the context of assertions of His almighty power and continuing presence with us (Matthew 28:18ff)? We can never be content with not growing both in depth and in numbers. Ordinarily, faithful churches should grow, and "failure" should be carefully scrutinized.

Pace or imprudence?

Third, we are concerned with the confusion of proper pace with prudence. On the one hand we are concerned with interminable delays in instituting worship reforms. Some ministers and sessions seem to be waiting perpetually for the right time. They've been waiting to introduce metrical psalm-singing, yet 10 years have now passed. There are no psalters in the pews. They're not even singing the metrical psalms found in the hymnal. They're not even photocopying the easy psalms found in modern versions such as the *Trinity Psalter* (there are dozens and dozens of them!).

Some have been convinced for years that they should introduce *lectio continua* (i.e. sequential) Bible readings to their services, but they haven't. Why not? Some realized years ago that their musicians and singer should not be up-front like stage performers, yet have done nothing to place them more appropriately on the side, or better, in the back. These hesitations are justified in the name of prudential pace of change, of course. Yet at times this caution borders on cowardice. Meanwhile, congregations are deprived of the sanctifying benefits of crucial elements of Reformed worship.

On the other hand, some others may be guilty of *imprudent haste*. They make the same mistakes as the ecclesiastical radicals. They evidence little or not *sensitivity* to the *culture* of the church.

Every church has a culture. That is, every church has accustomed ways of doing things. Every church has an ethos.

Everything in the church has a name on it. Someone started it, created it, donated it, approved it, and cherishes it. Before change can be implemented, the advocates of change must gain the trust of the people. Agents of change are wise to proceed carefully, sensitively, laying the theological/biblical groundwork for change, earning the right to make changes. Rush the process, and hurt, division, and loss of members inevitably results. Listen to the Apostle Paul's instructions to Timothy:

> *Do not rebuke an older man but encourage him as you would a father, younger men as brothers, older women as mothers, younger women as sisters, in all purity.* (1 Timothy 5:1–2)

Established members are to be treated like fathers and mothers. This means honoring their customs and practices, as well as honoring the persons (Exodus 20:12). As noted, in Savannah we tweaked the public services in ways hardly noticeable. We added psalms by singing them from the hymnal. We built on the Scripture reading before the sermon by adding a second reading. We subtly added prayer genres until we had established a "full-diet" of prayer. We preached as had always been done, but now the sermons were sequential expositions.

On the other hand, we tolerated a Chrismon tree in our place of worship for 15 Christmas seasons, and advent candle lightings for nearly as long. We still have a "Kirkin O' the Tartans" service with some highly dubious characteristics. These are wisdom issues. Don't rush, but don't delay either.

Specific concerns

Beyond the general concerns, we have specific concerns as well.

Reverential or liturgical?

First, we are concerned that the reverential is being confused with the liturgical, as if we need only borrow an item or two from the *Book of Common Prayer* and will have reformed our service. The temptation to take this route is easy enough to understand. There is so much silliness in worship today that a sharp backlash is understandable. Those wishing to escape the trivialities of our day can find a quick fix from Anglican services. The pendulum tends to swing from Willow Creek all the way to Canterbury's anglo-catholic wing, bypassing the balance found in Reformed worship. Liturgical responses, such as the *sursum corda*, the *Gloria*, and the *sanctus* are implemented, along with responsive readings, written unison prayers, litanies, plus the external trappings of crosses, candles, liturgical colors, clerical stoles and collars, and the liturgical calendar, especially Advent and Lent.

Once I showed the Rev. Dr. William Ralston, former English professor at the University of the South and Rector of St. John's Episcopal Church of Savannah, a bulletin from a liturgically-minded Presbyterian church. He laughed out loud, scoffing at the mishandling of the liturgy by Episcopal wannabees. Lesson: Presbyterians make poor Anglicans, even as we make poor Charismatics.

Liturgical prayers and responses tend to squeeze out free prayer. Among the great strengths of historic Reformed worship is its tradition of passionate and targeted free prayer. Similarly the liturgical calendar tends to squeeze out the *lectio continua*, both reading and preaching, as calendar themes usurp sequential commitments. Reverential worship is found in the solemnity with which the elements are handled, not in the degree to which the episcopal is mimicked. Don't settle for a superficial fix that consists primarily of form.

Depth or length?

Those of us fleeing from the banalities of contemporary worship above all don't want to be shallow. Whatever we do in worship, it must not be superficial. We wholeheartedly agree with John Stott that sermonettes will breed Christianettes. No 30-second prayers for us. We pray for 10 to 15 minutes. No sermonettes for us. We deliver 45–60 minutes of tightly-reasoned biblical exposition. Our services last from 1–1/2 to 1–3/4 hours.

This lengthening of the parts of the service, and the service as a whole, we believe, is a mistake. The long prayers, long sermons, and long services are a trial for most of God's people. Some of them eventually will drop out of the Sunday evening service, finding it "too much" to endure what seems like an endless evening service after an endless morning service. Still others will give up all together and move to a church where the services are less stressful.

Length, it needs to be said, does not equal depth. Some of the most successful mega-church pastors preach long sermons. The difference is their messages are only puddle deep. Length is a wisdom issue. It is wiser, we believe, to pray for 5 minutes, preach for 30 minutes, and meet for 1 to 1–1/4 hours. These are target numbers and so necessarily imprecise. However, we recommend remaining in the range of those figures, that is, 5 minute but not 10 minute prayers, 30 minute but not 45 minute sermons, 1 hour but not 1–1/2 hour services.

One can stick with the longer times. However, the likely result will be a small, remnant church that doesn't experience much growth. Remnant churches do an excellent job of catching whales, or spiritual giants, but typically a poor job of catching spiritual guppies. Let's not forget that at some point along the time spectrum the law of diminishing returns sets in. Perhaps some are convinced that that only would be after a two-hour sermon, a one-hour prayer, and a four-hour service, as with the Puritans. Still, *at some point long has become too long.* When exactly that point is reached is a wisdom issue about which we must think very carefully.

Fervency or frequency?

Third, we are concerned that fervency is being confused with frequency. This concern has particularly to do with the Lord's Supper. Among a number of *serious* pastors and *serious* churches weekly communion has become common. It is widely regarded as a sign of spiritual *seriousness*, particularly understandable in the content of the silliness of so much of today's church.

Yet weekly communion has never been a practice of the Reformed church, whether on the continent of Europe, among the Puritans of England, the Scottish Presbyterians, or their New World descendants (though it has had its advocates—see Chapter V, "Sacraments"). The verdict of the Reformed church has been that *careful* observance is to be preferred to *weekly* observance, that *intensity* was to take priority over *frequency*. Consequently, "communion seasons" were developed in which the Lord's Supper clearly came to play a central role in the life of the church. In the context of the covenant meal commitments to Christ were made and renewed. The mutual obligations of God and His people were sealed and confirmed. Don't confuse the *importance* of the Lord's Supper with the *frequency* of administration. Both history and contemporary observation deny a necessary connection between the two. Indeed, denominations which practice weekly communion struggle with rote and mindless participation. Further anecdotal evidence is that many Reformed churches practicing weekly communion are forced by time constraints to rush its administration. Infrequent (i.e. monthly) communion allows for greater focus, greater intensity, and greater emphasis to be placed on communion when it is served, and make it less likely that its observance will be routine.

Spirit or form?

Fourth, we are concerned that right spirit is being confused with right form. Given the dearth of substantial prayer today, we understandably are eager to utilize the six basic prayer genres, the "full-diet" of prayer: praise, confession of sin, thanksgiving, intercessions, illumination, and benediction. So we may have put the *form* in place. However, what about the *context* of those prayers? What about their *delivery*? We may have the correct form and yet our prayers may be insipid: meandering, cliché, indistinct. They may lack passion or urgency.

Given the dearth of truly expository preaching, we understandably are eager to load our sermons with rich biblical content. However, too often our sermons are not sermons but lectures, delivered without urgency, without application, without exhortation, and without obvious relevance to ordinary people. We're doing the right thing. Yet the heart of the matter, the spirit with which the matter is undertaken, is neglected. Our preaching (and praying) should be persuasive and passionate or they will fall flat, and fail to accomplish that for which we have hoped worked all of our lives.

Primary means or only means?

The English-speaking Reformed church identifies three *primary* means of grace, the word, sacraments, and prayer (see *Shorter Catechism #88*). These properly receive our focus, our attention, our energy, our resources, our emphasis. Yet this does not mean that we can ignore everything else. We are concerned that the primary means of grace may be emphasized at the expense of *relationships*. Some Reformed pastors may be tempted to hide in their studies, and thereby neglect the kitchen table, the coffee house, and the counseling room.

Linger long after services. Be the last to leave. Be available for questions and conversation. Pastor the people. Alec Motyer recalls a minister whose "position gave him the right to preach; but Monday to Saturday, he was not purchasing the right to be heard."[3] Healthy relationships, or more to the point, our pastoral care, is crucial, if our ordinary means ministry is to be received. "The diligent pastor," says Motyer, "is the most welcome preacher."[4]

We are concerned that the primary means of grace may be emphasized at the expense of *facilities*, concern for which we now return. In 1841 the Independent Presbyterian Church of Savannah had a beautiful "meeting house," but no restrooms, classrooms, nurseries, or offices. By 1871 classrooms for Sunday School had been added. Not until 1928 were offices and restrooms, a kitchen and fellowship hall added. Not until 1950 were nurseries. At any point along the way the objection might have been raised, "Why should we spend all this money to add restrooms (or nurseries, etc.). We've never had them before and we've done fine." The

---

3 Motyer, *Preaching?*, 134.
4 Ibid.

reason the money should be spent is because expectations change over time. The *luxuries* of one generation become the *necessities* of the next. Of course, one could do without any of the above. Yet, would it be wise? Would it enhance the ministry of the church to ignore the expectation that the church will have classrooms for Sunday School, nurseries for infants and young children, and restrooms for all? We think not. It is important for the church to keep pace with these expectations. We'll never change what we do in the worship services themselves. Our worship practices are determined by Scripture. However, the circumstances of our services, and the circumstances surrounding our services, are determined by Christian prudence (*Westminster Confession of Faith*, I.7). If this generation expects heating in the winter, we better provide it. If this generation expects air conditioning in the summer, we better provide it. If this generation expects nurseries and restrooms, we better keep pace with those expectations.

We are concerned that the primary means of grace may be emphasized at the expense of *public engagement.* The issue we raise is that of communication. The Apostle Paul went to Mars Hill, the public forum in Athens, for the exchange of ideas (Acts 17:16–34). He joined the discussion. Where is the equivalent of that forum today? The internet hosts a rich, diverse, energetic exchange of ideas. Luddites beware. We ignore it to the detriment of our ministry. Get the church's resources, ideas, convictions, doctrinal positions out there in today's forum. Join the debate. Join the discussion. One is wise to be cautious about over-engagement with the blogosphere. We know of those who have become obsessively involved, even compulsively involved with social media. Still, engagement at some level is an effective way of getting out one's message.

For generations the church bell signaled that the church service was about to begin. Again, the internet has become an important way of communicating the times and locations of one's church program. Utilize it. As Albert Mohler, President of Southern Seminary in Louisville, Kentucky, has said, among the younger generation, if a church does not have a web site, it does not exist.

We are concerned that the primary means of grace may be emphasized at the expense of *prudent church staffing*. We can learn from the business world in this area. When do businesses add employees? When doing so expands the work that can be done and in effect pays for itself. Employees are added when the current staff has reached its maximum work load and there is potential to do more with more staff. So it is with the church. When should a secretary or minister or youth director be added to the church staff? When doing so pays for itself by expanding the reach and effectiveness of the ministry. It pays for itself because it results in more "customers" and happier ones.

Finally, we are concerned that primary means of grace may be emphasized at the expense of important *church programs*. We are absolutely convinced that the bulk of the church's ministry of saving souls and sanctifying saints takes place in the morning and evening services of the Lord's Day. The whole church (not a part), assembled under the primary and ordinary means of grace (the word, sacraments, and prayer), as administered by those called to do so, is the God-ordained means of building the church. Yet does this preclude youth work? What about college ministry? What about ministry among singles in a world with declining rates of marriage? None of these specialized, targeted ministries should usurp the role of the public assembly on the Lord's Day. Yet they can play an important role in ministry, especially in outreach, and should be given careful consideration.

Let us walk, work, and worship carefully, "not as unwise but as wise," that Jesus might build His church in such a way as it becomes His instrument in battering down the gates of hell (Ephesians 5:15; Matthew 16:18).

❧ Chapter 9 ❧

Epilogue: Final Considerations

"It's for the sake of the children." Every time we hear a politician say that, we grab hold of our wallets. Cynical politicians hide behind "the children" whenever selling unjustifiable social spending or policy. If a program is "for the children," who can argue against it?

Still, we want to close this work by asking, what is best "for the children?" What impact does the worship of the Reformed church have on those "nourished by her help and ministry," as Calvin might have put it.[1] Think of a child born into a traditional Reformed church, who spends his or her first 18 years under its ministry. Compare that with the impact made by the new forms of worship upon children reared in those contexts. We've heard the horror stories and read the articles about teenagers brought up

---

1 Calvin, *Institutes*, IV.i.i., 1012.

in seeker churches who don't know the Apostles' Creed or the Ten Commandments, who don't know "Amazing Grace" or "Holy, Holy, Holy," or who don't even know the Doxology or the Lord's Prayer. What will be the cumulative impact of historic Reformed worship on those who participate Sunday morning and evening in its services for their first 18 years?

Scripture

First, they will be *exposed to vast portions of Scripture*. They will have heard much of the Bible *read* aloud. Significant portions will have been *preached* (perhaps 30–60 books of the Bible will be read or preached through their childhood and youth!). The Psalter will have been *sung* through frequently. Public *prayers* will have repeated the scriptural language of praise, confession, thanksgiving, petition, and blessing many times over. The children of traditional Reformed churches will have been exposed to exceptional quantities of Scripture in their 18 years. Other children will have been sprinkled with Bible; our children will have been immersed in it. Isn't this what all Christian parents want for their children? Since the means of sanctifying our children is the truth, and since God's word is truth, the amount of Scriptural content in a service is no mean consideration when choosing a church (John 17:17). If the scriptural content is what parents want for their children, historic Reformed worship and ministry is able to deliver.

Gospel

Second, our children will be *exposed to the gospel* at least twice in every service, both in the structure of the service (the cycle of praise–confession of sin–forgiveness–means of grace) and in Christ-centered preaching. Both implicitly and explicitly, by the liturgy and the sermon, by the prayers and songs, by readings and sacraments, the gospel will be driven home to the hearts of our children, week-in and week-out, Sunday morning, Sunday evening, for 18 years. Yet this will be done not in tired, worn out formulas of yesteryear, but in newly-composed and organized variety as rich as Scripture itself. Gospel principles and realities will be instinctive for our children.

Church

Third, the use of historic orders of service, traditional hymns, and historic creeds will underscore the point that *our children belong to something larger than themselves*. They will be rooted in something older than the present moment. Tradition will be for them not a thing to be despised but cherished. Each week they will link hands with the past, as they worship as their forefathers did, using the very language that our ancestors used hundreds and even (in the case of the psalms) thousands of years ago (2 Timothy 1:3). Moreover, because historical Reformed worship doesn't target the young, our young people will grow up in churches more likely to consist of a healthy cross-section of the generations. They will grow up known by and accountable to more than their immediate peers, and their peers' parents. Our out-of-town college students receive regular communication from sixty to eighty-year-old members of our church who have watched them grow up and love them. Parents, do you want your children to learn the great Creeds, the great hymns, the Lord's Prayer, the Ten Commandments, the Doxology, the Gloria Patri? Do you want them to grow up singing "Praise the Lord, the Almighty," "O Sacred Head Now Wounded," and the Easter classic, "Christ the Lord is Risen Today?" Do you want your children to mature in the context of a multi-generational church where young and old know and interact with each other? Historic Reformed worship preserves this communion of all the saints.

In addition, our children will also link hands with fellow believers across the nation, and even around the world. As our families travel and find themselves out-of-town on Sundays, they will find Reformed churches that worship "just like we do at home." As our children mature, leave for college, or find employment in other communities, they will find compatible spiritual homes in sister Reformed churches. This hope, of course, assumes that Reformed denominations will begin to aspire to a greater degree of uniformity in their worship practices, as we are urging. Appearances at the present make this hope seem vain indeed. The current situation, where Reformed denominations have no "brand-recognition," where the service at any given Reformed church may mimic that of an Episcopal, Revivalistic Baptist, Charismatic, Traditional Presbyterian, or Anglo-Contemporary church, means such linkage of hands is highly improbable. Currently it is more likely that our children will disregard denominational affiliation and the theological commitments that such affiliation entails and choose a church home where the worship suits their style preferences. Still, one can hope. As Timothy Quill observes, "A common liturgy unifies and strengthens the bond between congregations who share the same confession."[2] Historic Reformed worship, practiced throughout our churches, will demonstrate to our children that they belong to a national, even international, communion of like-minded, and like-worshiping saints, whose practices are rooted not in the whims of the local worship leader, but historic Reformed convictions.

---

2   Quill, Liturgical Worship," in Pinson (ed.), *Perspectives on Christian Worship*, 39.

Spirit

Our children will grow up with a keen awareness of both their dependence upon Christ from salvation and growth, and their dependence upon the Holy Spirit for all spiritual progress and health. The emphasis on the Scripture (by which we come to faith, are born again, and are sanctified) and on prayer, unparalleled in the new forms of worship, will underscore their absolute spiritual dependence upon Christ (John 15:1–5). Moreover, this point will be made in the context of the conviction that discipline, restraint, order, and self-control are the fruit of the Spirit's work, rather than the ecstatic, the ostentatious, and the unpredictable. They will develop a piety more characterized by Puritan integrity and sobriety than by pop-superficially and Pentecostal excess.

God

Finally, in a narcissistic, self-absorbed culture our children will experience in every service what it means to be God-centered. The message that God, not themselves, not humanity collectively, but God, is at the center of all things, is unlikely to be learned *if they do not learn it in their church's worship services*. Reformed worship emphatically makes this point, humbling worshipers before God each time they gather.

Hopefully we can now see that our decisions about worship are much more than matters of style and taste. The impact of weekly worship upon our children's spiritual self-awareness, both for good or ill, is enormous. The ability of the adult generation to communicate to the next generation Scripture's content and story, the message of our accountability to God, the problem of sin, our need of Christ, our dependence upon the Holy Spirit, and our identity as members of the body of Christ, is to a significant degree *dependent upon how we choose to worship*. Parents, what do you want for your children?

This question is another way of asking, what do we, the present generation, wish to pass along to succeeding generations as we look ahead hundreds of years into the future. Past generations have bequeathed to us a rich collection of hymns, metrical psalms, prayers, and orders of service, as well as a rich tradition of Bible reading, preaching, and praying. What will we bequeath to the future? Which way of worship and ministry, historic Reformed, or the new forms, is more likely to pass on the substance of the gospel and the richness of the biblical, that is, Reformed faith?

Christians today are in growing numbers in search of tradition, of rootedness, or worship that is "more than a glorified Bible study." Young neo-traditionalists are seeking to "reconnect with the historical church" and find a worship that is directed toward God and not "all about me."[3] This is what the media reports. If this is what Christians truly seek (and I think they do, whether they know it or not) they need not go to Rome or Canterbury, to Antioch or Hollywood, but will find a "sweet home" in Geneva, in Edinburgh, in Westminster and New England, in the heritage of worship found in the Reformed tradition.

---

3   Tolson, "A Return to Tradition" in *U.S. News & World Report,* Volume 143, Number 22, December 24, 2007, 42–47; Chris Armstrong, "The Future Lies in the Past," *Christianity Today,* Vol. 52, No. 2, February 2008, 23–29.

❧ Appendix A ☙

The following is a document which we have used to describe what we do in worship and why we do it. It includes item-by-item explanations of our order of service, as well as general biblical, theological, and historical background. We publish it as a pamphlet which we make available to our visitors. Permission is granted to reproduce it as long as credit is given.

Our Order of Service

Welcome to the Independent Presbyterian Church. We are pleased that you have chosen to worship with us today. Our service is a classic worship service in the tradition of Reformed (or Presbyterian) Protestantism. Given the diversity of styles of worship today, what we do is unfamiliar to many of our visitors. We offer the following booklet as an aid in understanding the meaning of each part of the service.

Before we explain each item let us make some general comments.

The Setting of Our Worship

The architecture and furnishings of a church building may either reinforce the congregation's message or detract from it. Our church building is a gift to us from past generations, and is a classic example of the architecture of Reformed Protestantism. The exterior "looks like a church," which we see as a positive virtue. It tells the onlooker that this is a house of worship, not a bank, or theater, or a retail outlet. The interior displays beautiful craftsmanship employing the finest materials. Yet notice the absence of religious art: no pictures, statues, or religious symbols. The architectural focal point, the pulpit, underscores our theological conviction: the word of God takes the central place in our worship without competition from extraneous visual stimuli. More broadly, decorative simplicity aids worshipers in giving their undistracted attention to the three primary means of grace (i.e. growth): the word, sacraments, and prayer. The pews are placed as they are in order to gather the congregation around the pulpit, baptismal font, and the Lord's Table.

The Elements of Our Worship

Our worship is simple, consisting of the few biblical elements that God has commanded. Our approach to worship means that:

We read and preach the Word—Approximately a chapter is read in each service in addition to the portion upon which the sermon is to be based. Normally our sermons are sequential, verse-by-verse expositions of whole books of the Bible.

We pray the Word—Our prayers are filled with the praises, the confessions, and the promises of Scripture. We offer a full-diet of prayer in each service.

We sing the Word—We incorporate at least one metrical Psalm

(the biblical Psalms translated and rhymed for singing) in each service. We also sing biblically rich hymns.

We receive the Visible Word—The sacraments of baptism and the Lord's Supper are the word of God made visible and perceivable by our senses.

Our services join together that which is so often separated: reverent worship and biblical preaching. We see this as the distinctive benefit of our ministry: God-centered worship and Bible teaching at the same place and at the same time.

The Order of Worship

The design of our worship, both morning and evening, is driven by what one might call "gospel logic."

1. A cycle of *praise* (call to worship / prayer of praise / hymn / *Gloria Patri* / Creed); is followed by ...

2. A cycle of *confession* (recitation of the Law of God / confession of sin / assurance of pardon / collection); which is followed by ...

3. A cycle *employing the means of grace* (intercessory prayers / sacraments / Scripture reading / sermon); which is followed by ...

4. A cycle of *thanksgiving and blessing* (concluding hymn / benediction)

This is essentially the pattern of Isaiah 6, the Lord's Prayer, and the gospel itself. In knowing the true God (in praise), we know ourselves (as sinners), our need (for grace), and give thanks for His gifts in Christ. Sometimes each element is distinct. Sometimes they are combined (as in the morning "pastoral prayer," where confession, pardon, and supplication are together in a "great prayer").

The Day of Worship

We worship on Sunday because the first day of the week is the Lord's Day, the Christian Sabbath, a day devoted to worship and rest. We worship twice on Sunday, following the pattern of the morning and evening sacrifice of the Old Testament and the devotions that flow from them. Morning and evening Lord's Day prayer have been standard for the Christian church from the beginning. Sunday morning is somewhat more formal in tone, with more "fixed forms." Robes are worn by the ministers not as priestly attire (pastors are not priests), but as a simple covering while performing sacred duties. Similarly, we encourage our members to wear their "Sunday best," that is, that they dress nicely and neatly, as they do for other important occasions. Visitors are warmly welcomed to come as they are.

We trust that you will find at the Independent Presbyterian Church two well-ordered services that are offered in "spirit and truth" (John 4:23), conducted with "reverence and awe" (Hebrews 12:28), and characterized by both emotional discipline and holy joy (Psalm 2:11; 1 Corinthians 14:32, 40).

Appendix A—Our Order of Service 343

The Lord's Day Morning Worship

"Let us show gratitude, by which we may offer to God an acceptable service, with reverence and awe." Hebrews 12:28

The Silent Prayer Upon Entering the Sanctuary
(We provide a different prayer for each week of the year for meditation as you prepare for worship. They are slightly expanded versions of the collects [short succinct prayers] from the Book of Common Prayer.)

The Prelude
(The prelude is part of the meditative environment we seek to establish prior to the call to worship.)

The Welcome and Announcements
(Announcements are handled before the call to worship so as not to interfere with the flow of the service.)

The Call to Worship
(The call marks the beginning of our worship as the congregation is called to the happy task of worshiping the Triune God. Sometimes this is sung by the choir, sometimes spoken by the ministers.)

The Hymnal
(This is a vigorous, energetic hymn of praise that focuses on the attributes and works of God.)

The Invocation and Lord's Prayer
(The invocation is a prayer of praise that calls upon God to be present

among us by His Spirit and bless us. It concludes with the Lord's Prayer.)

> Our Father who art in heaven, hallowed be Thy name. Thy kingdom come. Thy will be done on earth, as it is in heaven. Give us this day our daily bread. And forgive us our debts, as we forgive our debtors. And lead us not into temptation, but deliver us from evil: For Thine is the kingdom, and the power, and the glory, forever. Amen.

The Apostles' Creed

(The Creed is the oldest Christian confession of faith, with roots in the second century, and provides the means by which we affirm our Christian identity and faith. Because the churches of Christ have all affirmed this Creed for centuries, its use also demonstrates our unity with the whole church, past and present:)

> I believe in God the Father Almighty, Maker of heaven and earth:
>
> And in Jesus Christ His only Son, our Lord; who was conceived by the Holy Ghost, born of the Virgin Mary, suffered under Pontius Pilate, was crucified, dead, and buried; He descended into hell*; the third day He rose again from the dead; He ascended into heaven, and sitteth on the right hand of God the Father Almighty; from thence He shall come to judge the quick and the dead.

Appendix A—Our Order of Service   345

> I believe in the Holy Ghost; the holy catholic church;†
> the communion of saints; the forgiveness of sins; the
> resurrection of the body; and the life everlasting. Amen.

* this refers to the realm of the dead, not the place of punishment.

† "catholic" means "universal" church, the true church in all times and places.

The Gloria Patri

(This Trinitarian ascription of praise dates to the fourth century. It has played an important role in combating unitarianism. We sing it to several different tunes.)

> Glory be to the Father, and to the Son, and to the Holy Ghost;
> As it was in the beginning, is now, and ever shall be, world
> without end. Amen, Amen.

The Pastoral Prayer

(This is a comprehensive prayer of confession of sin and intercession, and follows the five-fold pattern of intercession found in Scripture [e.g. 1 Timothy 2:1ff]: (1) for civil authority; (2) for Christian ministry; (3) for all peoples; (4) for the sanctification of God's people; (5) for the afflicted.)

The Baptism

Baptisms are administered upon request of Christian parents (we practice infant baptism) and new believers (if never previously baptized). All those who are baptized are initiated into the membership of the church. Baptism is no mere ceremony, but a means of grace, blessing, and growth for believers and their children.

The Scripture Reading
(We read roughly a chapter of Scripture, sequentially, through books of the Bible, in each service, in addition to the portion of Scripture to be preached.)

The Psalter
(We sing a psalm in each service and work our way through much of the Psalter each year.)

The Collection
(A simple collection is taken for the support of the work of the church. It is not an "offering" that is presented to God on the altar, and for this reason is not brought forward with ceremony.)

The Choral Anthem
(The choir and organ are in the back, not up front as though they were entertainers, and are part of the congregation, not clergy. The primary task is to support and enrich the congregation's singing.

The Doxology
(The doxology was written by Thomas Ken in 1709, and perhaps has done more to popularize the doctrine of the Trinity than all the theological books ever written. It is typically associated with the tune Old Hundredth [Geneva Psalter, 1562] but is used in our services with a number of other tunes.)

> Praise God from Whom all blessings flow; praise Him all creatures here below. Praise Him above, ye heav'nly host, praise Father, Son, and Holy Ghost. Amen.

Appendix A—Our Order of Service 347

The Dismissal (Children ages 4 & 5 may leave for a separate service)

(We encourage children to stay for the entire service from as young an age as possible. The criteria for determining if our children should stay or leave is their ability to sit quietly and not be a distraction to those around them. We provide a "children's church" in which 4 and 5 year olds are encouraged to learn by heart the various fixed-forms in our services [e.g. Creed, Lord's Prayer, Doxology, Gloria Patri, Ten Commandments].)

The Sermon

(Normally our sermons are sequential and expository, verse-by-verse through books of the Bible.)

The Lord's Supper

The Lord's Supper is a covenantal meal ("this is the new covenant in my blood") which seals or finalizes covenantal commitments. Each time we partake we renew the covenant, recommit ourselves to Christ, even as He reaffirms the efficacy of His atoning death on our behalf. It is normally administered in the morning on the first Sunday of each quarter (January, April, July, October). We believe in the "true presence" of Christ in the supper, that is, His spiritual presence. We enjoy fellowship with the ascended Christ at the Table (1 Corinthians 10:16) and partake of spiritual food to the nourishment of our souls (1 Corinthians 10:3).

The Hymnal

(The closing hymn is normally related thematically to the sermon.)

The Benediction and Response (sung by all)

(The benediction is a prayer for the blessing of God upon the

congregation as it departs. A brief response by the congregation follows.)

The Postlude
(A final, beautiful selection is played on the organ as the congregation departs.)

Appendix A—Our Order of Service 349

The Lord's Day Evening Worship

"God is spirit, and those who worship Him must worship in spirit and truth." John 4:24

Preparation
(For a period of about 15 minutes before the beginning of the service we prepare for worship by singing hymns. As is the case in the morning, we place the announcements before the call to worship so as not to interfere with the flow of the service.)

Hymn Sing

Announcements

Praise
(As is the case in the morning service, the opening prayer and hymn focus on the attributes and works of God. The hymn is a vigorous song of praise.)

Call to Worship and Prayer of Praise

Hymn

Confession of Sin, Pardon, and Thanksgiving
(Having praised God we move on to the confession of our sins. We make liturgical use of the Ten Commandments in the evening as a preparation for the confession, a practice rooted in the synagogue and early church, and revived by the Protestant Reformers in the sixteenth century. A comprehensive prayer of confession is offered

350 *Serving with Calvin*

followed by scriptural assurance for all of the benefits that we receive in Christ.)

> Minister: God spake all these words saying, I am the Lord thy God, which have brought thee out of the land of Egypt, out of the house of bondage.
>
> All: 1. Thou shalt have no other gods before me.
> 2. Thou shalt not make unto thee any graven image.
> 3. Thou shalt not take the Name of the Lord thy God in vain.
> 4. Remember the Sabbath day, to keep it holy.
> 5. Honor thy father and thy mother.
> 6. Thou shalt not kill.
> 7. Thou shalt not commit adultery.
> 8. Thou shalt not steal.
> 9. Thou shalt not bear false witness.
> 10. Thou shalt not covet. [Exodus 20:1–17]
>
> Hear also the words of our Lord Jesus, how he saith: Thou shalt love the Lord thy God with all thy heart, and with all thy soul, and with all thy mind. This is the first and great commandment. And the second is like unto it: Thou shalt love thy neighbor as thyself. On these two commandments hang all the law and the prophets. [Matthew 22:37–40]

Appendix A—Our Order of Service 351

Reading of the Law of God

The Prayer of Confession of Sin

Assurance of Pardon

Prayer of Thanksgiving

Collection

Provision for Life and Growth
(*Also known as the "means of grace," this cycle [following the cycles of praise and confession] employ the ordinary means given by God to the church by which to sanctify the saints and grow the church.*)

Scripture Reading
(*Normally a chapter is read in addition to the text upon which the sermon is to be based. This means that regularly two full chapters will have been read in our services on a given Sunday.*)

Intercessory Prayer
(*We see prayer as an important part of our ministry to our own people and to the world. This fourth prayer of the service is a prayer that is primarily petitionary, that is, an intercessory prayer.*)

Psalter
(*A second metrical psalm of the Sunday is sung.*)

Prayer of Illumination
(*This is a prayer for the aid of the Holy Spirit in understanding the Scripture as it is read and preached. It is based on scriptural example*

352 *Serving with Calvin*

[e.g. Psalm 119:12, 17, 18, 27, etc.] and the practice of the early church. It demonstrates our dependence upon the Holy Spirit.)

Scripture & Sermon
(As is the case in the morning, normally our sermon is expository, taking us verse-by-verse through a book of the Bible.)

The Lord's Supper
The Lord's Supper normally is administered in the evening service on the first Sunday of the months in which it is not administered in the morning (that is, February, March, May, June, August, September, November, December, and Maundy Thursday). At the Table we enjoy a spiritual meal ("the Lord's Supper"), fellowship with Christ ("Communion"), and give thanks ("Eucharist") for our salvation in Christ Jesus.

Thanksgiving and Blessing
(The concluding cycle of response includes a hymn that is normally related to the theme of the sermon and the concluding blessing upon the congregation.)

Hymn

Benediction

Conclusion: *Worship and Ministry*
Worship is both our highest priority and greatest privilege as believers. We give it careful and focused attention at Independent Presbyterian Church. Worship also shapes our ministry. Because we worship twice on Sunday and our services are filled with biblical content, our weekday schedule is relatively uncluttered. Bible study,

Appendix A—Our Order of Service

prayer, fellowship, and discipleship are not activities that must be scheduled for weekdays (and weeknights). They occur richly in our Sunday services. Christian growth is not something that must be pursued through retreats, camps, conferences and frenetic weekday activity, but through the ordinary services of the church.

354

❧ Appendix B ❦

The following charts may help in summarizing what *Worshipping with Calvin* and *Serving with Calvin* attempt to teach.

Old School	New School
Piety	Personality
Faithfulness	Format
Substance	Style
Character	Techniques
Prayer	Program
Theology	Therapy
Minister	Life coach
Ministry	Marketing

Communion

Is	Is Not
meal	mass
supper	sacrifice
table	altar
pastor	priest
gift of God	offering to God

Solas

Scriptura	fide
Christo	gratia
Deo gloria	

Appendix B—Charts

	Contemporary	Liturgical	Reformed
reading	verses preached	*lectio selecta*	*lectio continua*
preaching	topical	expository selective or topical	expository sequential
praying	little	written comprehensive (six types)	free/ studied comprehensive (six types)
singing	choruses	classic hymns	metrical psalms and classic hymns
sacraments	infrequent	weekly	frequent

Strength of Worship of Reformed Protestantism

God-centered
Word-filled
Gospel-structured
Spirit-dependent
Church-aware

The Worship of Reformed Protestantism

Read	word	*lectio continua*
Preach	word	expository & sequential
Sing	word	psalms & hymns
Pray	word	full diet of 6 prayer genres
See	word	Lord's Supper & baptism

Appendix B—Charts

Marketing the Church (or Churching the Market?)

	Secular Marketing Principles:	Church Marketers	Historic Ministry
Market:	Identify desired market	Target ministry for Saddleback Sam, Willow Creek Wally, young, white-collar, professionals	Identify existing "market;" i.e. who lives in neighborhood, not a demographic slice of the neighborhood
Ministry Products:	Design product according to needs & tastes of targeted market	Soft-rock music; talk show format; felt-needs sermons; unchurchy setting	Conduct historic forms of ministry tailored to character of neighborhood without targeting a subset of the neighborhood: • historic hymns & psalms • expository preaching • *lectio continua* reading • full diet of prayer • frequent sacraments
Promotion:	Design promotion according to needs and tastes of targeted market	"cool" advertising for target market	Promotional materials that appeal broadly to neighborhood, not a group within the neighborhood.

360

Bibliography of Cited Works[1]

1. Original Sources[2]	323
Reformation	323
Post Reformation	324
2. Background Reading	326
3. History of Worship	328
General	328
Early, Medieval & Orthodox	328
Reformation	329
Post-Reformation	329
Modern & Contemporary Discussion	330
Reformed & Presbyterian Worship Today	332
4. Practice of Worship	334
Pastoral Theology	334
Preaching	335
Reading Scripture	337
Prayer	337
Church Song	338

---

1   For more complete bibliography, see *Worshipping with Calvin*.

2   See also below, "Practice of Worship" for some original sources classified by topic.

361

Serving with Calvin

Sacraments   339
Setting of Worship   340

Bibliography

1. Original Sources

Reformation

Calvin, John. *Preface to the Psalter*, 1543 in McKee, E. A. (ed.) *John Calvin: Writings on Personal Piety*. New York: Paulist Press, 2001.

_____. *Institutes of the Christian Religion—Vol. 1 & 2,* in John T. McNeill (ed.) The Library of Christian Classics, Volume XXI. Philadelphia: The Westminster Press, 1960.

Luther, Martin. 'On the Babylonian Captivity of the Church', in James Atkinson (ed.), *Three Treatises*. Philadelphia: Fortress Press, 1970.

Nixon, Leroy, translator. John Calvin's *Sermons from Job*. (Grand Rapids, Michigan: William B. Eerdmans Publishing Co., 1952)

Thompson, Bard. *Liturgies of the Western Church*. Philadelphia: Fortress Press, 1961.

Zwingli, Ulrich. "Of Baptism" in G.W. Bromiley, *Zwingli & Bullinger* in John Baillie, et. al. (ed.) *The Library of Christian Classics*, Vol. XXIV. Philadelphia: The Westminster Press, 1953.

Post Reformation

Bannerman, D. *et. al. A New Directory for Public Worship of God.* Edinburgh: Macriven & Wallace, 1898.

Baxter, Richard. Thompson, J. M. Lloyd, Ed. *The Autobiography of Richard Baxter*, Everyman's Library, edited with Introduction, Appendices and Notes. 1696, London: J.M. Dent & Sons Ltd), 1931.

_____. "A Christian Directory" in *The Practical Works of Richard Baxter*, Vol 1. 1673; Ligonier, PA: Soli Deo Gloria Publications, 1990.

Burroughs, Jeremiah. *Gospel Worship: or the Right Manner of Sanctifying the Name of God in General.* 1648, Pittsburgh, PA: Soli Deo Gloria Publications, 1990.

Bruce, Robert. *The Mystery of the Lord's Supper: Sermons on the Sacrament preached in the Kirk of Edinburgh by Robert Bruce in A.D. 1589*, ed. Thomas F. Torrance. 1958; Ross-shire, Scotland: Christian Focus Publications, 2005.

Charnock, Stephen. *The Existence and Attributes of God.* Volumes I and II, 1682, 1853; Grand Rapids, MI: Baker Books, 1996.

Doolittle, Thomas. *A Treatise Concerning the Lord's Supper.* 1709, Morgan, PA: Soli Deo Gloria, 1998.

Edwards, Jonathan. *The Works of Jonathan Edwards*, Vol. 1. 1834, Edinburgh: The Banner of Truth Trust, 1974.

Edwards, Jonathan. *The Works of Jonathan Edwards*, Vol. 7: The Life of David Brainerd. Yale University Press, 1985.

_____. *Treatise Concerning the Religious Affections*, Select Works of Jonathan Edwards, Vol. III. 1746, London: The Banner of Truth Trust, 1961.

Gillespie, George. *A Dispute Against English Popish Ceremonies Obtruded on the Church of Scotland.* 1642; Dallas, TX: Naphtali Press, 1993.

Gurnall, William. *The Christian in Complete Armour: A Treatise of the Saints' War Against the Devil.* 1662 and 1665; Edinburgh: Banner of Truth Trust, 1964.

Henry, Matthew. "A Church in the House," "A Communicant's Companion" and "Treatise on Baptism" found in *The Complete Works of Matthew Henry.* 2 vols. Edinburgh: J. Fullarton & Co., 1855. Reprint Grand Rapids: Baker Book House, 1979. Second reprinting, Grand Rapids: Baker Book House, 1997.

_____. *A Method for Prayer.* Ed. J. Ligon Duncan, III. 1710, Greenville, South Carolina: Reformed Academic Press, 1994.

_____. *Family Religion: Principles for Receiving a Godly Family.* Ross-shire, Scotland, UK: Christian Focus Publications, 2008.

Owen, John. "A Discourse Concerning Liturgies, and Their Imposition," in *Sermons to the Church: The Works of John Owen,* Volume XV, William H. Goold (ed.). 1965, Carlisle, Pennsylvania: The Banner of Truth Trust, 1990.

Spurgeon, C.H. *Till He Come: A Collection of Communion Addresses.* Fearn, Ross-shire: Christian Focus Publications, n.d..

Swinnock, George. "The Incomparableness of God in His Being, Attributes, Works, and Word," in *The Works of George Swinnock,* Volume IV. Edinburgh: Banner of Truth Trust, 1992.

"The Directory for the Publick Worship of God" in *The Westminster Confession of Faith and the Larger & Shorter Catechisms.* Glasgow: Free Presbyterian Publications, 1985.

Vincent, Nathanael. *Attending Upon God Without Distraction.* 1695; Grand Rapids, Michigan: Soli Deo Gloria Publications, 2010.

Vines, Richard and Edmund Calamy, *et. al. The Puritans on the Lord's Supper,* ed. Don Kistler. Morgan, PA: Soli Deo Gloria, 1997.

366　　　　　　　　　*Serving with Calvin*

Watts, Isaac. *A Guide to Prayer*. 1715, Edinburgh: The Banner of Truth Trust, 2001.

Westminster Confession of Faith. Glasgow: Free Presbyterian Publications, 1985.

2. Background Reading

Armstrong, John (ed.). "The Evangelical Fall from the Means of Grace," in *The Compromised Church*. Wheaton, IL: Crossway, 1998.

Bloom, Allan. *The Closing of the American Mind*. New York: Simon & Schuster, 1987.

Boice, James Montgomery, *Whatever Happened to the Gospel of Grace?* Wheaton, IL: Crossway Books, 2001.

Calhoun, David. *Splendor of Grace*. Greenville, SC: A Press Printing, 2005.

Colson, Charles. *The Body: Being Light in the Darkness*. Dallas: Word Publishing, 1992.

Edgar, William. *Truth in All its Glory: Commending the Reformed Faith*. Phillipsburg, NJ: P&R Publishing, 2004.

France, R. T. *Matthew*, Tyndale New Testament Commentaries. Grand Rapids: Eerdmans Publishing Co., 1989.

MacDonald, Gordon. "How to Spot a Transformed Christian," in *Leadership Journal*, Summer 2012.

Hahn, Scott. *Rome, Sweet Home*. San Francisco: Ignatius Press, 1993.

Johnson, Terry L. *The Family Worship Book*. 1998, Geanies House, Fearn, Ross-shire, Great Britain, 2003.

Kevan, Ernest. *The Grace of Law: A Study in Puritan Theology*. London: The Carey Kingsway Press Limited, 1964.

Lewis, C. S. *The Screwtape Letters*. 1951; New York: MacMillan Publish Co., Inc., 1975.

MacArthur, John Jr. *The Gospel According to Jesus*. Grand Rapids, MI: Zondervan, 1988.

MacDonald, Gordon. "How to Spot a Transformed Christian," in *Leadership Journal*, Summer 2012.

McGrath, Alister E. *Intellectuals Don't Need God and Other Modern Myths*. Grand Rapids, MI: Zondervan Publishing, 1993.

Metaxas, Eric. *Bonhoeffer: Pastor, Martyr, Prophet, Spy: A Righteous Gentile vs. the Third Reich*. Nashville, TN: Thomas Nelson, 2010.

Motyer, J. Alec. *Looking to the Rock: An Old Testament Background to Our Understanding of Christ*. Leicester, England: Inter-Varsity Press, 1996.

Murray, Iain. H. (ed.). *A Day's March Nearer Home, Autobiography of J. Graham Miller*. Edinburgh: The Banner of Truth Trust, 2010.

Murray, John. *Principles of Conduct*. London: The Tyndale Press, 1957.

_____. *Redemption Accomplished and Applied*. Grand Rapids, MI: Wm. B. Eerdmans Publishing Co., 1955.

Myers, Kenneth A. *All God's Children and Blue Suede Shoes*. Wheaton, Il: Crossway Books, 1989.

Packer, J.I. *A Quest for Godliness: The Puritan Vision of the Christian Life*. Wheaton, IL: Crossway Books, 1990.

_____. *Faithfulness and Holiness: The Witness of J. C. Ryle*. Wheaton, IL: Crossway Books, 2002.

_____. *Hot Tub Religion*. Wheaton: Tyndale House Publishers, 1987.

_____. "Theology and Wisdom," in J. I. Packer & Sven K. Soderlund (eds), *The Way of Wisdom: Essays in Honor of Bruce K. Waltke*. Grand Rapids: Zondervan Publishing House, 2000.

Pattison, Robert. *The Triumph of Vulgarity: Rock Music in the Mirror of Romanticism*. New York: Oxford University Press, 1987.

Postman, Neil. *Amusing Ourselves to Death*. New York: NY: Penguin Group, 1985.

The Book of Church Order of the Presbyterian Church in America. Office of the Stated Clerk, Sixth Edition, 2005.

Warfield, B. B. "The Prodigal Son," in *The Saviour of the World: Sermons Preached in the Chapel of Princeton Theological Seminary*. New York: Hodder and Stoughton, 1913.

Watson, Thomas. *The Ten Commandments*. 1959; London: The Banner of Truth Trust, 1970.

Wells, David F. *God In the Wasteland: The Reality of Truth in a World of Fading Dreams* (Grand Rapids: Michigan: Wm. B. Eerdmans Publishing Co., 1994

_____. *The Courage to Be Protestant: Truth-lovers, Marketers, and Emergents in the Postmodern World*. Grand Rapids, Michigan: William B. Eerdmans Publishing Co., 2008.

3. History of Worship

General

Davies, J. G. (ed.). *The New Westminster Dictionary of Liturgy & Worship*. Philadelphia: The Westminster Press, 1986.

Early, Medieval & Orthodox

Jungmann, Joseph A.S.J. *The Early Liturgy: To the Time of Gregory the Great*, Liturgical Studies Volume VI. Notre Dame, Indiana: University of Notre Dame Press, 1959.

Reformation

Duncan, Ligon, ed. "Westminster and the Sabbath," in *The Westminster Confession into the 21st Century: Essays in Remembrance of the 350th Anniversary of the Westminster Assembly.* Ross-shire, UK: Christian Focus, 2004.

Eire, Carlos M. N. *War Against the Idols.* Cambridge: Cambridge University Press, 1986.

Gaffin, Richard B. Jr. *Calvin and the Sabbath.* Ross-shire, UK: Christian Focus, 1998.

Johnson, Terry L. *The Case for Traditional Protestantism.* Edinburgh: Banner of Truth Trust, 2004.

McKee, Elsie Ann (ed.). *John Calvin's Writings on Pastoral Piety.* The Classics of Western Spirituality. New York: Paulist Press, 2001.

Old, Hughes O. *The Patristic Roots of Reformed Worship.* Zurich: Theologischer Verlag, 1970.

Pak, G. Sujin. *The Judaizing Calvin: Sixteenth-Century Debates over the Messianic Psalms.* Oxford: University Press, 2010.

Thomas, Derek. *Calvin's Teaching on Job: Proclaiming the Incomprehensible God.* Geanies House, Ross-shire, Scotland: Christian Focus Publications, 2004.

Post-Reformation

Bonar, Andrew A. *Robert Murray M'Cheyne: Memoir and Remains.* London: Banner of Truth, 1966.

Bostwich, David. "The Character and Duty of a Christian Preacher," in John Brown (ed.), *The Christian Pastor's Manual.* 1826; Morgan, PA: Soli Deo Gloria Publications, 1991.

Chapell, Bryan. *Christ-Centered Worship.* Grand Rapids, MI: Baker Publishing Co., 2009.

Erskine, John. "The Qualifications Necessary for Teachers of

Christianity," in John Brown (ed.), *The Christian Pastor's Manual.* 1826; Morgan, PA: Soli Deo Gloria Publications, 1991.

Garretson, James M. *Princeton and Preaching.* Edinburgh: The Banner of Truth Trust, 2005.

Haslam, David. "Quotes from Robert Murray M'Cheyne," http://web.ukonline.co.uk/d.haslam/mccheyne/rmmquotes.htm

Kuyper, Abraham. *Our Worship,* ed. Harry Boonstra.1911; Grand Rapids: William B. Eerdmans Publishing Co., 2009.

Puckett, David L. *John Calvin's Exegesis of the Old Testament,* Columbia series in Reformed Theology. Louisville, Kentucky: Westminster John Knox Press, 1995.

Modern & Contemporary Discussion

Armstrong, Chris. "The Future Lies in the Past," *Christianity Today*, Vol. 52, No. 2. February 2008.

Baker, Anthony D. "Learning to Read the Gospel Again," *Christianity Today*, Vol. 55, No. 12, December 2011.

Belcher, Jim. *Deep Church: A Third Way Beyond Emerging & Traditional.* Downers Grove, Ill: InterVarsity Press, 2009.

Brown, Frank Burch. "Worship Mismatch" in *Christian Century*, Vol. 126, No. 5, March 10, 2009.

_____. *Good Taste, Bad Taste, and Christian Taste: Aesthetics in Religious Life.* New York: Oxford University Press, 2000.

Buss, Dale. "Less Seeking, More Thrills," *The Wall Street Journal*, June 27, 2008.

Carson, D. A. (ed.). *Worship by the Book.* Grand Rapids, Michigan: Zondervan, 2002.

Due, Noel. *Created for Worship: From Genesis to Revelation to You.* Geanies House, Fearn, Ross-shire, Scotland: Christian Focus Publications, 2005.

Eastman, Fred and Louis Wilson. *Drama in the Church: A Manual of Religious Drama Production*. 1932; New York: Samuel French, 1942.

"Fuller Seminary's Brehm Center for Worship, Theology, and the Arts." *Fuller Focus*, Fall 2004, Vol. 12, No. 3

Hawkins, Greg and Cally Parkinson. *Reveal: Where Are You?* Barrington, Illinois: Willow Creek Association, 2007.

Kallestad, Walt. "'Showtime!' No More," in *Leadership Journal. net*, http://www.christianitytoday.com/le/2008/fall/13.39.html, posted November 26, 2008.

Kauflin, Bob. *Worship Matters: Leading Others to Encounter the Greatness of God*. Wheaton, IL: Crossway Books, 2008.

Lawrence, Michael and Mark Dever. "Blended Worship" in J. Matthew Pinson, *Perspectives on Christian Worship: 5 Views*. Nashville, Tennessee: B & H Academic, 2009.

McCarthy, Rebecca. "Gwinnett's 12Stone church features glitzy amenities, Starbucks." *Atlanta Journal Constitution,* January 22, 2008.

Pinson, J. Matthew. *Perspectives on Christian Worship: 5 Views*. Nashville: Broadman & Holman Publishers, 2009.

Plantinga, Jr., Cornelius and Sue A. Rozeboom, *Discerning the Spirits: A Guide for Thinking about Christian Worship Today*, Calvin Institute of Christian Worship Liturgical Studies Series. Grand Rapids, Michigan: Wm. B. Eerdmans Publishing Co., 2003.

Pope, Randy. *The Prevailing Church: An Alternative Approach to Ministry*. Chicago: Moody Press, 2002.

Reeder, Harry. *From Embers to a Flame: How God Can Revitalize Your Church*. Phillipsburg, NJ: P&R Publishing, 2004.

Tolson, Jay. "A Return to Tradition," in *U.S. News & World Report*. Volume 143, Number 22, December 22, 2007.

Vande Bunte, Matt. "Sunday night services a fading tradition," *Christian Century*, October 19, 2010, Vol. 127, No 21.

Warren, Rick. *The Purpose Driven Church*. Grand Rapids, Michigan: Zondervan, 1995.

Webber, Robert. *Blended Worship: Achieving Substance & Relevance in Worship*. Peabody, MA: Hendrickson, 1994.

_____. *Evangelicals on the Canterbury Trail*. Wilton, Connecticut: Morehouse-Barlow, 1985.

Williams, Donald T. "Durable Hymns" in *Touchstone: A Journal of Mere Christianity*, Vol. 22, No. 6, July/August 2009.

Reformed & Presbyterian Worship Today

Clark, R. Scott. "Letter and Spirit: Law and Gospel in Reformed Preaching" in R. Scott Clark (ed.)., *Covenant, Justification, and Pastoral Ministry*. Phillipsburg, New Jersey: P & R Publishing, 2007.

Clark, R. Scott. *Recovering the Reformed Confession: Our Theology, Piety, and Practice*. Phillipsburg, NJ: P&R Publishing, 2008.

Clowney, Edmund. "Declare His Glory Among the Nations," message from Urbana 76, found at http://www.urbana.org/_artciles.cfm?RecordID=879.

Dennison, Charles G. "Worship and Office," in Mark R. Brown, ed., *Order in the Offices*. Classic Presbyterian Government Resources: Duncansville, PA 1993.

Frame, John M. *Worship in Spirit and Truth: A Refreshing Study of the Principle and Practice of Biblical Worship*. Phillipsburg, NJ: Presbyterian & Reformed Publishing, 1996.

Godfrey, W. Robert. "The Offering," *The Outlook* 41. Nov. 1991.

Hart, D.G. *Recovering Mother Kirk: The Case for Liturgy in the Reformed Tradition*. Grand Rapids, Michigan: Baker Book House, 2003.

_____ and John R. Muether. *With Reverence and Awe: Returning to the Basics of Reformed Worship*. Phillipsburg, NJ: P&R Publishing Company, 2002.

Horton, Michael. *A Better Way: Rediscovering the Drama of God-Centered Worship*. Grand Rapids, Michigan: Baker Books, 2002.

Johnson, Terry L. *Leading in Worship* (Oak Ridge, TN: The Covenant Foundation, 1996); *Leading in Worship, Revised and Expanded Edition* (Powder Springs, Georgia: Tolle Lege Press, 2013.

_____. *Reformed Worship: Worship that Is According to Scripture: Revised & Expanded. 2000*; Welwyn Garden City, EP Books, 2015.

Leith, John H. *Introduction to the Reformed Tradition,* Revised Edition. Atlanta, GA: John Knox Press, 1981.

Macleod, Donald. *Presbyterian Worship: Its Meaning and Method*. Richmond, VA: John Knox Press, 1965.

Meyers, Jeffrey J. *The Lord's Service: The Grace of Covenant Renewal Worship*. Moscow, ID: Canon Press, 2003.

Old, Hughes O. *Worship: That is Reformed According to Scripture.* 1984; Louisville: Westminster John Knox Press, 2004.

Rayburn, Robert. *O Come Let Us Worship: Corporate Worship in the Evangelical Church*. Grand Rapids: Baker Book House, 1980.

Ryken, Philip G., Derek W. H. Thomas, and J. Ligon Duncan, III (eds.). *Give Praise to God: A Vision for Reforming Worship*. Phillipsburg, New Jersey: P&R Publishing, 2003.

Still, William. *Congregational Record and Bible Readings*. Gilcomston South Church of Scotland, Aberdeen, February 1989.

4. Practice of Worship

Pastoral Theology

Baxter, Richard. *The Reformed Pastor.* 1656, rprt; Edinburgh: The Banner of Truth Trust, 1974.

Blaikie, William G. *For the Work of the Ministry: A Manual of Homiletical and Pastoral Theology* (1896; Birmingham, Alabama: Solid Ground Christian Books, 2005).

Bridges, Charles. *The Christian Ministry; With an Inquiry into the Causes of Its Inefficiency; With an Especial Reference to the Ministry of the Establishment.* London: Seeley, 1849.

Brown, John. *The Christian Pastor's Manual.* Ligonier, 1826, Pennsylvania: Soli Deo Gloria, 1991.

Fairbairn, Patrick. *Pastoral Theology: A Treatise on the Office and Duties of the Christian Pastor.* 1875; Audubon, New Jersey: Old Paths Publications, 1992.

James, John Angell. *An Earnest Ministry: The Want of the Times.* 1847, Edinburgh: The Banner of Truth Trust, 1993.

Johnson, Terry L. *The Pastor's Public Ministry.* Greenville, SC: Reformed Academic Press, 2001.

_____. *Worshipping with Calvin.* Darlington, England, EP Books, 2014.

Miller, Samuel. *Letters on Clerical Manners.* Philadelphia, Presbyterian Board of Publication, 1852.

Murphy, Thomas. *Pastoral Theology: The Pastor and the Various Duties of His Office.* 1877; Audubon, New Jersey: Old Paths Publications, 1996.

Plummer, William S. *Hints & Helps in Pastoral Theology.* 1874; Harrisonburg, Virginia: Sprinkle Publications, 2003.

Shedd, W.G.T. *Homiletics and Pastoral Theology.* 1867; Edinburgh: The Banner of Truth Trust, 1965.

C. H. Spurgeon, *Commenting and Commentaries*, New Updated Edition (1876; Grand Rapids: Kregel Publications, 1988)

_____. *Lectures to My Students: A Selection from Addresses Delivered to the Students of The Pastors' College, Metropolitan Tabernacle*. London: Passmore and Alabaster, 1881.

Still, William. *The Work of the Pastor*. Aberdeen: Didasho Press, 1976.

Preaching

Alexander, James W. *Thoughts on Preaching: Being Contributions to Homiletics*. 1864; Edinburgh: The Banner of Truth Trust, 1975.

Beecher, Henry Ward. *Yale Lectures on Preaching*. New York: Fords, Howard, and Hulbert, 1893.

Broadus, J. A. *On the Preparation and Delivery of Sermons*, Revised Edition. 1870; Nashville: Broadman Press, 1944.

Brooks, Phillips. *Lectures on Preaching Delivered before the Divinity School of Yale College In January and February*. 1877, New York: E. P. Dutton and Company, 1907.

Brosend, William. "Enough About Me: There is no I in Preach," in *Christian Century*, Vol. 127, No. 4, February 23, 2010.

Carrick, John. *The Imperative of Preaching: A Theology of Sacred Rhetoric*. Edinburgh: The Banner of Truth Trust, 2002.

Chapell, Bryan. *Christ-Centered Preaching: Redeeming the Expository Sermon*. Grand Rapids: Baker Books, 1994.

Dabney, Robert L. *Sacred Rhetoric or Course of Lectures on Preaching*. 1870; Edinburgh; The Banner of Truth Trust, 1979.

de Witt, John R. "A Few Thoughts on Preaching," *The Banner of Truth Trust Magazine*. Issue 588, October 2012.

Dale, R. W. *Nine Lectures on Preaching*. London: Hodder and Stoughton, n.d.

Eby, David. *Power Preaching for Church Growth: The Role of Preaching in Growing Churches*. Ross-shire, Great Britain: Christian Focus Publications, 1996.

Ferguson, Sinclair. "Evangelical Exemplar," *Tabletalk*. February 1999

Hunt, Arthur W., III. *The Vanishing Word: The Veneration of Visual Imagery in the Postmodern World*. Wheaton: Crossway Books, 2003.

Johnson, D. E. *Him We Proclaim: Preaching Christ from All the Scriptures*. Phillipsburg, New Jersey: P&R Publishing, 2007.

Lloyd-Jones, D. Martyn. *Preaching and Preachers*. Grand Rapids, Michigan: Zondervan, 1971.

Logan, Jr., Samuel T. *The Preacher & Preaching: Reviving the Art in the Twentieth Century*. Phillipsburg: New Jersey: Presbyterian & Reformed Publishing Company, 1986.

Motyer, J. Alec. *Preaching? Simple Teaching on Simply Preaching*. Ross-shire, Scotland: Christian Focus Publications, 2013.

Mouw, Richard J. "Preaching Worth Pondering," *Fuller Focus* 5. November 1996.

Murray, Iain H. "'Expository Preaching'—Time for Caution," *The Banner of Truth Magazine*, February 2010, Issue 557.

_____. "Raising the Standard of Preaching: Notes of a Memorable Address," in *The Banner of Truth Magazine*. Carlisle, PA: The Banner of Truth Trust, March 2011, Issue 570.

Porter, Ebenezer. *Lectures on Homiletics and Preaching, and on Public Prayer; Together with Sermons and Letters*. New York: Flagg, Gould and Newman, 1834.

Stott, John R. *Between Two Worlds: The Art of Preaching in the Twentieth Century*. Grand Rapids, Michigan: William B. Eerdmans Publishing Company, 1982.

Taylor, William M. *The Ministry of the Word.* 1876; Harrisonburg, Virginia: Sprinkle Publications, 2003.

Willimon, William H. *Preaching and Leading Worship.* Philadelphia: The Westminster Press, 1984.

Reading Scripture

Logan, Samuel T., Jr., Editor. *The Preacher and Preaching: Reviving the Art in the Twentieth Century.* Phillipsburg, NJ: Presbyterian and Reformed Publishing Company, 1986.

Old, Hughes O. *The Reading & Preaching of the Scriptures in the Worship of the Christian Church, Volume 3: The Medieval Church.* Grand Rapids: Eerdmans Publishing Company, 1999.

_____. *The Reading and Preaching of the Scriptures in the Worship of the Christian Church, Volume 6: The Modern Age.* Grand Rapids: William B. Eerdmans, 2007.

Prayer

Boa, Kenneth. *Handbook to Prayer: Praying Scripture Back to God.* Atlanta: Trinity House Publishers, 1993.

Cogan, Donald. *The Prayers of the New Testament.* New York: Harper and Row Publishers, 1967.

Johnson, Terry L. *When Grace Comes Alive: Living Through the Lord's Prayer.* Ross-shire, Scotland: Christian Focus Publications, 2003.

Lockyer, Herbert. *All the Prayers of the Bible.* Grand Rapids: Zondervan Publishing House, 1959.

Miller, Samuel. *Thoughts on Public Prayer.* 1844, Harrisonburg, Virginia: Sprinkle Publications, 1985.

Old, Hughes O. *Leading in Prayer: A Workbook for Ministers.* Grand Rapids, Michigan: William B. Eerdmans Publishing Company, 1995.

_____. "The Psalms as Christian Prayer. A Preface to the Liturgical Use of the Psalter." Unpublished manuscript, 1978.

Powlison, David. "Praying Beyond the Sick List," in *By Faith*. Issue 8, April 2006.

Pratt, Richard. *Pray With Your Eyes Open*. Phillipsburg, NJ: Presbyterian and Reformed Pub. Co., 1987.

Robertson, O. Palmer. *A Way to Pray*. Edinburgh: Banner of Truth Trust, 2010.

Scroggie, W. Graham. *Paul's Prison Prayers*. 1921, rprt.: Grand Rapids: Kregel Publications, 1981.

Church Song

Begbie, Jeremy S. *Resounding Truth: Christian Wisdom in the World of Music*. Grand Rapids: Baker Academic, 2007.

Berry, Mary. "Hymns," in *The New Westminster Dictionary of Liturgy and Worship,* ed. J. G. Davies. Philadelphia: Westminster Press, 1986.

Blanchard, John, Peter Anderson, Derek Cleave. *Pop Goes the Gospel: Rock in the Church*. Darlington, England: Evangelical Press, 1989.

Gordon, T. David. *Why Johnny Can't Sing Hymns: How Pop Culture Rewrote the Hymnal*. Phillipsburg, New Jersey: P&R Publishing, 2010.

Holloway, Carson. *All Shook Up: Music, Passion, & Politics.* Dallas: Spence Publishing Company, 2001.

Johansson, Calvin. *Discipling Music Ministry: Twenty-First Century Directions*. Peabody, MA: Hendricksen, 1992.

Johnson, Terry L. Compiler & Ed. *Trinity Psalter*. 1994; Pittsburgh, PA; Crown & Covenant Publications, 1997.

Kidd, Reggie M. *With One Voice: Discovering Christ's Song in Our Worship*. Grand Rapids: Baker Books, 2006.

Makujina, John. *Measuring the Music: Another Look at the Contemporary Christian Music Debate.* Salem, Ohio: Schmul Publishing Co., 2000.

Noll, Mark. "Deep & Wide: How My Mind Has Changed," *Christian Century,* June 1, 2010, Vol. 127, No. 11, 32.

Olaskey, Marvin. "Joyful Noises," *World.* March 8/15, 2008.

Stapert, Calvin R. *A New Song for an Old World: Musical Thought in the Early Church,* The Calvin Institute of Christian Worship Liturgical Studies. Grand Rapids: William B. Eerdmans, 2007.

Williams, D. T. "Durable Music," *Touchstone: A Journal of Mere Christianity,* Volume 22, Number 6, July/August 2009.

Sacraments

Alexander, J. W. *God is Love.* 1860; Edinburgh: The Banner of Truth Trust, 1985.

Letham, Robert. *The Lord's Supper: Eternal Word in Broken Bread.* Phillipsburg, New Jersey: P&R Publishing, 2001.

Old, Hughes Oliphant. *Holy Communion in the Piety of the Reformed Church* (Powder Springs, Georgia: Tolle Lege Press, 2013

Old, Hughes O. *The Shaping of the Reformed Baptismal Rite in the Sixteenth Century.* Grand Rapids: Eerdmans, 1992.

Schmidt, Leigh Eric. *Holy Fairs: Scottish Communions and American Revivals in the Early Modern Period.* Princeton, New Jersey: Princeton University Press, 1989.

Still, William. *Child Rearing Within the Covenant of Grace.* Aberdeen, Didasko Press, n/d.

Warfield, B.B. "The Posture of the Recipients at the Lord's Supper," in John E. Meeter, *Selected Shorter Writings of Benjamin B. Warfield—II.* Phillipsburg, New Jersey: Presbyterian & Reformed Publishing Co., 1973.

Witvliet, John, D. *Worship Seeking Understanding.* Grand Rapids: Baker Book House Company, 2003.

Setting of Worship

Bess, Philip. *Till We Have Built Jerusalem: Architecture, Urbanism, and the Sacred.* Wilmington, Delaware: ISI Books, 2006.

Biéler, André. *Architecture in Worship.* Edinburgh & London: Oliver & Boyd, 1965.

Bruggink, Donald J. and Carl H. Droppers. *Christ and Architecture.* Grand Rapids: Eerdmans, 1965.

Drummond, A. L. *The Church Architecture of Protestantism: An Historical and Constructive Study.* Edinburgh: T & T Clark, 1934.

Gobel, David. "Reforming Church Architecture," in *New Horizons Magazine*, February 2011, Vol. 32, No. 2.

Jeremias, Joachim. *The Eucharistic Words of Jesus.* London: SCM Press, 1966.

Nichols, James H. & Leonard J. Trinterud. *The Architectural Setting for Reformed Worship*, Revised Edition. Chicago, Illinois: Presbytery of Chicago, 1960.

Index

Genesis

Genesis 12:1	122
17:1	122
17:7	213
17:17	264
18:23–33	212

Exodus

15:1–18	212
19:18	147
20:1–17	350
20:12	324
23:19	74
25–31	116
29:38–43	67
32:11–14	212
33:12–17	212
34:6–7	206
34:8	77, 223

Leviticus

26:33ff	207
27:34	147

Numbers

6:24–26	227
11:10–15	212
14:11–19	212
14:18	207
18:29–30	74

Deuteronomy

4:8	122
18:15	146
30:1–5	207

Joshua

15–21	116

1 Samuel

2:1–10	207, 213, 239

2 Samuel

7:1ff	146
7:18–29	213

1 Kings

3:6–9	213
8:22–53	213
8:54–61	213
19:12–13	223

2 Kings

19:14–19	213

1 Chronicles

1–9	116
15:22	74
16:8–43	67
28:21	74
29	211
29:11–13	212
29:11–22	67

2 Chronicles

6:1–42	67
6:4–7	67
6:14–42	213
6:40–42	207, 239
23:13, 18	67

29:11–20	213
29:20–28	67
30:9	207
30:16–20	67
30:21	67
34:12	74

Ezra

3:3	67
9:5–15	67, 213

Nehemiah

1:5–11	213
7:7–73	116
8:1–18	67
8:8	128
9	207
9:3–38	67
9:5–27	213
9:17, 31	207

Psalms

1	155
2	141, 207, 239
2:11	87, 342
3	237
4	237
5	237
5:3	68
6	237
8	75, 141

Index

10	237	78:2	147
13	237	86:11–12	227
16	141	88	237
19	50, 75	88:13	68
19:7–13	164	89:1	236
19:8, 10	153	92:2, 4	236
22	141	93	75
22:1	207, 239	95:2	75
23	102, 237	95:5	87
25	237	96	67
29	75	96:1–2a	80
31:5	207, 239	96:2b–3	80
32	237	96:4	80
33	75	96:4–6	236
33:3	74	96:6, 9	94
34:14	192	96–100	75
42:2	21	100:2	75
43:3	212	100:4	74
45	141	101:1	236
46	75	103	226
48	75	103:8	207
51	212, 225, 237	103:8, 10–12	226
59:16	68	104	75
63:1	68	105	67
64	237	106	67
65	75	110	141, 147
66	75	111	75
66:18	79	111:4	207
72	141	112:4	207
73:17–19	21	113	75
77	237	114	75

116:5	207	7:6	51
117	75	7:6–23	103
118	141	10:5–6	103
118:22	147	12:11	103
118:26ff	147	23:1–2	103
119	50	25:6–7	103
119:11	153	27:18	103
119:12, 17, 18, 27	352	27:18, 23	51
119:18	227	27:23	103
119:33	227	28:19	51
119:105	153		
119:147	68		

Ecclesiastes

130	237	5:2	216
132:8–9	207, 239	12:13	145

Isaiah

135	75		
136	75		
141:1–2	67	4:2	94
143	237	6	223
145:9	207	6:5	77
145–150	75, 237	6:10	147
146	207, 239	9:1–2	147
		35:5ff	147
		40:3	147

Proverbs

1:8	153	42:1–21	147
1–9	153	52:7	94
3:1	153	59:2	79
4:2	153	61:1	147
5:23	153	62:11	147
6:6–11	51		
6:20, 23	153		

Jeremiah

7:2	153	8:11	225

Index   385

		Matthew	
8:22	120, 238		
9:23–24	120	1:1–2:12	146
32:16–25	213	2:6	147
		2:18	147
Daniel		3:1–3	147
3:18	175	3:13–17	147
9	212	4:1–11	147
9:1–19	213	4:15–16	147
9:5ff	207	4:17	153
		5	160
Hosea		5:1–2	124
11:1	147	5:3, 5	49
		5:3–16	165
Joel		5–7	158
2:13	207	5:7	147
2:28–32	123	5:17–48	165
		5:31–32	127
Jonah		5:43–48	164
4:2	207	6:1–18	165
		6:7	216
Micah		6:19–34	165
5:2	147	7:7–8	140, 209
		7:16–20	168
Habakkuk		7:20	153
1:12–17	213	7:21–23	173
		7:21ff	139
Zechariah		7:22	163
4:12	25	7:24–27	50, 103
9:9	147	7:28–29	124
		8:43–44	159
		9:1–8	202

386   *Serving with Calvin*

9:16–17	50, 103	4:5	57
9:36–38	227	4:26–29	320
10:29–30	209	6:41	179
11:1–6	147	7:34	179
12:18–21	147		
12:20	173	**Luke**	
12:46	146	1:46–55	207, 213, 239
13	124	1:68–79	213
13:14–15	147	2:29–32	213
13:19,23	124	3:3, 18	153
13:35	147	5:8	77
13:51	124, 180	6	158, 160
16:18	24, 74, 323, 332	6:27ff	159
16:24–25	49, 171	6:43–45	153, 168
20:25–28	49	6:46	173
20:28	226	10:8	179
21:5	147	11:1	207
21:9	147	16:31	65
21:42	147	17:32	161
22:37–40	350	22:29–30	262
22:39–40	159	23:46	179, 207, 239
22:44	147	24	121
26:26–27	259	24:16, 25–27, 31–32	121, 122
27:46	207, 239	24:27	127, 148
28:18–20	174	24:31	179
28:18ff	323	24:31, 33, 35	122
28:20	158	24:32	179
		24:45	179

Mark

1:14–15	153		
2:25	160	1:29	146

John

Index

387

1:46	321
2:19–22	146
3:1ff	162
3:16	140, 208
4:20–24	109
4:23	342
4:24	349
5:46	148
6:35	145
8:12	154
8:32	154
8:56	160
13:34–35	159
14:15, 21	150
15:1–5	44, 155, 337
15:1–11	45
15:5	45
15:12, 17	159
15:26–27	123
16:14	266
17:17	67, 155, 295, 334
20:1, 19, 26	70
21:25	135

Acts

2:6, 11	123
2:17	123
2:38	153, 264
2:42	23, 109
3:24	148
4:23–31	109

4:24–30	207, 213, 239
6:1–5	34
6:1–6	71
7:37	146
11:4	180
16:14	179
16:34	179
17:2–4	179
17:16–34	330
17:28	193
18:4	179
18:26	180
19:8	179
20:7	70
20:11	189
20:19–20	123
20:20, 27	126
20:27	126, 148
26:20	153

Romans

1–11	152
1:16	44, 128, 129, 322
1:18ff	94
1:26	51
2:14–16	94
3–5	163
3:8	152
3:20	173
3:21ff	149
3:31	168

4	143	14:3–9, 19	159
4:11	257, 264	15:5, 7, 14	159
5	160		

1 Corinthians

5:1	226		
5:1–11	152	1:17	108
6	163	1:18	128, 317
6:1–14	162	1:21	108, 128, 129, 295
6:1–23	152	1:22–23	317
6:4	163	1:22–24	148
6:12, 14	163	1:23	108
7	163	1:24–25	317
7:14–25	152	2:1	318
8	163	2:1–2	148
8:1	226	2:1–4	108
8:3	154	2:1–5	128, 318
8:4	168	2:2	27, 108, 318
8:12–17	152	2:3	318
8:12ff	169	2:4	108, 179, 319
8:28	209	2:5	108, 319
8:28–30	167	2:14	227
8:32	149	3:1ff	234
8:37	170	3:6	315
9–11	163	3:6–8	24
10:15	94	3:7	179, 315
10:17	67, 208, 279, 295, 296	3:10	26, 27, 316
11:11–21	71	3:11	26, 316
12:9–10	159	3:12–13	316
12–16	152, 163	3:14–15	317
13:8	168	4:16	161
13:8–10	159	5–7	159
13:13	100	6:9–10	163

Index

6:18	174
6:20	149
7:5	192
7:14	264
9:24–27	169
9:27	171
10:1–14	161
10:2	147
10:3	347
10:16	347
11:1	161
11:1–16	159
11:13	53
11:14	51
11:23–34	31
11:24–25	259
11:27–29	265
11:27ff	202, 271
12:25	159
13	160
14:14–1	202
14:15	242
14:17, 19	203
14:25	85
14:32, 40	342
14:34–38	159
15:10	171
15:57	170
16:2	70

2 Corinthians

1:3–4, 11	227
1:12	45
1:20	147
2:14–3:6	44
2:16	47
3:5	47
4:4–5	148
4:12	49
5:14ff	150
5:17	162
5:21	226
8–9	159
12:7–10	44
12:10	170
13:14	227

Galatians

1–5:12	152
2:11–14	71
2:15	72
3:1	292
3:28	23, 73
5:13	159
5:13–6:18	152
5:14	159
5:19–21	163
5:21	139, 163
5:22–23	160, 226
5:22–24	162
5:24	49

6:2	159, 208	5:5–20	159
6:7	139	5:15	332
		5:15–18	51
Ephesians		5:15ff	51
1	202	5:19	242
1:1–23	213	5:21	159
1–3	152	5:21–6:4	71
1:3	151	5:21–6:9	159
1:11	209	5:21ff	149
1:15–23	212	6:1–3	140
1:17–21	53	6:1ff	258, 264
2:1–10	163	6:10	170
2:8–9	140		
2:10	170	**Philippians**	
2:13–22	72	1	202
3:18	227	1–4	152
3:18–19	212	1:9–11	53, 212, 213
4	160	2:1–4	160
4:2, 32	159	2:5–11	152
4–6	152	2:6–8	149
4:7–13	82	3:4–10	152
4:11ff	124	3:12–14	171
4:17–6:20	169	4:6–7	137
4:17–24	124	4:8	54, 94
5:1–4	159	4:8–9	74, 160
5:1–17	214	4:13	170
5:1ff	226		
5:2	159	**Colossians**	
5:3	53	1	202
5:3–4	100	1–2	152
5:4	54	1:9–11	212

Index

391

1:9–12	53, 213
1:27–2:7	156
1:28	189
1:29	170, 171
2:2–3	51
2:3	145, 151
2:11	264
2:16–23	159
3	160
3:1–4, 6	169
3–4	152
3:5–7	159
3:8–9	159
3:13, 16	159
3:15	100
3:16	123, 237, 242
3:18–4:1	159
3:18–25	71
3:22–25	159
4:4–6	159

1 Thessalonians

1:10	137
2:10	45
2:11–12	192
4:1–8	159, 192
4:9	159
4:11	159
4:18	159
5:17	174
5:22	174, 192

2 Thessalonians

3:6	192
3:6–12	159
3:11–13	193

1 Timothy

1 Timothy	211
1:5	166
1:12–16	167
1:17	212
1:18	179
2:1–2	227
2:1, 3–4	227
1 Timothy 2:1–8	166
2:5–6	167
2:9	54
2:9–10	100
1 Timothy 2:9–15	167
2:9–17	159
2:10	53
3	32, 34, 44, 160, 172
3:1–13	167
3:3	162
3:6	30, 32
3:15	167
3:16	167
4:1–5	159
4:5	266
4:7–8	44
4:12	161
4:13	115

4:16	44	4:3	166
5:1–2	324	4:6–8	123
5:1–16	72, 159	4:17	180
5:8	159		
6	174		

Titus

6:2	123, 167	1	32, 34, 44, 160, 172
6:3	167	2:1	53, 87
6:6–10, 17–19	159	2:1–10	159
6:9–19	72	2:2–8	72
6:11	191	2:8	161
6:11–14	191	2:9–10	71
6:15–16	212	2:11–12	171
6:17–19	192		
6:20	228		

Hebrews

		Hebrews	152
		1:1–3	146

2 Timothy

		2:17–18	234
1:3	335	3, 4	161
1:6	85	4:12	155
1:11	123	4:14–16	146
1:12, 14	228	4;15–16	234
1:13	123	4:16	203
1:16–18	159	5:1–10	146
1:22	159	5:11–6:2	234
2:1–26	169	6	163
2:2	30, 124	6:11	161
2:22	174, 191	6:12	161
3:15	128, 166	6:13–10:25	146
3:15–4:5	123	7:27	279
3:16	166	9:2–5	109
3:16–17	128, 166	10	163
4:2	166, 178		

Index

393

10:10, 12	279
10:24	159
11	143, 161
11:1–12:2	161
11:7	122
12:1–3	160
12:10–11	164
12:14	164
12:28	61, 87, 343
13	159
13:5	209
13:20–21	227

James

1	208
1:5	208
1:19, 26	159
1:22	173
2	140
2:1–9	72
2:14–26	168
2:14ff	192
3:1–12	159
3:11–12	168
4:1–3, 7–10	140
5:1–6	72, 159
5:10–12, 18	160
5:13–18	227
5:13–20	202
5:16	159
5:17–18	143

1 Peter

1 Peter	152
1:15–16	226
1:16	208
1:22	159
1:23	155
2:1–2	155
2:11–12	159
2:13–3:7	159
2:21	160
2:21–24	149
2:24	225
3:7	53
3:10a	136
3:10b	136
3:11	137, 192
3:13	136
4:1–5	159
4:9	160
5:1–5	162
5:3	161

2 Peter

2 Peter	152
1	160
1:3	151
1:5–7	45
1:8	45
3:10–13	136

1 John

1:6–10	140	
1:7	160	
1:7–2:2	149	
1:9	208, 225	
2:7ff	159	
2:15–16	226	
3:11, 23	159	
3:16	160	
3:16–17	149	
3:17	159	
4:7	159	
4:10–11	160	
4:11	149	
4:19	150	
5:2	153	
5:14–15	208	

2 John

5	159

Jude

4	171

Revelation

1:10	70, 107
1:17	78
4:8–5:14	213

Index of Names

A

Addison, Joseph	244
Alexander, Archibald	42, 210
Alexander, J. W.	42, 269
Ambrose	97
Aristotle	96, 100
Augustine of Hippo	97, 98, 99, 103, 108, 147, 193, 240

B

Bacharach, Burt	195
Bach, Johann Sebastian	230, 245
Baird, Dr. James	125, 189, 305
Bannerman, Douglas	84
Barna, Frank	24
Barth, Karl	99, 283, 289
Baxter, Richard	39, 68, 78, 83, 84, 91, 182, 189, 190, 232, 251, 253, 262, 266, 312
Beach Boys, The	196, 240
Beatles, The	195
Beecher, Lyman	43
Beethoven, Ludwig van	119
Begbie, Jeremy	103, 240
Begbie, Jeremy S.	96
Bernard of Clairvaux	289
Beza, Theodore	83
Blaikie, William G.	34, 43, 84, 200, 205, 216, 219, 220
Blanton, Joseph Edwin	282
Blues Brothers, The	245
Boa, Kenneth	215
Boice, James M.	133, 244
Bonhoeffer, Dietrich	99, 238, 295
Brahms, Johannes	244
Bridges, Charles	42
Broadus, John	206
Brooks, Phillips	43, 183
Brosend, William	63

Brown, Frank Burch 102, 103
Brown, John 43
Bruce, A. B. 84
Bruce, Robert 130, 252, 269
Bruggink, Donald J. 275, 276, 280, 282, 284
Bubba 245
Bucer, Martin 83, 125
Bullinger, Heinrich 130

C

Cage, John 102
Calamy, Edmund 271
Calvin, John 29, 56, 57, 69, 78, 83, 97, 98, 101, 103, 107, 113, 125, 130, 133, 140, 141, 142, 143, 144, 164, 177, 193, 194, 196, 207, 226, 240, 251, 257, 258, 260, 266, 285, 305, 333
Carrick, John 121, 158, 181
Carson, D. A. 30
Cartwright, Thomas 83
Chalmers, Thomas 194, 205
Chapell, Bryan 148
Charnock, Stephen 108, 257
Chrysostom, John 48, 97
Clark, Scott 67, 68, 69
Clowney, Edmund 86
Colson, Charles 175, 176
Cowper, William 230
Cyprian 68

Cyril of Jerusalem 130, 293

D

Dabney, R. L. 43, 205, 209, 218, 219, 221, 222
David, Hal 195
Dever, Mark 95, 246
Doddridge, Philip 230
Dominic 290
Doolittle, Thomas 130, 253
Driscoll, Mark 287
Droppers, Carl H. 275, 276, 280, 282, 284
Drummond, A. L. 276, 278
Due, Noel 38

E

Eastman, Fred 293
Eby, David 46
Edgar, William 101
Edwards, Jonathan 130, 189, 190, 193, 222, 223, 251
Eire, Carlos M. N. 286

F

Fairbairn, Patrick 88, 204
Farel, William 56
Ferguson, John 232
Ferguson, Sinclair 138
Fogelberg, Dan 194
Forsyth, P. T. 127

France, R. T. — 175

Francis of Assisi — 290

Fromm, Chuck — 229

G

Gaffin, Richard — 69

Gerhardt, Paul — 238

Getty, Keith — 243

Gillespie, George — 261

Gobel, David — 277

Godfrey, Dr. Robert — 33

Gordon, T. David — 100, 101, 231, 238, 241

Graham, Billy — 282

Greenham, Richard — 83

Gurnall, William — 46, 124, 133, 177

H

Handel, George Frideric — 230

Hart, D. G. — 85

Hauerwas, Stanley — 24

Haydn, Joseph — 244

Henry, Matthew — 75, 132, 204, 215, 256, 257, 258, 260, 301

Higgins, Jack — 194

Hodge, Charles — 193

Holloway, Carson — 96

Holst, Gustav — 244

Hulse, Erroll — 46

Hunt, Arthur W., III — 286, 287

Hybels, Bill — 19, 20, 24, 297

J

James, John Angell — 40

Jeremias, Joachim — 259

Johnson, Dennis E. — 51, 121, 145, 150, 154, 156, 161, 188, 189

Jones, Paul — 249

Jowett, J. H. — 135

K

Kallestad, Walt — 19

Kauflin, Bob — 21

Keller, Timothy — 93

Kelly, Dr. Douglas — 237

Kidd, Reggie M. — 245

Kimball, Dan — 246

King, Martin Luther, Jr. — 237

Knox, John — 78, 252, 312

Kuyper, Abraham — 30, 91, 118, 132, 184, 262, 288

L

Laidlaw, John — 84

Lawrence, Michael — 95, 246

Led Zeppelin — 119

Leith, John — 107, 285

Letham, Robert — 254

Lewis, C. S. — 194

Lloyd-Jones, D. Martyn — 120, 126, 133, 181, 189, 190, 193

Luther, Martin — 55, 56, 83, 101, 125, 143, 194, 233, 236, 249, 320

M

MacArthur, John 133, 168, 186, 196
MacDonald, Gordon 195
Macleod, Donald 76, 77, 272, 277
Manton, Thomas 188
Martin, Albert N. 180
Mason, Lowell 230
M'Cheyne, Robert Murray 46, 47
Melanchthon, Philip 83
Mendelssohn, Felix 230
Metaxas, Eric 238
Miller, J. Graham 200
Miller, Samuel 88, 90, 204, 211, 214, 219, 220
Mohler, Albert 331
Montgomery, James 236
Moody, D. L. 282
Motyer, Alec 47, 65, 89, 121, 122, 123, 124, 126, 132, 135, 139, 144, 145, 147, 178, 179, 180, 183, 188, 197, 322, 329
Mouw, Richard J. 63
Moynihan, Daniel Patrick 194
Murphy, Thomas 41, 88, 205, 208, 211, 219, 221
Murray, John 181

N

Newton, John 230
Nichols, James Hastings 280
Nietzsche 96

Nixon, Leroy 143
Noll, Mark 262

O

Oecolampadius, Johannes 125
Olasky, Marvin 242
Old, Hughes 107, 117, 125, 260
Owen, John 84, 85, 251

P

Packer, J. I. 46, 50, 118, 181, 187, 190, 223
Pak, G. Sunjin 141, 142
Palau, Luis 196
Perkins, William 83
Plantinga, Jr., Cornelius 86
Plato 96, 97, 98, 240
Pliny the Younger 68
Plumer, William S. 43
Pope, Randy 17, 18, 24, 27, 297
Porter, Ebenezer 41
Postman, Neil 194, 295
Powlison, David 201, 238, 239
Pratt, Richard L. 215
Presley, Elvis 248

Q

Quill, Timothy C. J. 239, 246, 336

R

Ralston, Rev. Dr. William 325

Rayburn, Robert G. 37, 76, 219, 269
Reeder, Harry 17
Rienstra, Ron 70
Ronne, Dave 286
Rousseau, Jean Jacques 96
Rozeboom, Sue A. 86
Rushdoony, Rousas J. 322
Ruth, Lester 101
Ryle, J. C. 70, 118, 180

S

Salmond, S. D. F. 84
Schlegel, Katarina von 239
Schmidt, Leigh Eric 18
Schoenberg, Arnold 102
Scroggie, W. Graham 215
Shedd, W. G. T. 36, 42, 217, 220, 221
Simeon, Charles 135
Simon & Garfunkel 64
Spurgeon, C. H. 43, 114, 118, 119, 120, 125, 130, 188, 196, 216, 220, 222, 251
Stapert, Calvin R. 97
Steinmetz, David C. 141
Still, William 49, 91, 120, 127, 265
Stott, John 120, 135, 175, 188, 196, 242, 326
Sunday, Billy 282
Swinnock, George 50

T

Taylor, William M. 43
Tertullian 68, 97
Thomas, Derek 141
Thomas, Geoffrey 187, 200
Toplady, Augustus 230
Torrance, T. F. 252
Townend, Stuart 243
Trajan 68
Trinterud, Leonard J 280

V

Vincent, Nathanael 21, 24, 25, 270, 271

W

Warfield, B. B. 134, 261
Warren, Rick 17, 19, 24, 27, 91, 100, 246, 247, 277, 297, 298, 300
Watson, Thomas 130, 153, 175
Watts, Isaac 75, 84, 204, 216, 217, 222, 228, 229, 230, 236
Wells, David 20, 39, 46, 194
Wesley, Charles 101, 230, 236, 249
Wesley, John 101, 236
Whitefield, George 220
Williams, D. T. 106, 232, 234, 236
Willimon, William 217
Wilson, Lewis 293
Witt, John R. de 181, 183, 187, 196
Witvliet, John D. 226

Wren, Sir Christopher 280

Z

Zwingli, Ulrich 55, 56, 83, 125, 264, 285